WESTERN GLORY

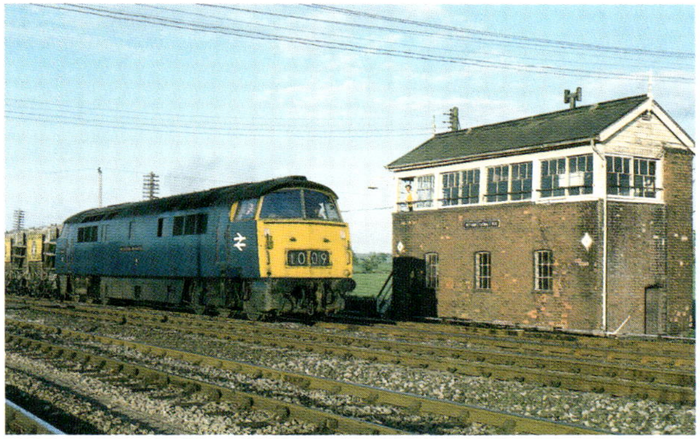

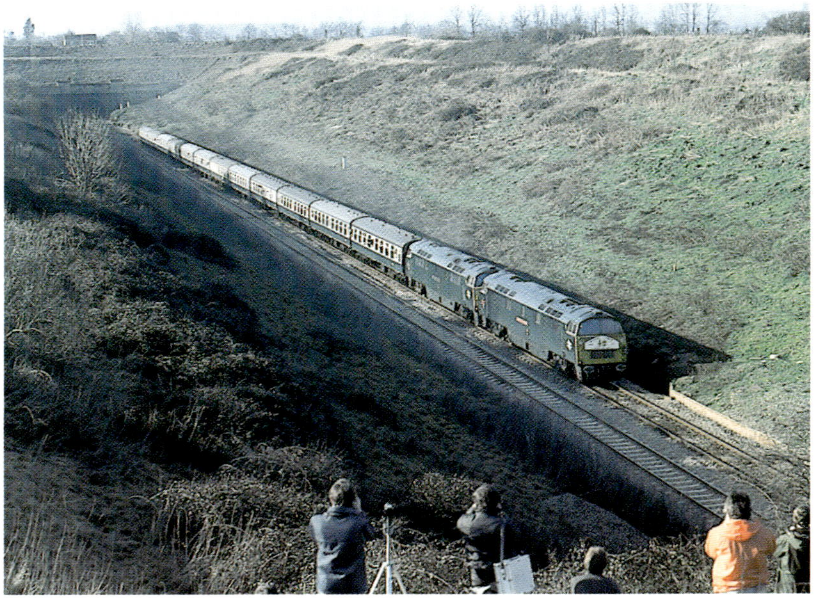

Western Tribute Railtour, Severn Tunnel East, February 26th, 1977.

WESTERN GLORY

Photographs of the Class 52 Westerns

January 1975 to February 1977

CHRIS CHAPMAN

Waterfront
a division of Kingfisher Productions

First published 2002 by Waterfront - a division of Kingfisher Productions
The Dalesmade Centre,
Watershed Mill, Settle,
North Yorkshire BD24 9LR

www.railwayvideo.com
www.westernglory.co.uk

ISBN 0-946184-99-2

British Library Cataloguing in Publication Data
A catalogue record for this book is available from the British Library

Book design and layout by Chris Chapman
Printed by Ian Allan Printing Ltd, Hersham, Surrey, KT12 4RG

DEDICATION

This book was written and compiled in memory of my Dad, Tom Chapman. He took many of the photographs in this volume, and without him it would never have seen the light of day.

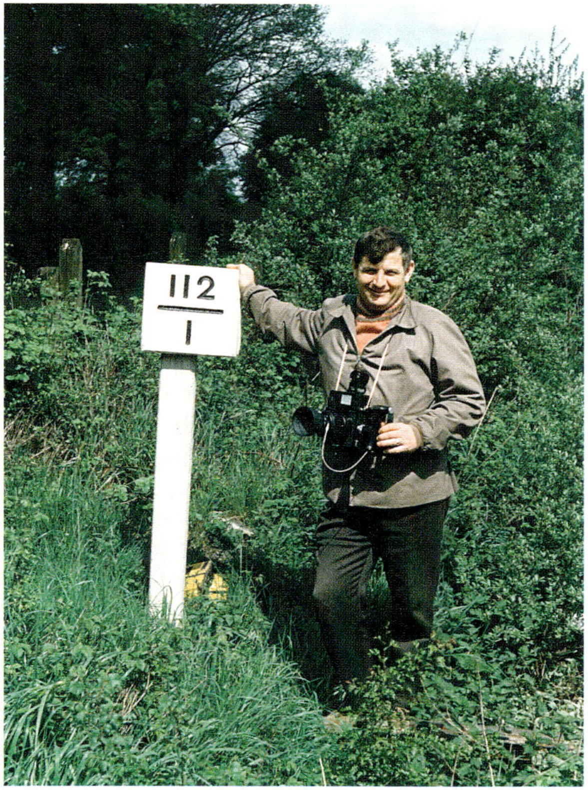

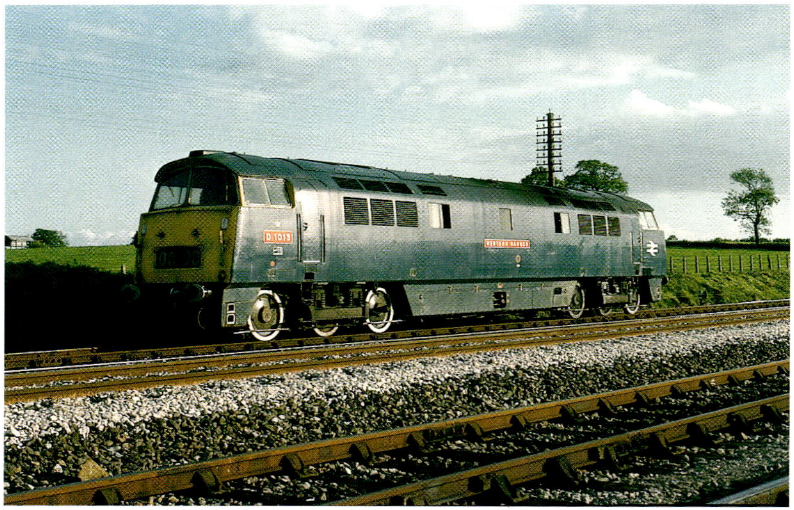

D1013 *Western Ranger*, Witham down refuge siding, May 1976.

CONTENTS

PREFACE

Thinking back through the years, it was a time when my Dad was working very hard and he enjoyed the escape into the countryside on evenings and weekends. Mum sometimes came with us - my sister wasn't the slightest bit interested - but with the benefit of hindsight I can see that he was spending a lot of time with me in cultivating interests, both in transport and photography. At first we explored the West of England main line between Westbury and Castle Cary, close enough to our North Somerset home for trips in the summer evenings and day trips at weekends. Although the WR main line between Bath and Bristol was closer to home than our chosen stretch of line, we preferred the West of England route for its semaphore signals. They were more informative for the railway photographer as well as being more photogenic! We recorded all the remaining Westerns that we saw – of the forty five locomotives still in service we missed only five. Some of those we photographed in black and white, only to lose the negatives in a darkroom fire in the eighties. We got to know the best vantage points for railway photography and quickly learnt that chatting to friendly signalmen held all sorts of fringe benefits for photographers keen to know where the next train from Penzance was, or if there were any specials running that day. Soon we were admitted to that secret, slightly mysterious place behind the door which still held a cast iron plate stating 'Great Western Railway. No unauthorised persons allowed in this box', and were introduced to the arcane intricacies of bell codes and block instruments. It also sparked off an interest in signalling which continues to this day; both in personal and professional capacities.

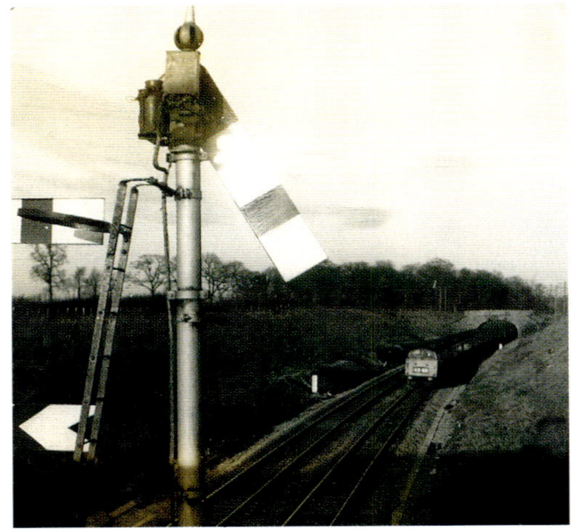

On Sunday 4th January 1975, D1022 *Western Sentinel* approaches Clink Road Junction, with the inner home 'down main to loop' signal clear for the 12.30 Paddington to Plymouth. Significant for being the first photograph I ever took of a Western.

Camerawise, Dad bought a Mamiya 'Universal' camera, using the 150 mm lens most often and a 6 x 9 film back which gave only eight shots per 120 roll-film. He also had to remember to cock the shutter and take the dark-slide out before every picture. I had my trusty Rolleiflex but soon realised it wasn't much use for taking pictures of express trains from overbridges with its standard focal length lens. Thereafter I used a Mamiya C220 with 180 and 250 mm lenses, until early 1976 when Dad bought a Minolta XE-1 35 mm camera with a variety of lenses and automatic exposure setting, a real innovation at the time. Winter evenings were useless for train photography in our usual haunts, which were mere wayside passing places as far as the railway was concerned. We consoled ourselves at Blatchbridge Junction with tins of baked beans and big soup all mixed up together and heated on the Baby Belling. In front of the coal stove, doors wide open and coals blazing, we made toast using the toasting fork (a bespoke accessory unique to each signalbox) and waited for the long summer evenings to return.

Our summer holiday that year was in August. We travelled from Silk Mill to Penzance, in our Bedford CF camper van, documenting Westerns and signalboxes down the line. As a birthday treat in September 1976, I was allowed to spend all night at Witham Box on the 22.00 to 06.00 nightshift with John Francis. Highlight of the night was seeing the 'Papers' – the 00.30 Paddington to Penzance News & Parcels – headed by a Western, rushing past on the Down Main at eighty mph, just after two in the morning.

The end of the Summer timetable in 1976 signalled the end of our Western chasing days. As the nights drew in, we saw very few Western hauled workings. The Westerns South Western railtour passed us at Blatchbridge in the pouring rain. The following weekend we went to Paignton North to meet John Francis who had moved to Newton Abbot as a relief signalman. The old level crossing gates were being replaced by lifting barriers which remain there today, superseding all else from the mechanical age. D1053 *Western Patriarch* was in the carriage sidings at Goodrington. We didn't realise it at the time but her next working, the 15.27 Paignton to Newton Abbot, would be the last ever Western hauled service train we photographed. After that, we only saw an occasional Western in the hours of darkness at our favourite haunts of Witham and Blatchbridge, the sound of the Maybach engines revealing the loco itself, seconds before the digits on the headcode panel identified the loco number.

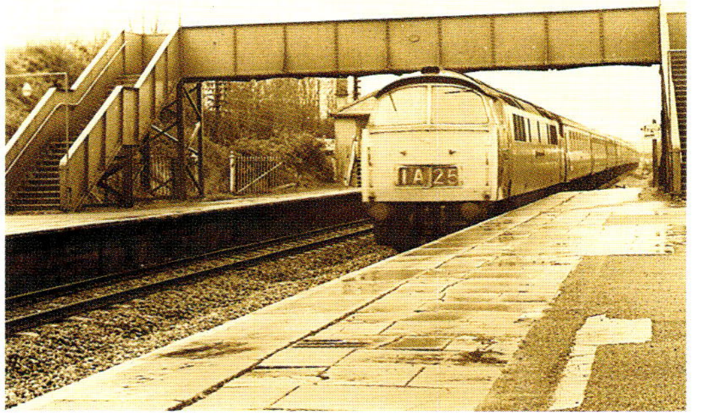

On the following Sunday, D1030 *Western Musketeer* passes Bruton, hauling the 09.30 Plymouth to Paddington.

Christmas 1976 came and went. A couple of months passed before 26th February; along with many others, we lined up near Pilning, waiting for the 'Western Tribute' railtour to emerge from the tunnel mouth and pass through Severn Tunnel East. My Dad considered this such an important event to capture that we used three cameras, Mum taking the third shot in her cameo role as a photographer for the day. Having got the shot, we dashed down the M5, stopping on the hard shoulder where the motorway passes over the railway between Worle Junction and Puxton. I got the shot on the Minolta but unfortunately Dad forgot to cock the shutter on the 'Universal', swearing as he realised his mistake and taking a shot much later than the decisive moment he had intended. We saw the railtour once more; that evening after darkness at Blatchbridge Junction. I made a tape recording from the box window, now lost in countless house moves, and Dad's attempt at night photography with our meagre flashgun as the train passed by resulted in an illuminated bufferbeam and little else apart perhaps from a startled driver. Over the years the slideboxes gathered dust, although some consideration was given to a book; but apart from the occasional glance I gave it no more thought, until my Dad died last year. It then seemed a very appropriate thing to do and the right time to do it; a project with a lot of happy memories.

Chris Chapman, Somerset, 2002

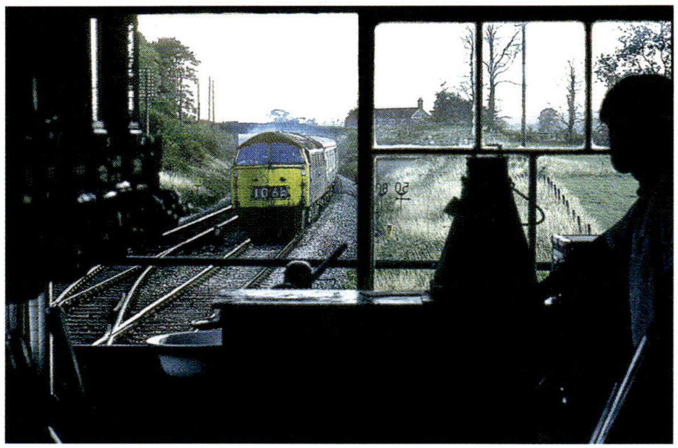

D1068 *Western Reliance* and Chris Burden, shortly before the signalbox shakes as the train passes by - Blatchbridge Junction, 1976.

ACKNOWLEDGMENTS

The task of sorting out some two hundred and fifty Western transparencies finally fell upon me in 2001. I picked up the small green filing cabinet that had for many years stored the medium format transparencies, and went through each one individually, trying to decipher my Dad's original filing system, without much success. The 35 mm Kodachrome slides were all still in their little yellow boxes. Many nights later, I had transferred them to slide projector magazines and edited them into a series of shots worthy of publication.

Most of the medium format transparency sleeves held meticulous notes, marked up at the time in my father's strong hand, usually with the locomotive name and often including the date and time the photograph had been taken. The rest he had placed to one side as being technically inferior, with some marked up in a childish hand by me, then in the middle of my secondary school years. In 1975, the trains still had headcodes but by 1976 the engine number was usually wound up on the headcode board, making loco identification simple but in many cases that year we didn't record what the train was. I started by tracking down a few of the dates using Mum's 1976 diary, with help from some of the signalbox train registers of the period. Our old friend Chris Burden had written Western numbers in the train register book for a few weeks during his turns of duty as signalman at Blatchbridge Junction in 1976; with Bernie Miles and Dave Richards doing the same thing at Fairwood Junction I was able to fill in a few more gaps. Fortunately we had been given some of these train registers and we saved them at the back of the garage in a tea chest. Apart from the mice they hadn't been touched for nearly twenty years, after removal there in 1983! Chris Burden provided us with a lot of support in our photographic endeavours, and he was instrumental in furthering my interest in railways to the professional stage. Like many railwaymen before him, he nurtured enthusiasm and turned it into railway service.

Help arrived from many directions. John Francis, then a signalman at Witham and subsequently Newton Abbot, answered my many operational queries in thorough detail. He also takes credit for being the person who, throughout the years pestered me on and off about doing something with the pictures! His advice on publishing and his critique of my captions were also invaluable. Charlie Beatson, funnily enough also a signalman at Witham and then Newton Abbot, but now living in Oregon, provided many thought provoking memories and lots of background information. Adrian Curtis, author of *Cast of Thousands*, proved unfailingly helpful after I phoned him out of the blue, and helped enormously in filling much of the hitherto missing detail about these images. Alex Hunt, also a Western enthusiast from the seventies and now a happy volunteer driver of D1010 *Western Campaigner* on the West Somerset Railway, contributed much needed detail from a locoman's perpective as well as contacting Bob Tiller, chairman of the Diesel & Electric Preservation Group, who very kindly sent his comprehensive history of *Campaigner* in preservation. Ian Wannell, signalman at Westbury North in the seventies and now based in Exeter, supplied invaluable reminiscences about the train working at Westbury in those days, and also helped to pin down dates of our visits there. Paul Dye furnished us with working timetables at the start of our Western chasing days, and introduced us to Adrian Vaughan, who sometimes held Merehead trips at his up branch inner home signal, the better for us to photograph them!

Finally, thanks to my wife Seona, who has remained cheerful in the face of endless slide shows, caption redrafts and gaffer's stories about the old days.

PART 1: WESTBURY to SOMERTON

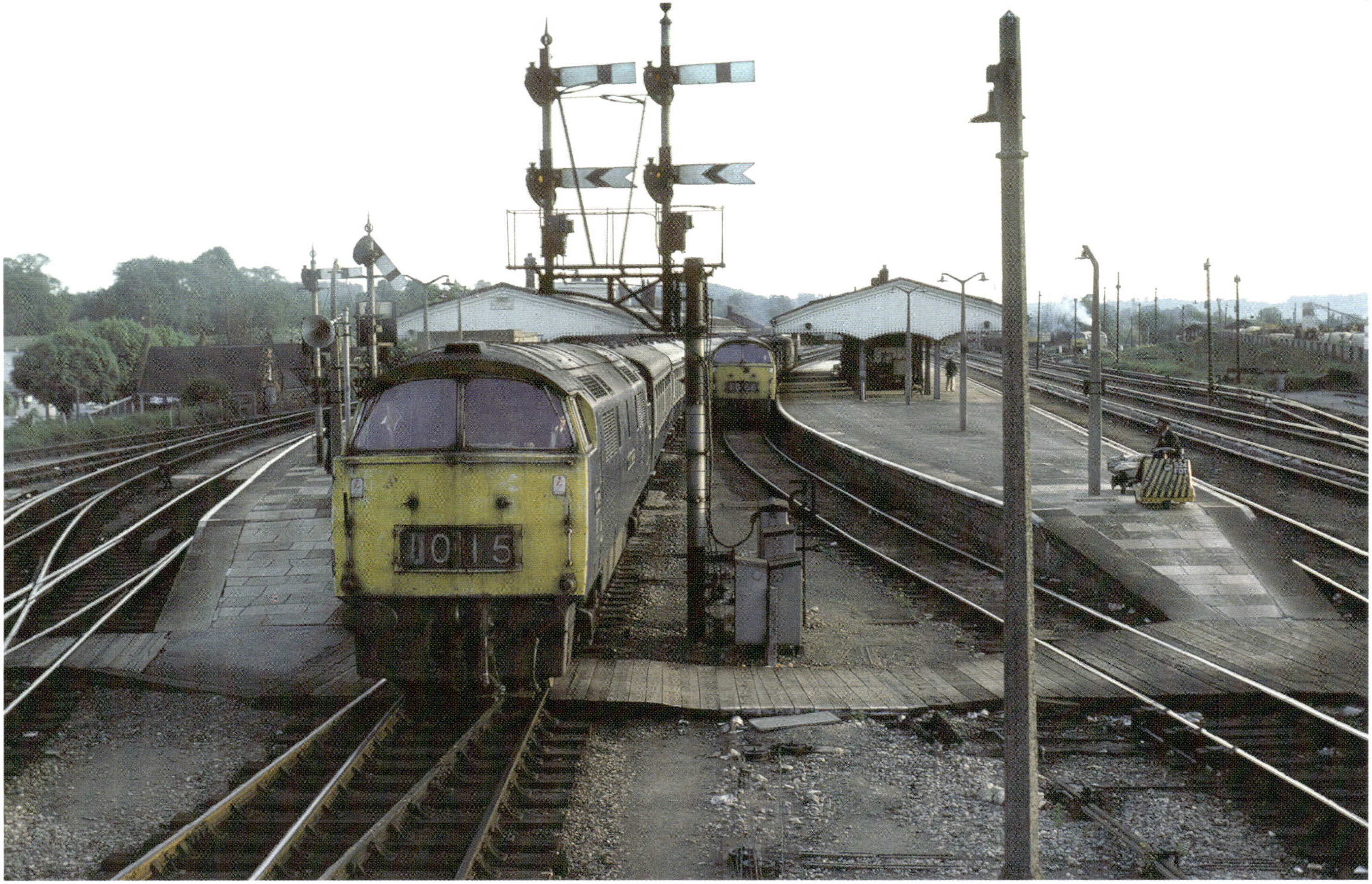

It is a glorious evening in the spring of 1976, towards the end of May, at about ten minutes to eight. Looking from the window of Westbury North signalbox, D1015 *Western Champion* is pulling the empty stock from the 17.45 Paddington to Westbury out of platform 2, having hauled the train down from London and run round it at Westbury. The stock was then propelled into the 'Long Road', an up siding adjacent to the diesel depot, where it was stabled until the following morning's use on the 06.40 to Paddington. Meanwhile, the Southern loco of the Pompey parcels, (the 17.22 Portsmouth & Southsea to Bristol Temple Meads) had come off the train as diagrammed. It was replaced by a fresh engine, D1056 *Western Sultan,* seen here awaiting departure from the Up Salisbury line to Bristol. Another Western can be seen on shed in the distance, whilst the station porter waits on his battery trolley with parcels from the Pompey for the parcel office on the down side.

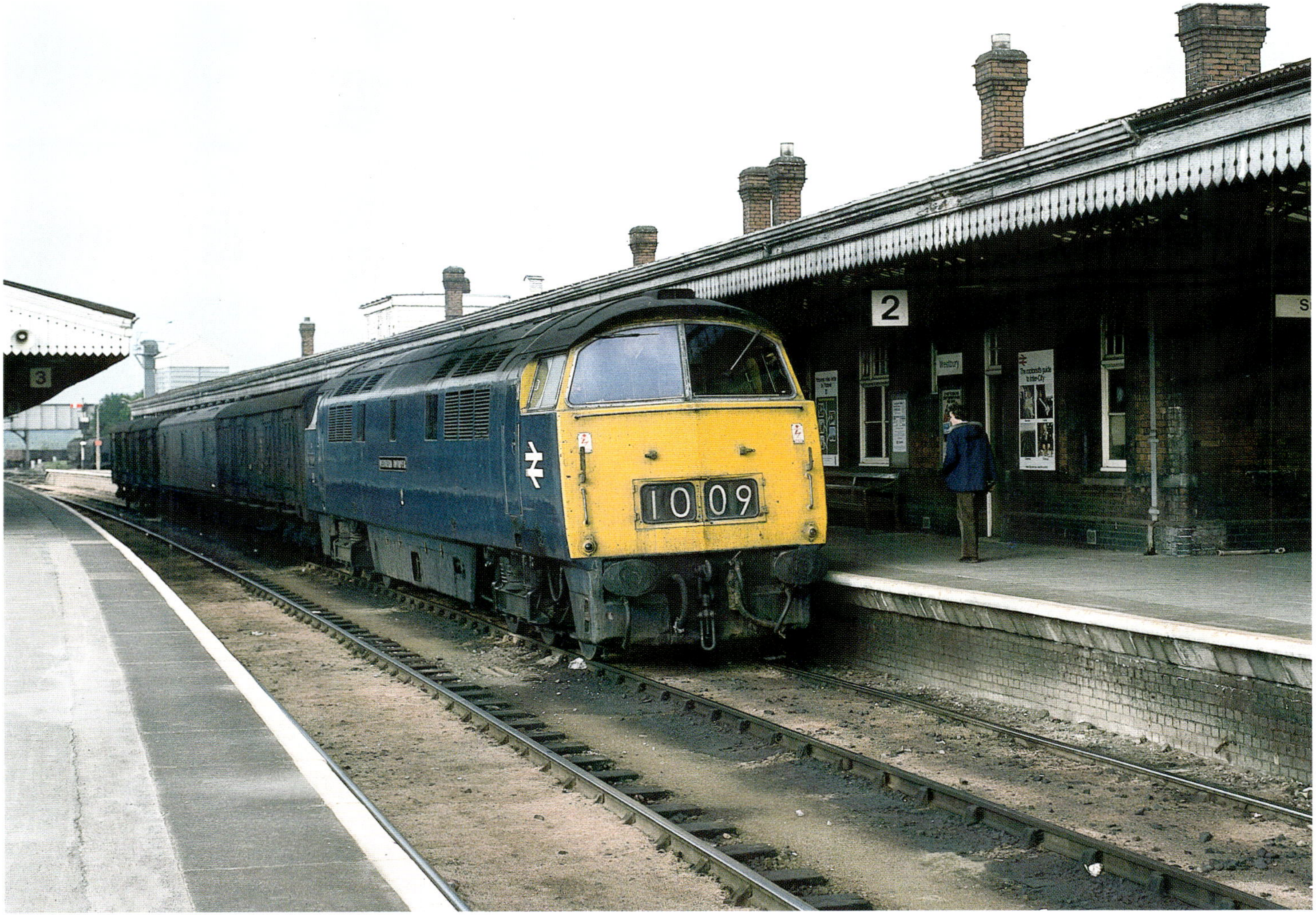

It seems remarkable to me that twenty five years ago there were parcels trains from Bristol to Salisbury, but so it was. The weekday service left Bristol Temple Meads at 04.30, stopping at Westbury for nearly an hour, but on Sundays it was booked to leave Bristol at 16.35, only stopping at Westbury for twenty minutes from 18.06 to 18.26. On a Sunday in May 1976, D1009 *Western Invader* is waiting in the Down Main platform at Westbury. The loco returned light from Salisbury, arriving back at Westbury at 19.55.

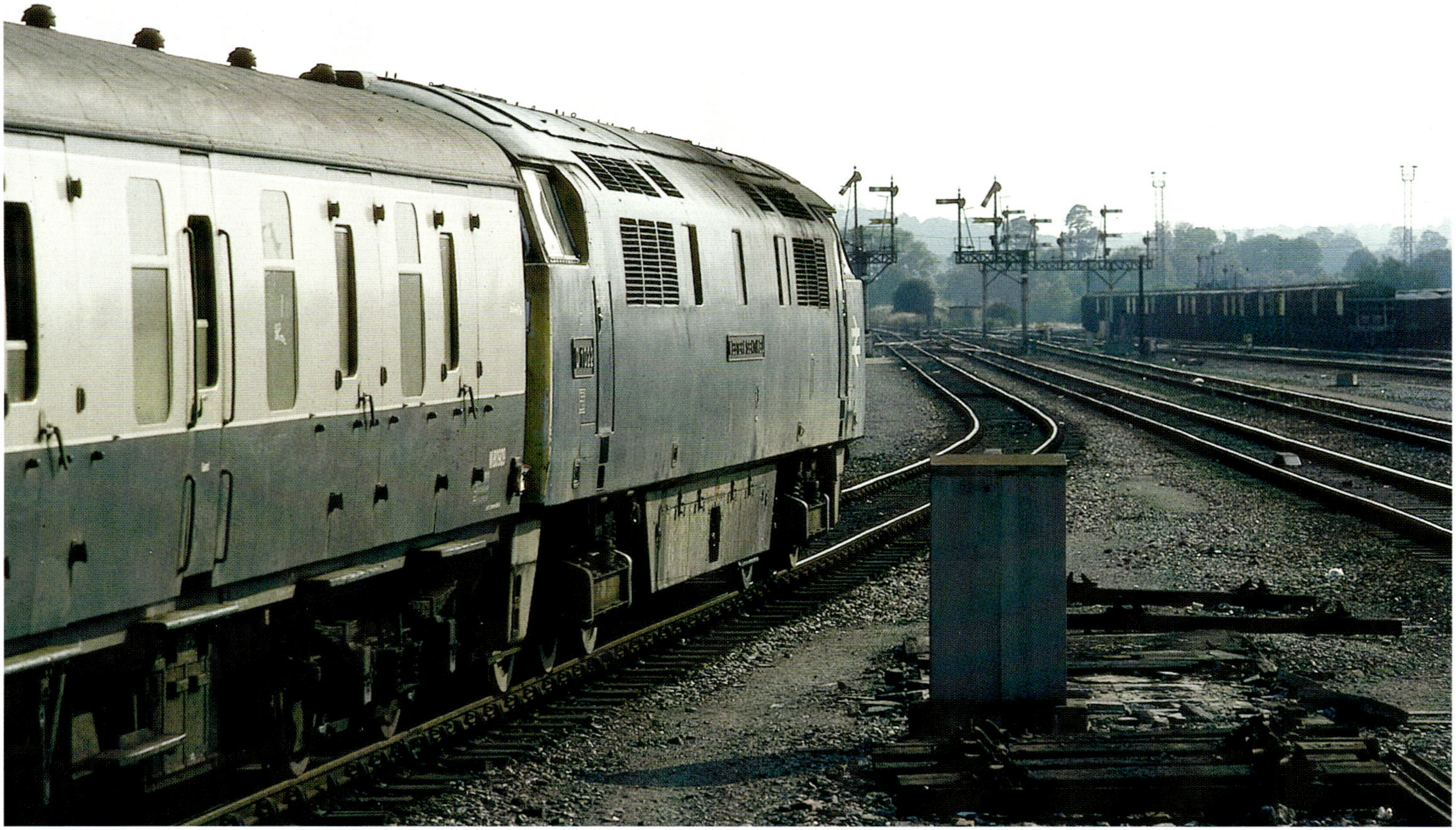

D1022 *Western Sentinel* departs from Westbury with the 16.35 Bristol parcels on Sunday, 8th August 1976. The South box Down Salisbury home signal is lowered but the driver of *Sentinel* will not know if he is 'right away' to Warminster until he starts to climb Dilton Marsh bank and ascertains the position of the starting signal, nearly half a mile in advance of the home. The Down Main home signal is also off, for the 17.52 Bristol Temple Meads to Weymouth stopping passenger, due at 18.34. Fairwood Junction's distant is still at caution as the 13.30 Penzance has not yet cleared the junction there, en route for London via the Westbury avoiding line. The Westbury North signalman would ring Fairwood Junction on the telephone circuit bell as the Weymouth left Westbury station, to let the signalman there that it was on the move, in case the Penzance was a little late and the stopper had a margin to clear Fairwood. The signalman there would then clear his signals and the motor operated distant would lower in time for the driver to see it before passing Westbury South.

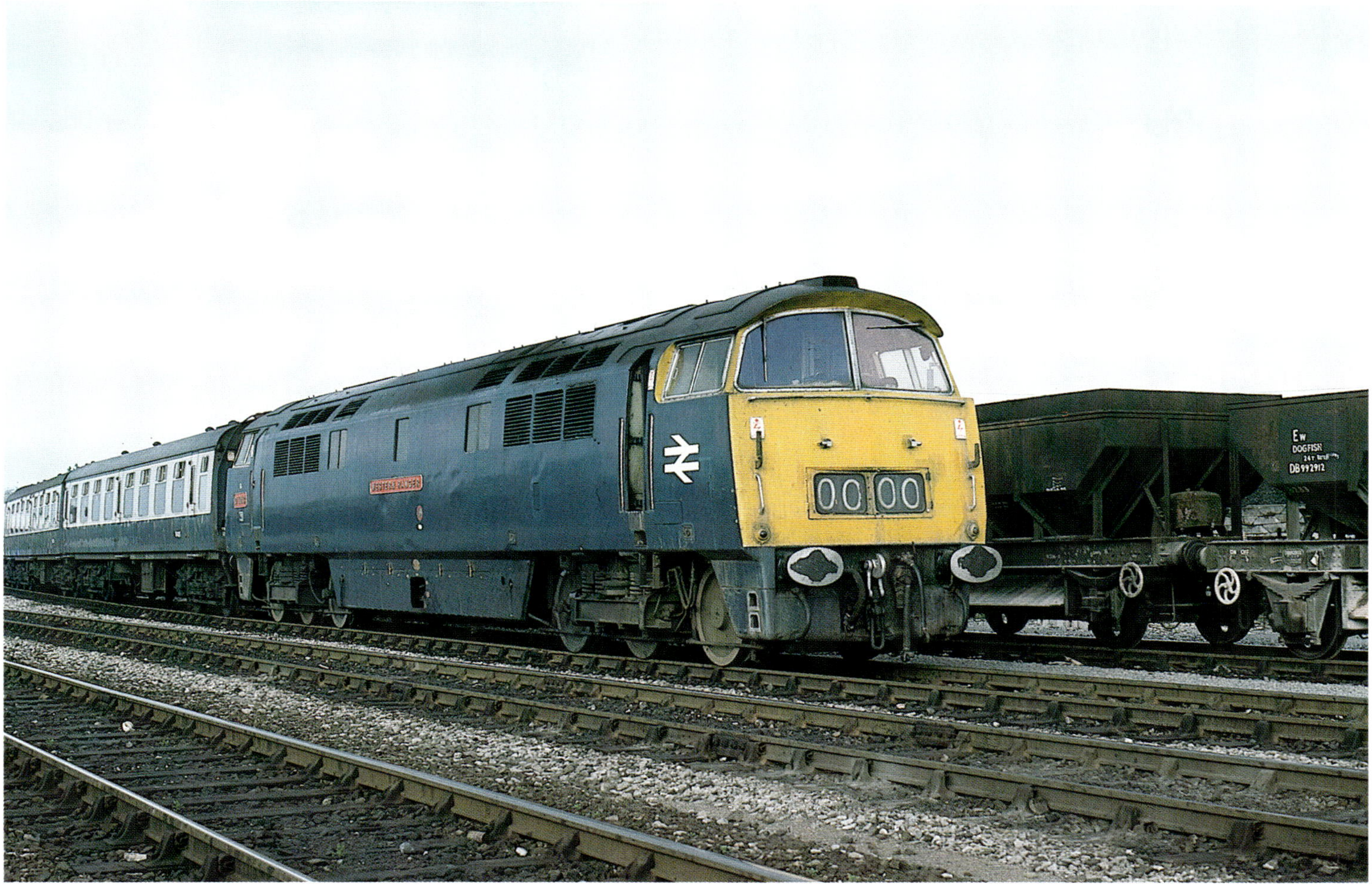

With engines shut down, D1013 *Western Ranger* waits on the Down Salisbury line at Westbury with a train of empty coaching stock in May 1976. The platforms at Westbury were too short for full length trains and it was usual for the locomotives of down trains to stop some distance towards Westbury South to avoid the stationary train fouling the point work at Westbury North. The new battery box clips fitted to the class after the derailment of D1007 *Western Talisman* at Ealing in 1973 are evident in this photograph.

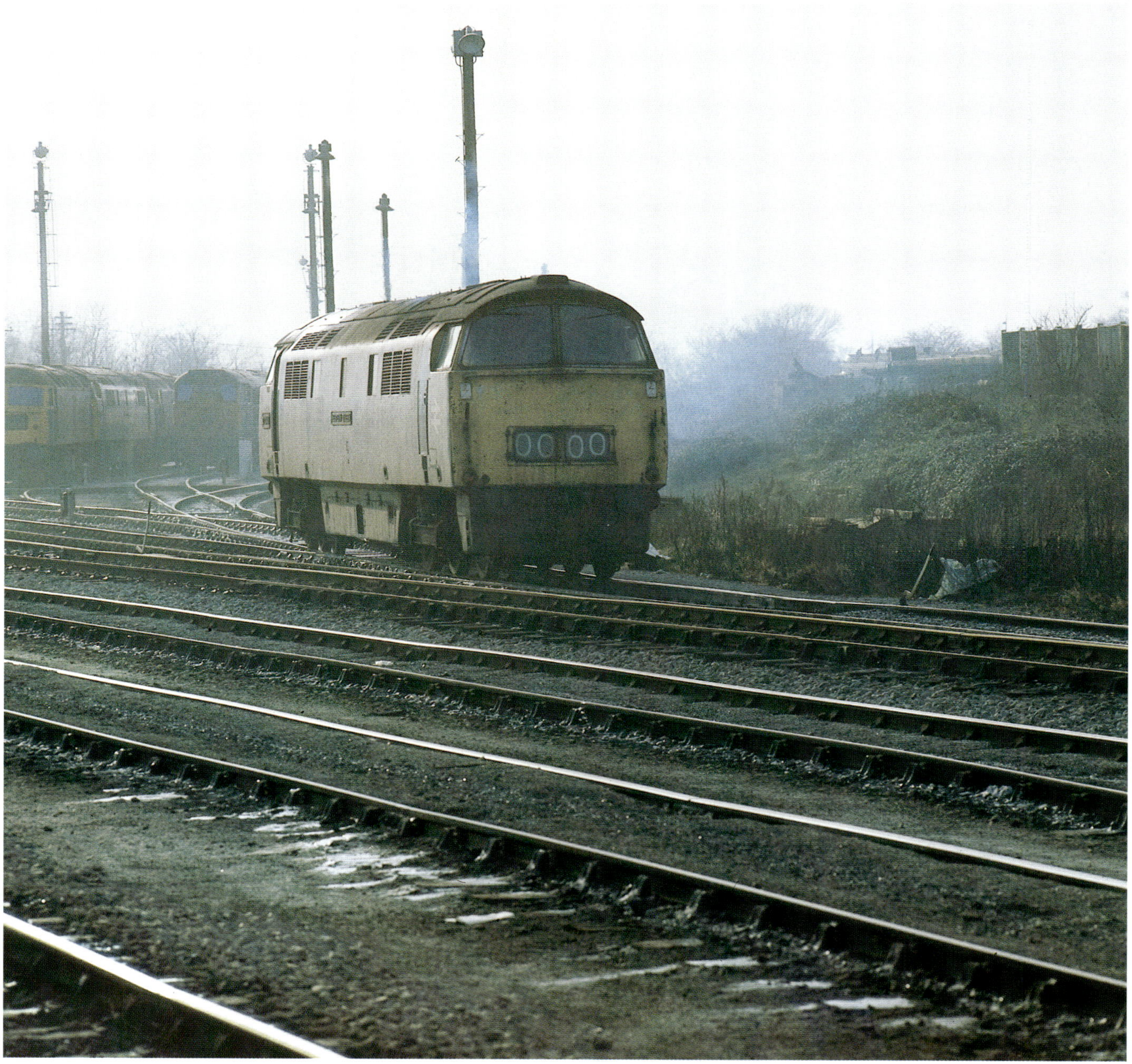

0000

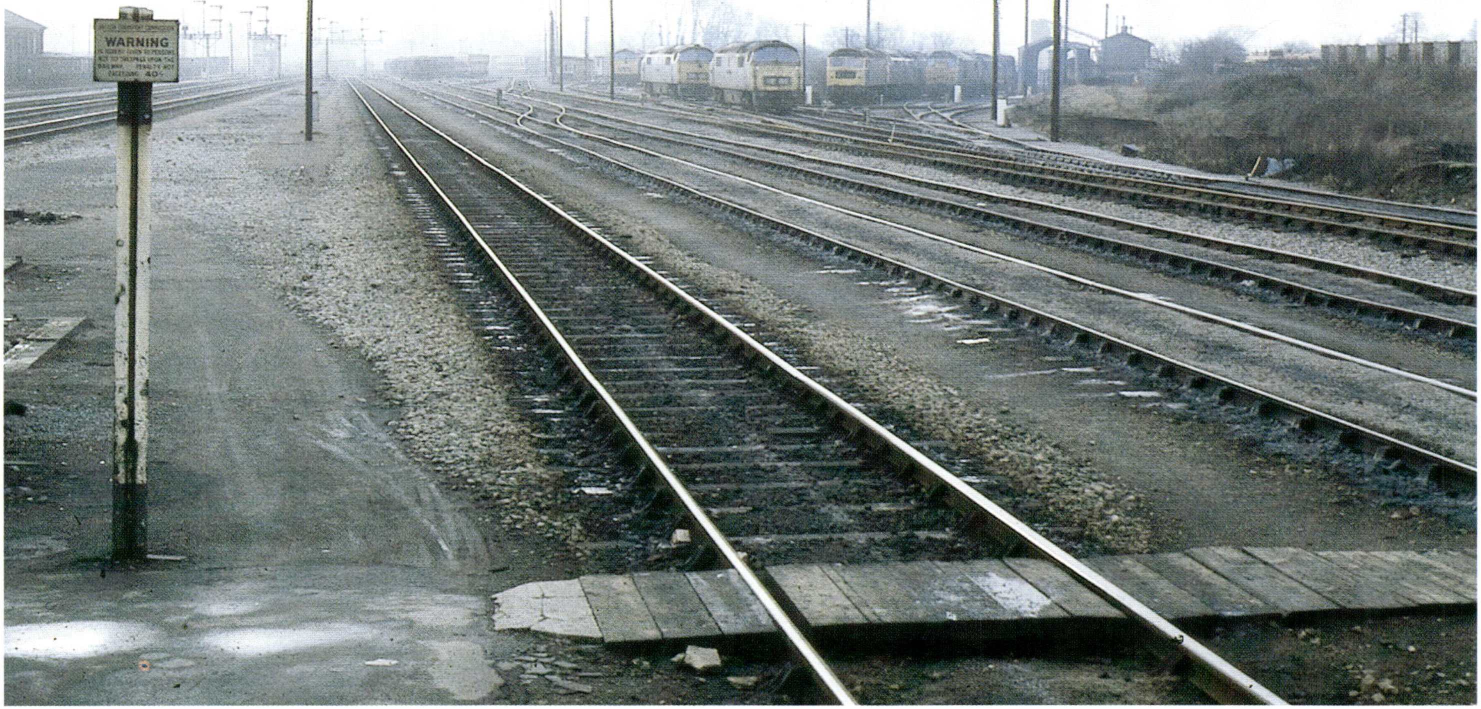

Opposite: in early 1976, D1040 *Western Queen* is stabled at Westbury depot, having been towed there by 46 028. Above: the steam era locoshed had been on the down side of the layout, accessible only via Westbury South; dieselisation brought the up side depot into use, the entrance to which was controlled from Westbury North box. Refuelling and light maintenance tasks were undertaken there. The writing on the wall came for the depot with the introduction of the class 59 locomotives in the mid-eighties, which have always been privately maintained at Merehead, working direct to the destination. At the time of the Westerns withdrawal, the quarries at Whatley and Merehead were reliant on a pool of locomotives for trip workings from the quarries to Westbury, as well as the ongoing diagrams to the various stone terminals at places such as Botley, Fareham, Brentford, Theale, Worcester, Wootton Bassett, Allington, Ardingly, Padworth, Acton, Bletchley, West Drayton, Thorney Mill, Basingstoke, Ipswich, Luton, Banbury,Northampton, Gloucester, Totton and Woking. The traincrews for the local trips were also based at Westbury and manned the diagrams to stone terminals throughout the south of England as well as some passenger turns of duty. This view shows the shed after D1040 *Western Queen* was stabled, with three other Westerns and sundry 47s and 31s on shed.

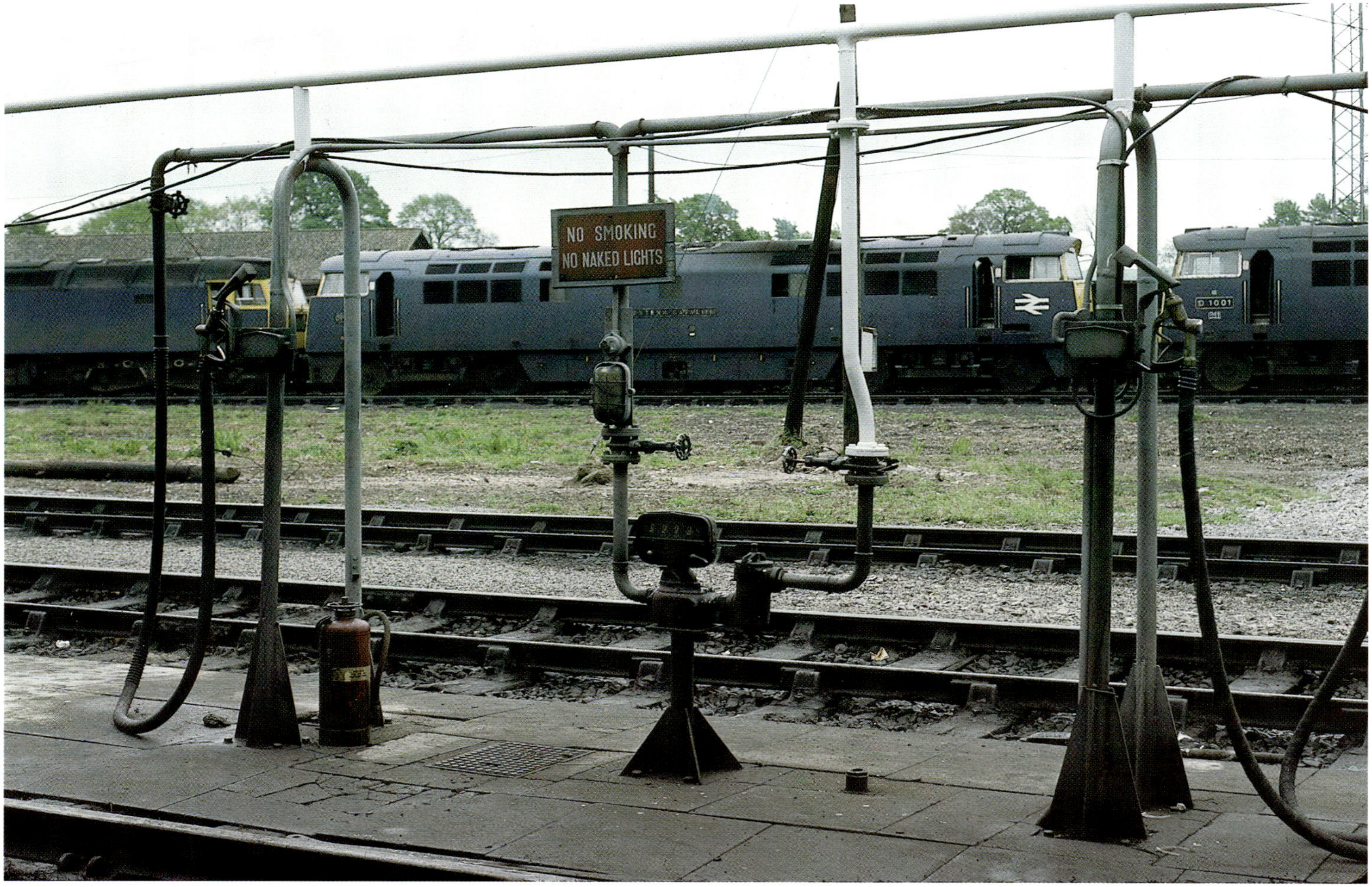

Fed up with tantalising glimpses from Westbury platform, and empty promises of a depot visit from a locoman, we threw caution to the winds one day, ignored the 'No Trainspotters Allowed' sign, and entered the depot with our cameras. We weren't thrown out, and came away with these photographs. Above: framed by the diesel pumps, D1021 *Western Cavalier,* D1001 *Western Pathfinder* and an unidentified 47. Opposite: just outside the depot building, D1013 *Western Ranger,* amidst the oil drums and brake blocks.

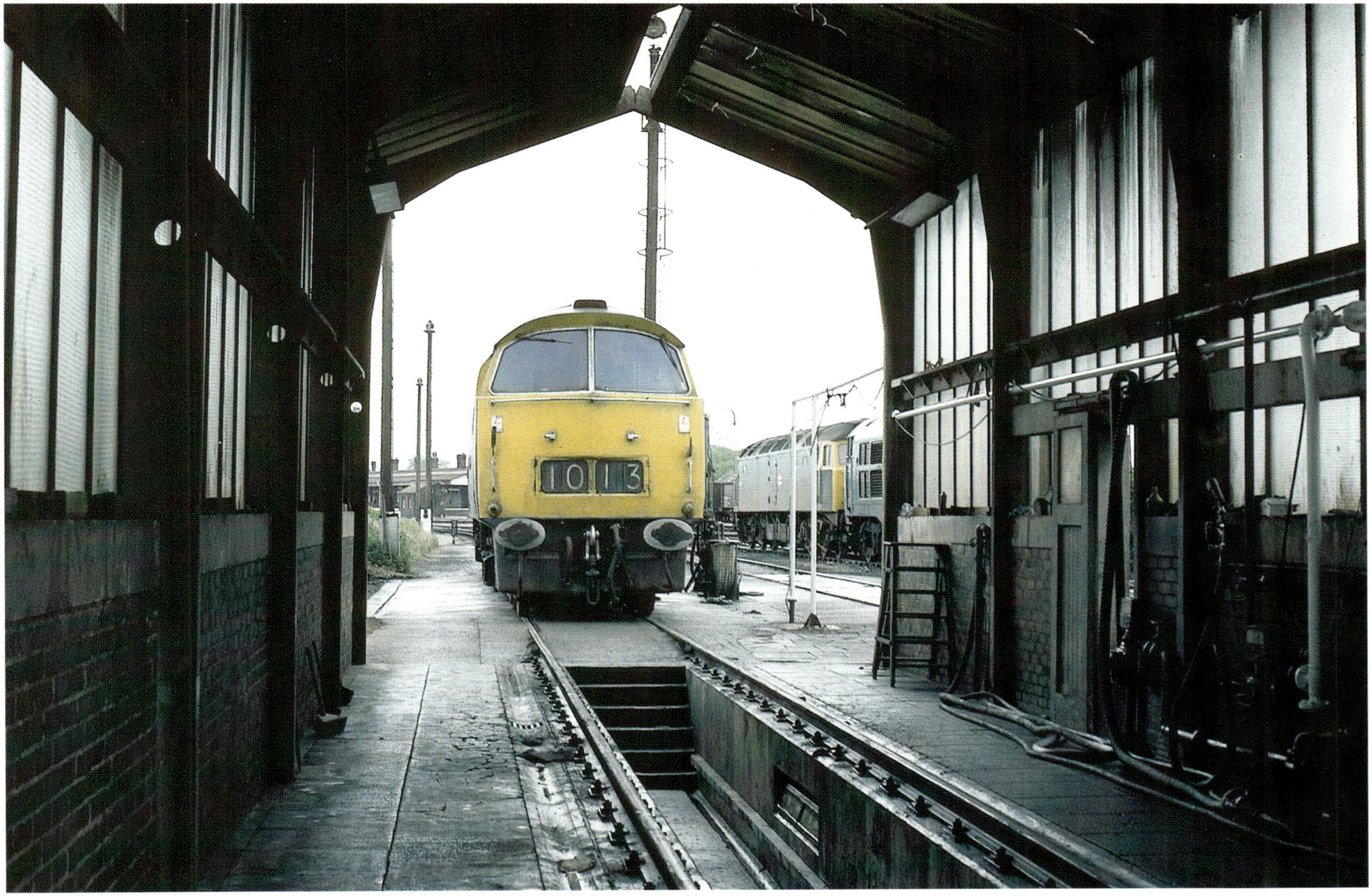
1013

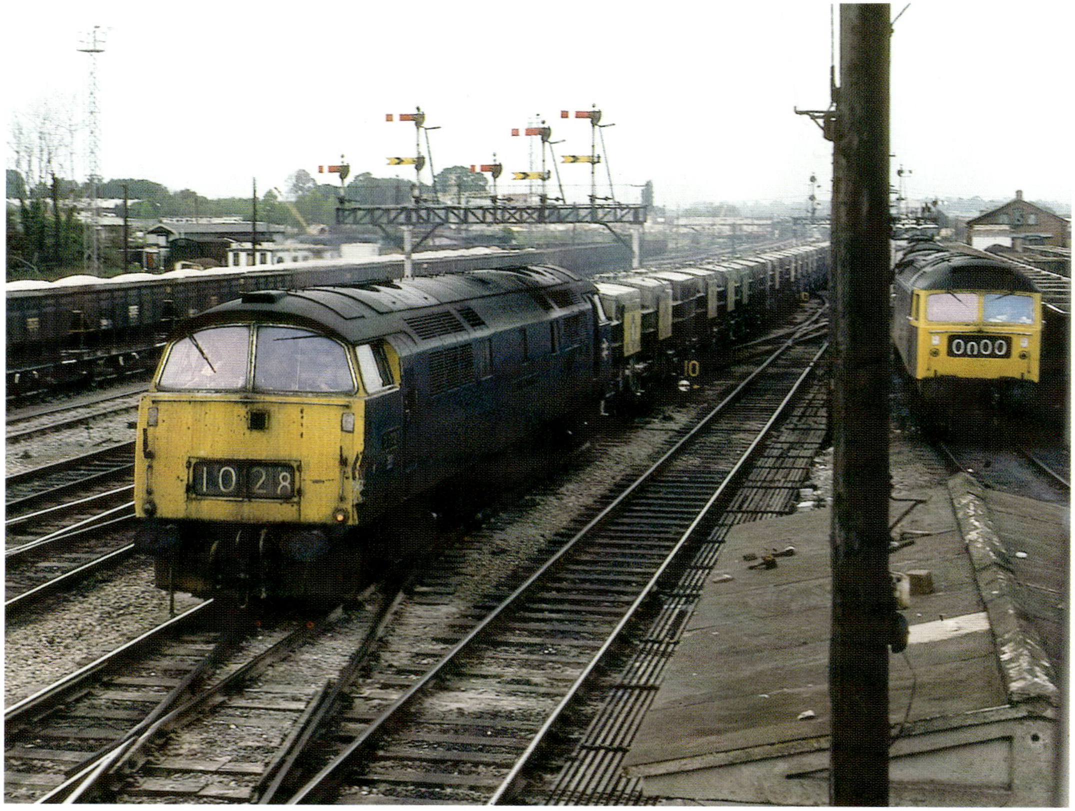

With the 'back board' off, signalling a clear run through Fairwood Junction, D1028 *Western Hussar* powers away from Westbury South hauling the 19.07 cement for Exeter Central on 17th June 1976. We rarely saw the return working - it arrived back at Westbury at 01.36 the following morning! Having taken all day to get to Westbury, a class 47 waits in the down reception with the 03.20 Carlisle to Eastleigh freight, timetabled to leave 19.10. The busy scene with loaded stone wagons in the up yard and empties on the down side was typical of the intensive use of the layout at Westbury in the mid nineteen-seventies.

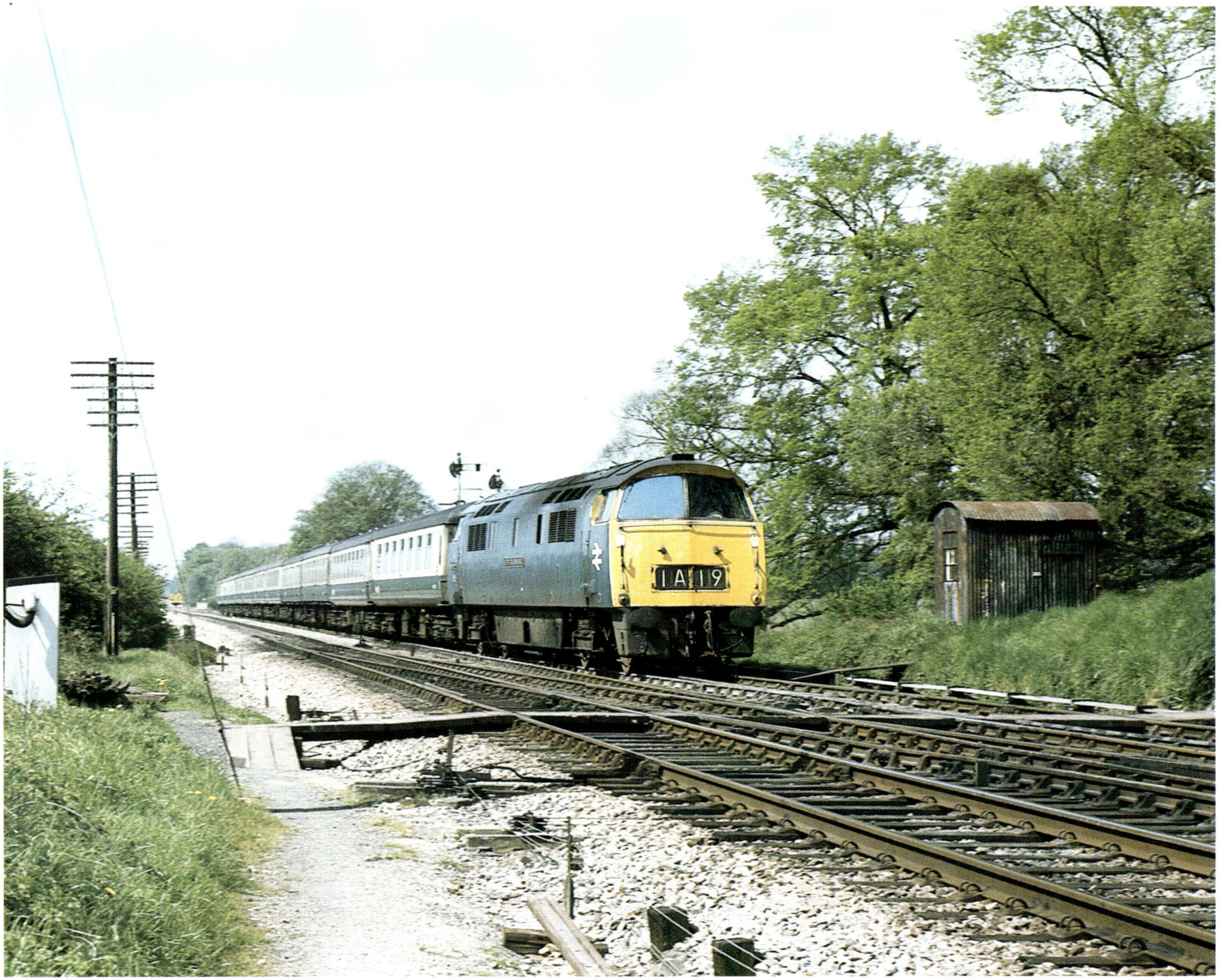

On Sunday, 11th May 1975 D1022 *Western Sentinel* turns into Westbury at Fairwood Junction with the 08.30 Plymouth to Paddington.

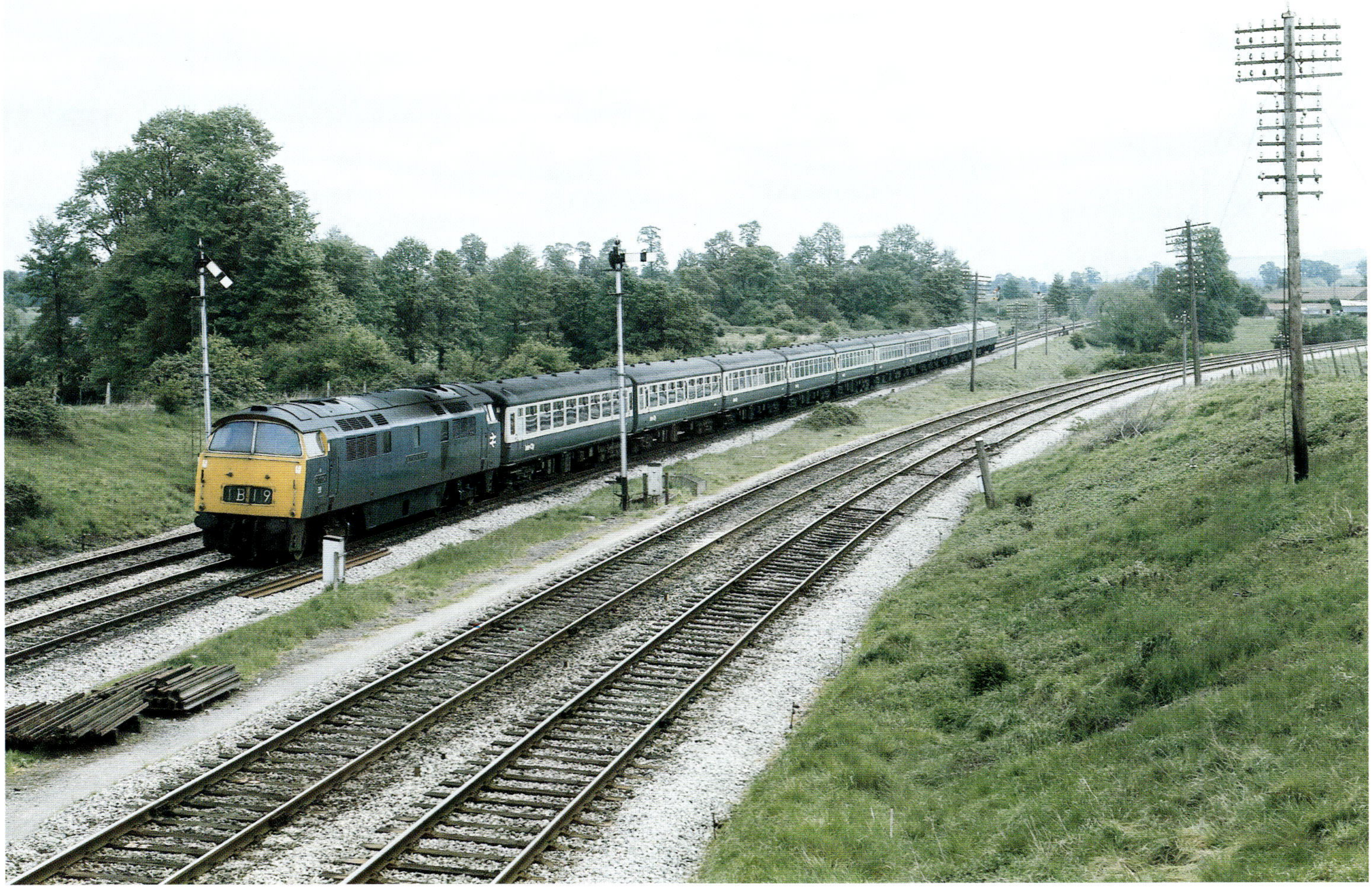

D1064 *Western Regent* passes Fairwood Junction's down main inner home signal with the 10.45 Paddington to Plymouth on Sunday, 11th May 1975. My father's transparency notes record the time as 12.26, making it five minutes early at Fairwood. This train ran non-stop through Westbury that year as the signalboxes at each end of the avoiding line were switched out of circuit on Sundays.

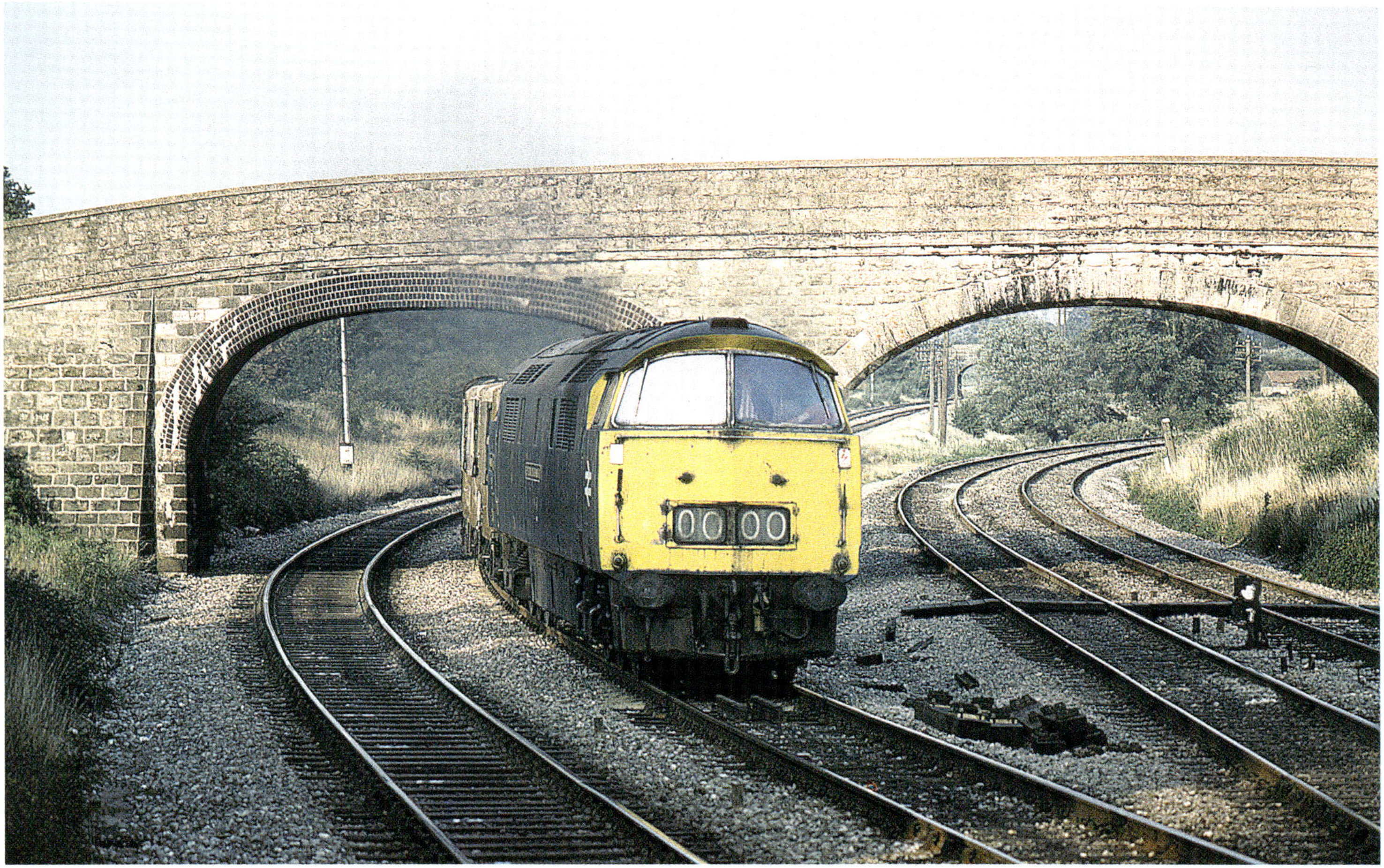

D1022 *Western Sentinel* has a spare traincrew in the leading cab in this shot at Fairwood Junction in the summer of 1976. When the avoiding line was built, the main line into Westbury was diverted under the new arch of the bridge, leaving the original arch for the fast 'avoider' to Heywood Road Junction. The foot crossing to the right of the picture was part of the official walking route to the signalbox, used by the signalmen who had motorbikes as well as those who cycled and walked. All was fine until one evening when the red light of Dave Richards' Honda was mistaken for a handsignal by an up train approaching the junction, seeing the signalbox in darkness and a wavering red light a hundred yards further on, getting smaller and smaller......

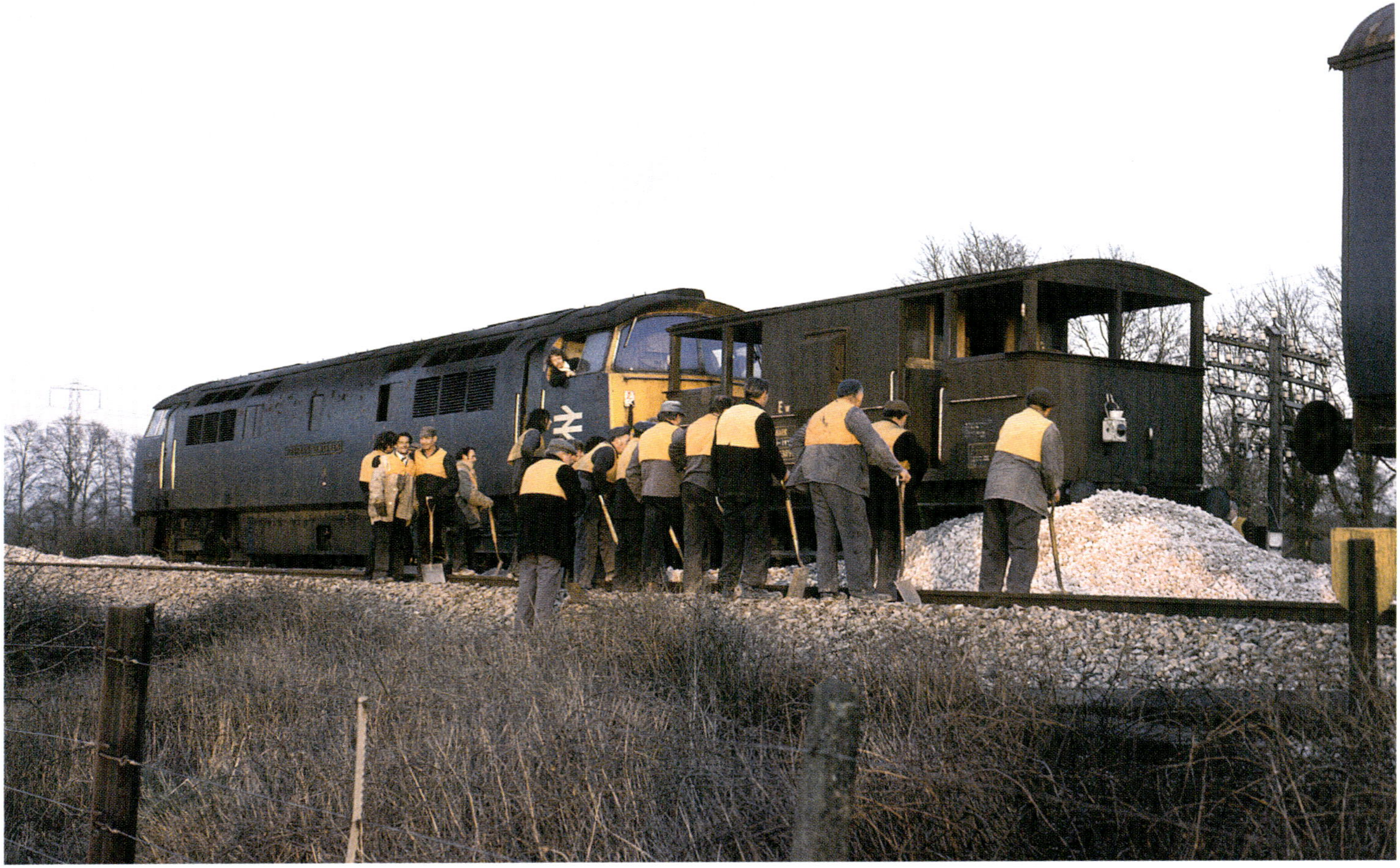

In the early months of 1976, we learnt of a weekend derailment at Berkley, near Clink Road's down distant signal. By the time we arrived, the crane had been used for rerailing and D1005 *Western Venturer* was ballast ploughing with a plough van. The Westbury track gang were out in force, but their supervisor, 'Mac', still had time to ham it up for the camera before all was back to normal for Monday's timetable.

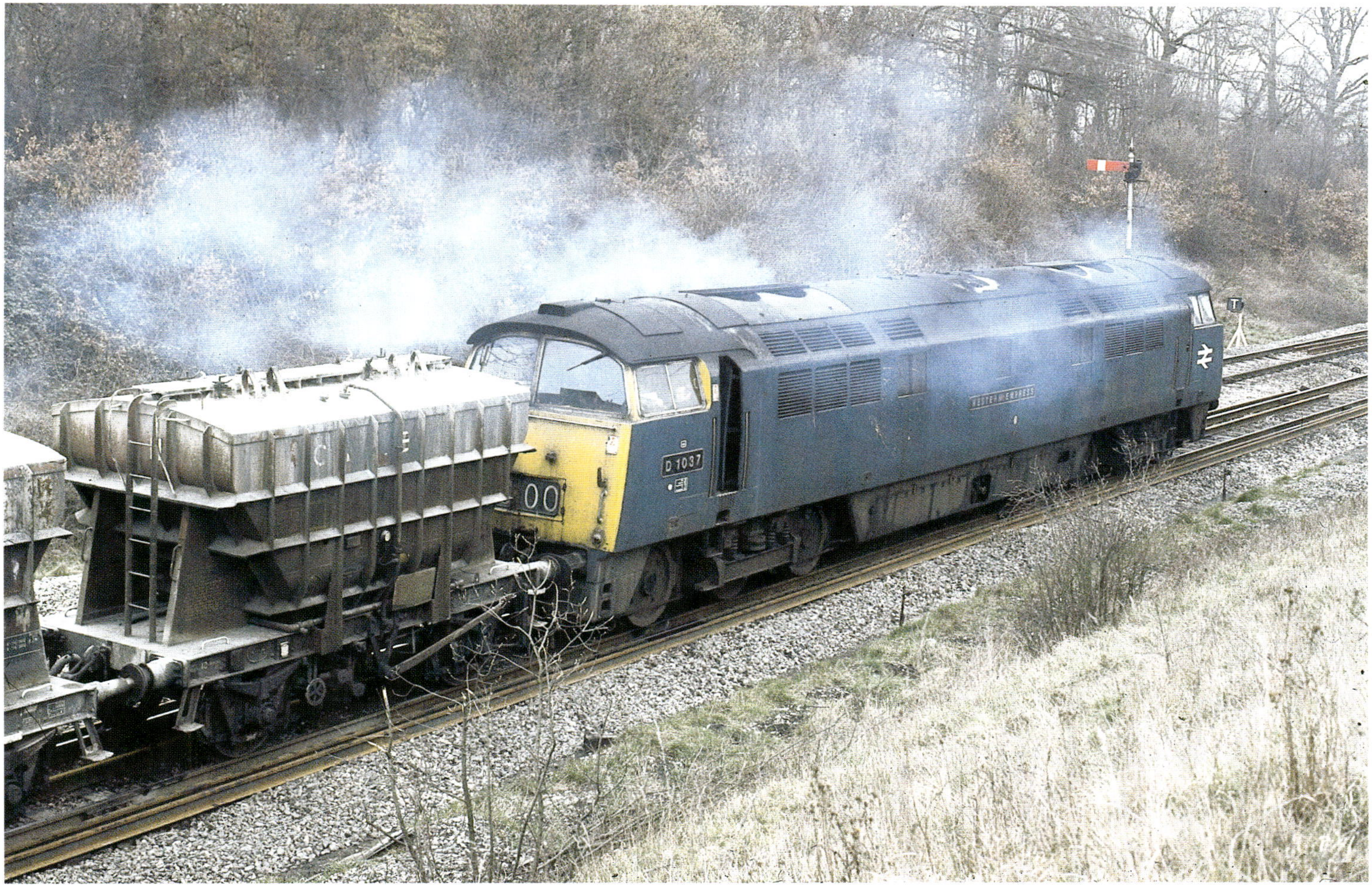

Smoke billows out from both Maybachs as D1037 *Western Empress* waits at Clink Road on a Sunday occupation early in 1976, the driver engrossed in the paper. Although this was a Permanent Way working, the cement wagons provided some brake force for the otherwise unfitted train. The rest of the consist included 'Mermaid' wagons, loaded with stone dust and ballast for the blanketing and reballasting of the up main, which was being relaid in advance of Clink Road Junction. There were also low-loaders for the diggers being used and a sleeping and messing van for the plant operators.

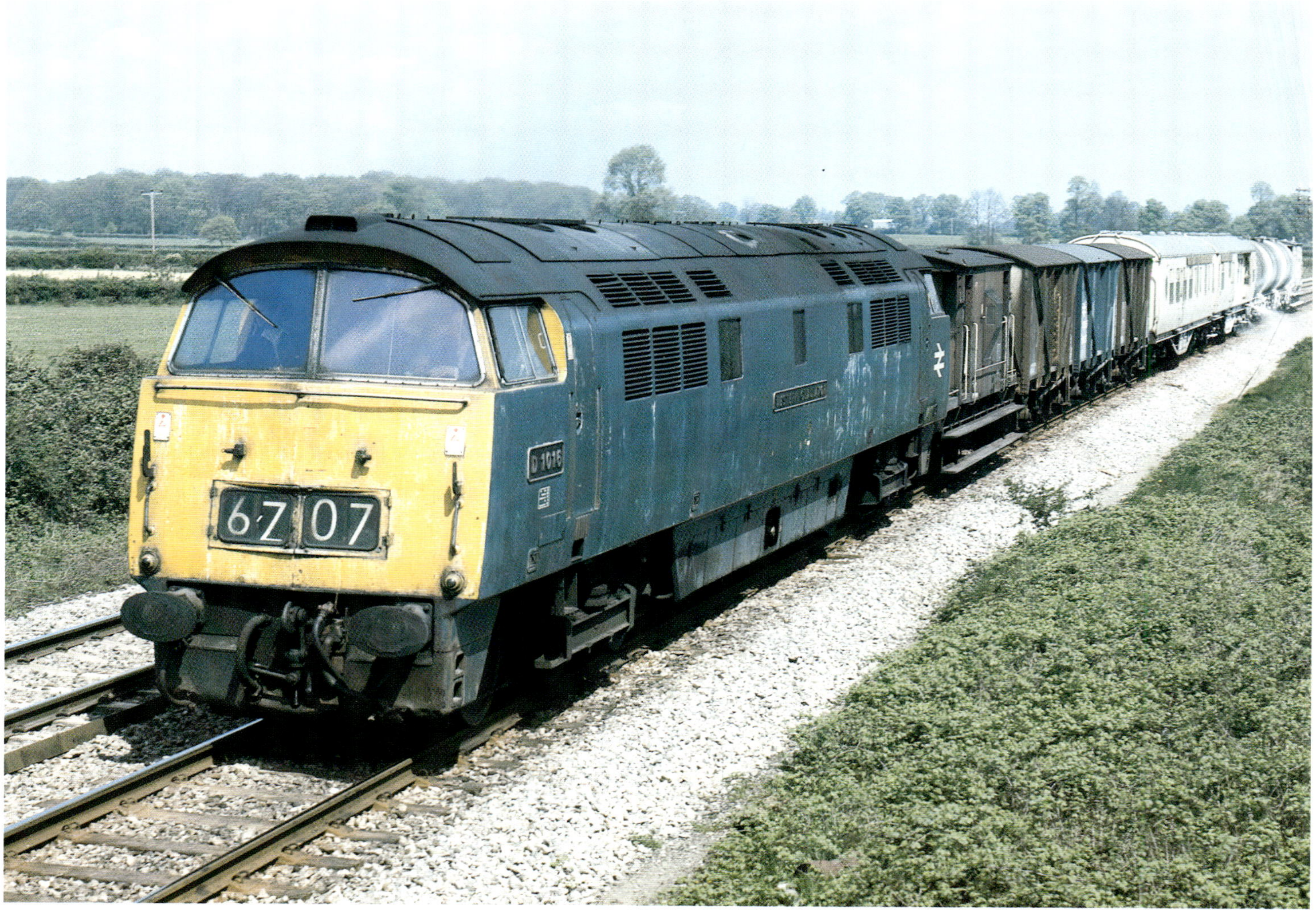

In less environmentally aware times, D1016 *Western Gladiator* heads Chipmans weedkiller train at Berkley, between Westbury and Frome. There was plenty of capacity in the timetable for this special working on Saturday, 26th April 1975, with just over another week to go before the summer service started.

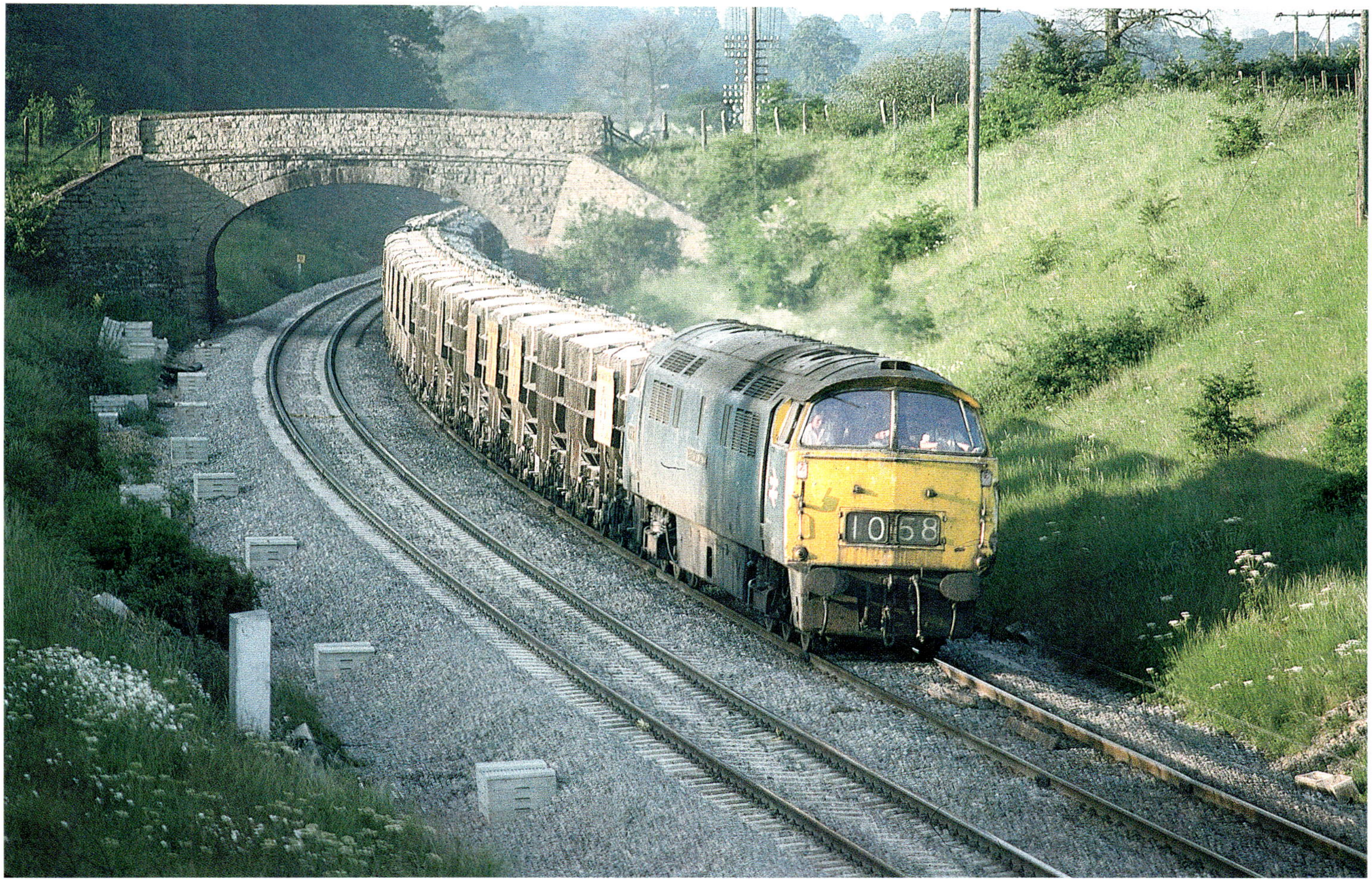

On Monday, 7th June 1976, D1058 *Western Nobleman* passes between the two bridges at Clink Road Junction, both built by the Wiltshire, Somerset & Weymouth Railway in 1850. The bridge from which this photograph was taken was a haven for Frome trainspotters, who saw a fair variety of traffic including the workings to and from both Whatley and Merehead quarries rattle through the junction. *Nobleman* is approaching with the 19.07 Westbury, a favourite train of ours as it was usually Western hauled in 1976, often the first 'Thousand' we saw having driven out after tea-time with our cameras. *Nobleman* had been on a Merehead trip that afternoon before working the cement and returned to Westbury to cover the same diagrams the next day.

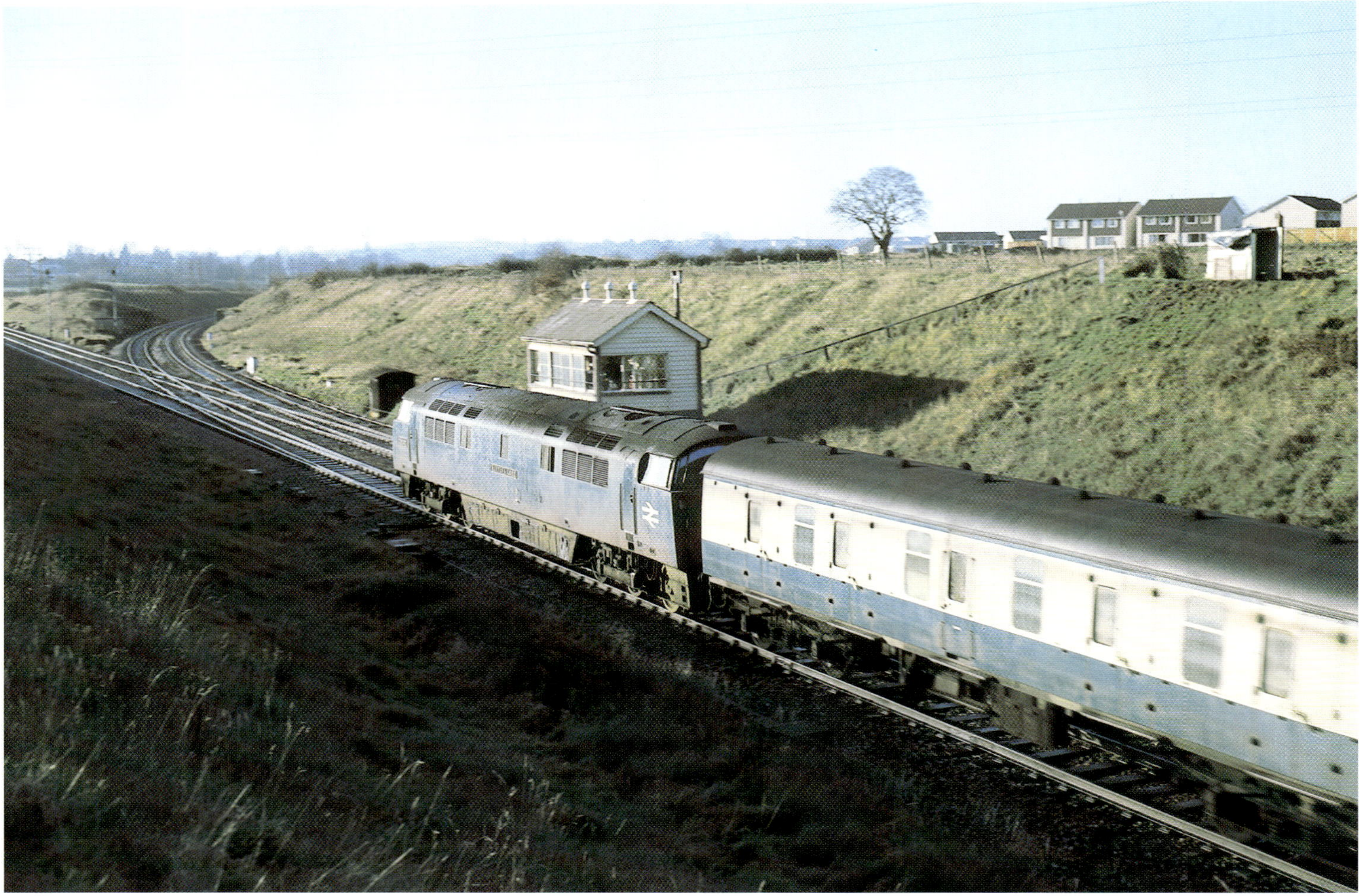

D1047 *Western Lord* passes Clink Road Junction with a down fast on a bright winter's morning late in 1975. The tiny shed at the top of the cutting was homemade for the on duty signalman's motorbike, as it was inadvisable to drive down the steep pathway to rail level. The signalman, having stoked up his fire at six that morning, is hot enough to let the windows open for a spot of fresh air as the Western takes the Frome 'avoider', the main lines into Frome curving away in the cutting to the right.

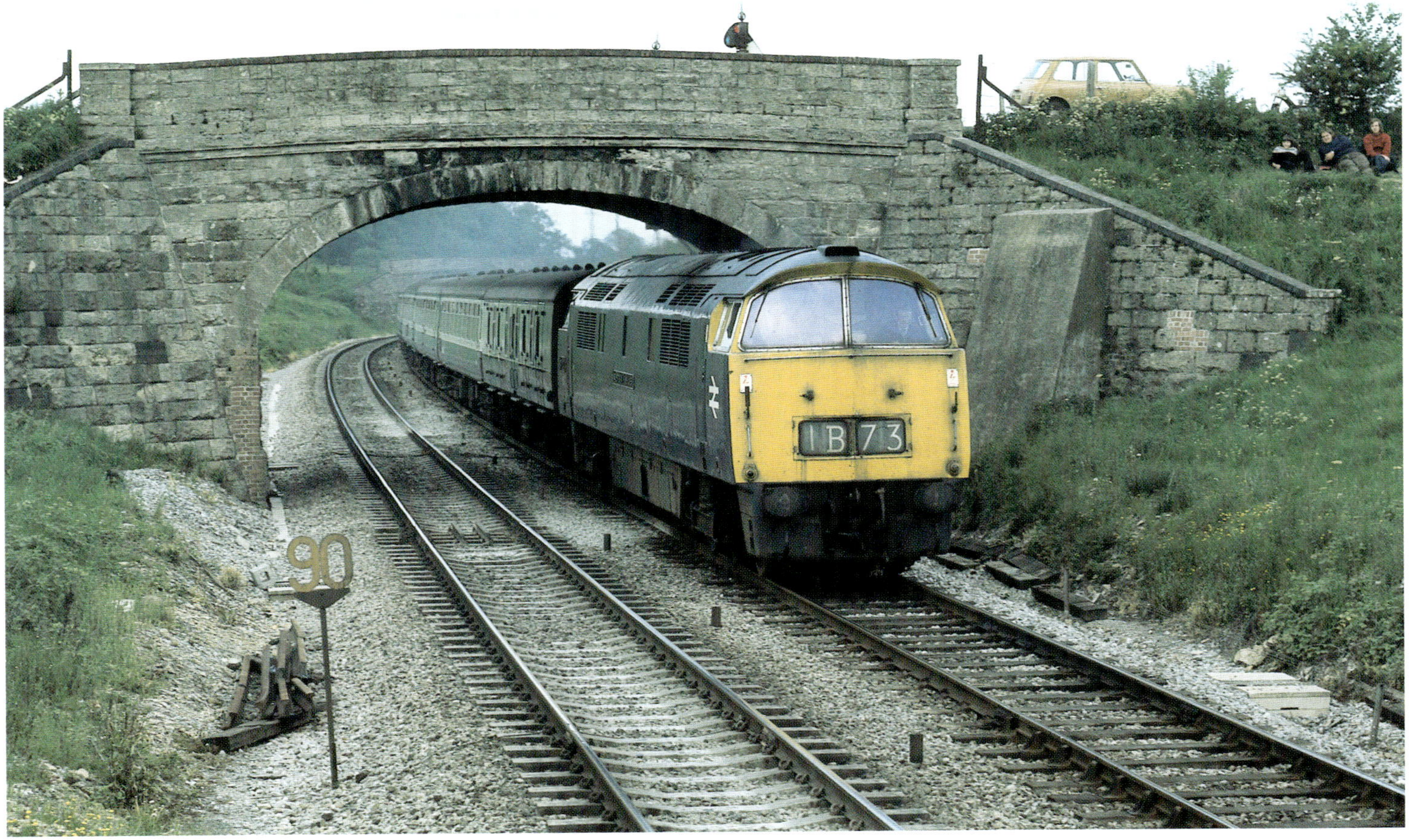

D1023 *Western Fusilier* roars under Clink Road overbridge, en route to Paignton with the 14.30 from Paddington on Saturday, 17th May 1975. This was the view of approaching trains from the signalbox, built during construction of the Frome cut-off line in 1933. Although the box was in a cutting, visibility was reasonable. With the trainspotters having a picnic and the block bells ringing out through the open windows of the box, it was a very pleasant place to spend a summer Saturday afternoon.

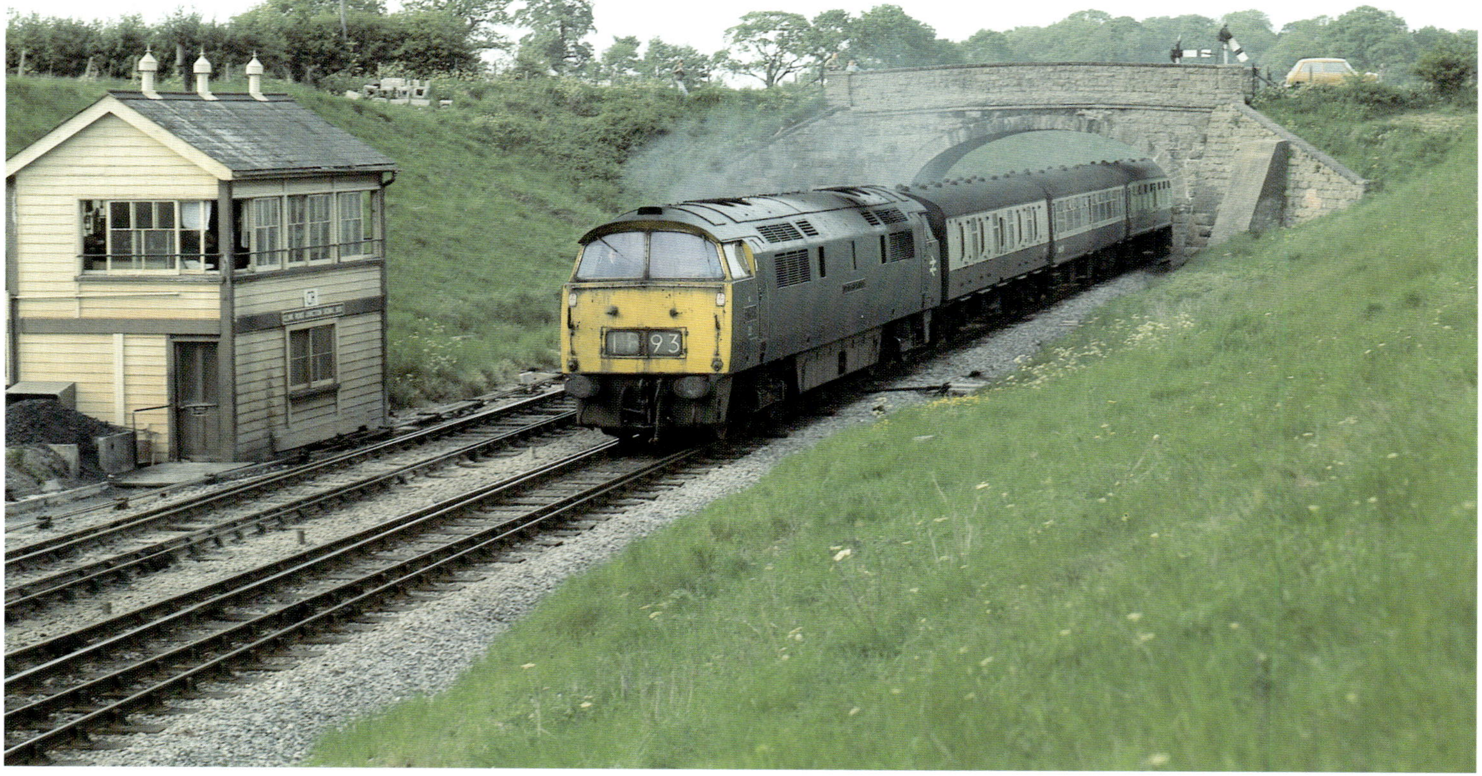

D1041 *Western Prince* hauls the 16.30 Paddington to Paignton past Clink Road Junction on a summer's evening in June 1975. The signalbox was very prone to shaking in the bow wave of air as up trains shot by on their way to Paddington. Tea stains can be seen on the front of the box where the signalmen habitually emptied out their teapot - occasionally on the head of an unsuspecting track patrolman!

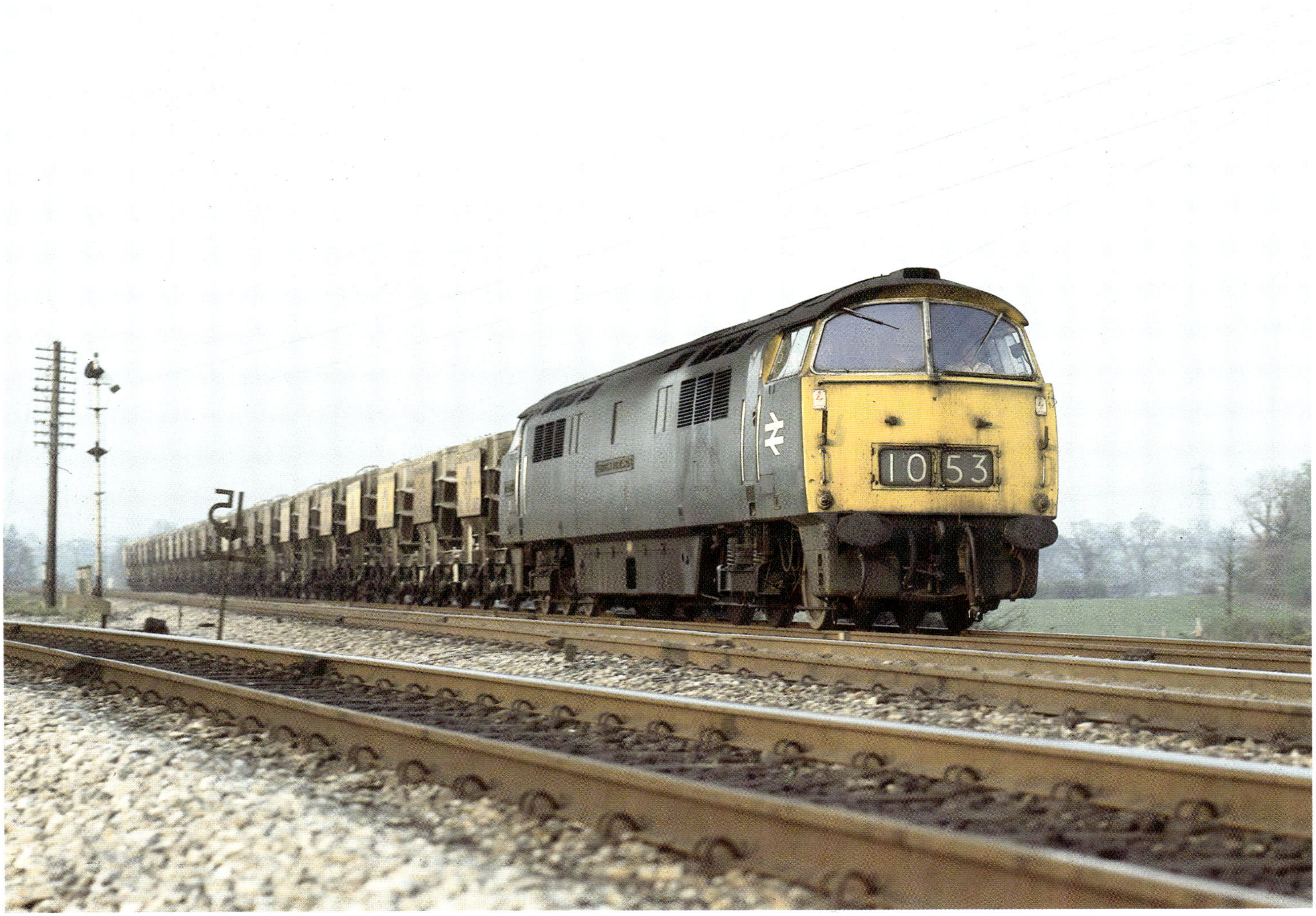

On Wednesday 19th May 1976, D1053 *Western Patriarch* comes off the Frome 'avoider' at Blatchbridge Junction with the presflos of the 19.07 Westbury to Exeter. It was commonplace for the cement to leave Westbury before time, and on this particular evening it passed Westbury South seventeen minutes early. Consequently it was checked behind the 17.30 Paddington to Penzance '*Golden Hind*' at Fairwood Junction as well as the 17.45 Bristol to Weymouth at both Clink Road and Blatchbridge Junctions, finally leaving Blatchbridge six minutes early at 19.16. Class 52s were permitted a gross weight of 1200 tons on this working, 80 tons greater than the allowance for a class 47.

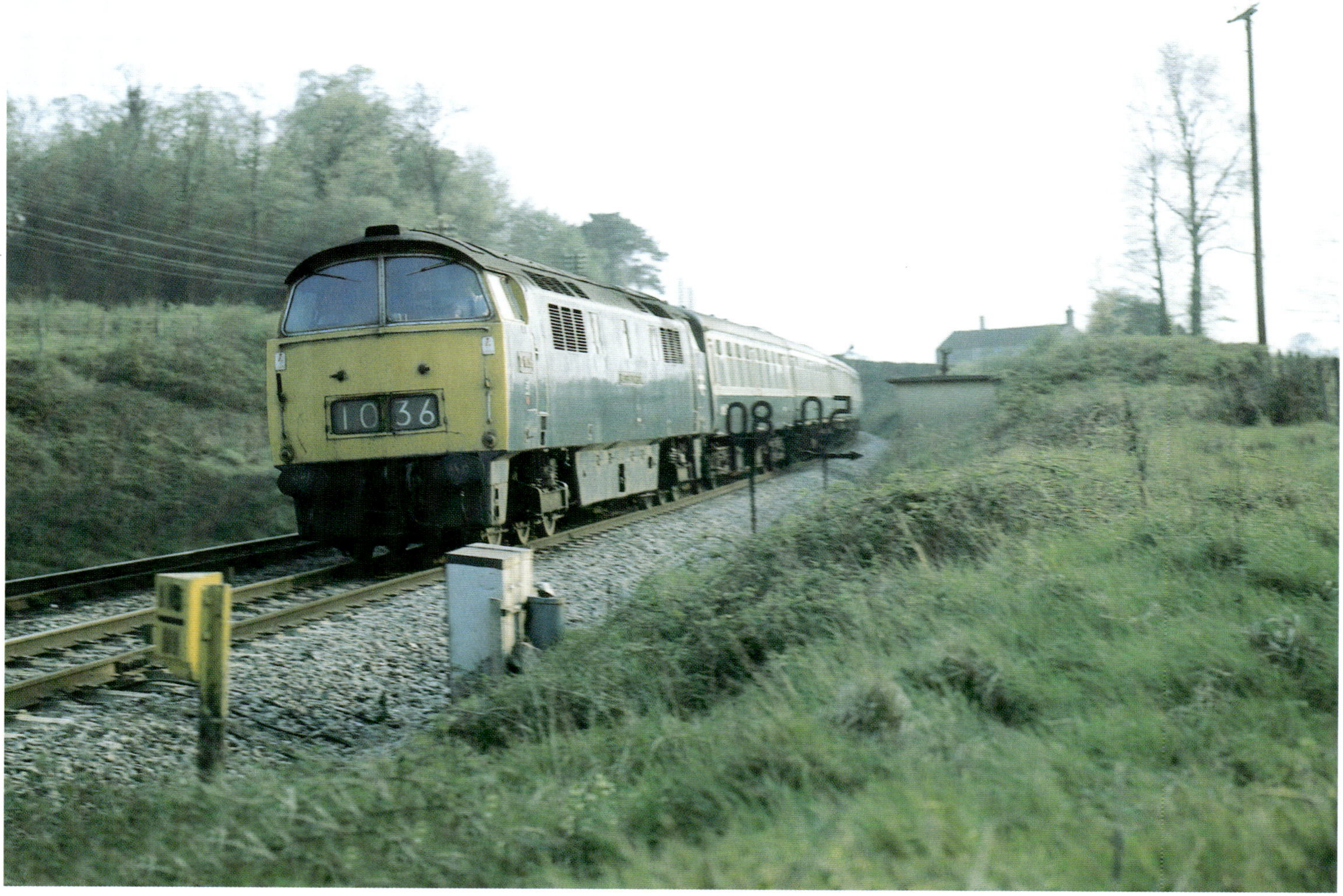

On Saturday, 8th May 1976, D1036 *Western Emperor* approaches Blatchbridge Junction with the 14.30 Penzance to Paddington. *Emperor* was the only Western to have the numberplates higher than the nameplates, easily recognisable as a consequence but one wonders whether they had a little trouble reading the plans when they fitted them at Crewe. Also that evening we saw D1054 *Western Governor* on the late running 15.30 Paddington and D1056 *Western Sultan* on the 15.55 Paignton. Had we been there that afternoon we would also have seen D1015 *Western Champion* on the Saturdays only 13.20 Weymouth to Birmingham. The down starting signal, just identifiable above the rear of the train, was lowered for the *Golden Hind* which was invariably hauled by a class 50 - it was 50 021 on this particular evening.

This photograph shows a shovelful of coal in mid-air, whilst Tony Page looks out from the window of Blatchbridge Junction signalbox. He was still in the first hour of his 13.20 to 22.00 late turn shift on Saturday, 29th November 1975. The traincrew are busy with their newspapers and the locomotive has been stopped on the main-to-main crossover with its engines shut down.

After the 12.15 Weymouth had cleared the single line section to Frome North, the coal movement was signalled as a 'freight train requiring to stop in section', leaving Frome at 13.47. Five minutes later, D1023 *Western Fusilier* arrived hauling a single coal wagon. Gerald Quartley, then station clerk at Frome, shovelled the coal from the wagon into the signalbox bunker. He had plenty of time to finish his work as the next train wasn't timetabled for over an hour. It was unusual to be able to photograph stationary trains at Blatchbridge and we took full advantage of the situation. The return working propelled the wagon into Frome, leaving Blatchbridge at 14.50, five minutes before Clink Road asked 'Is Line Clear?' for the 13.30 Paddington.

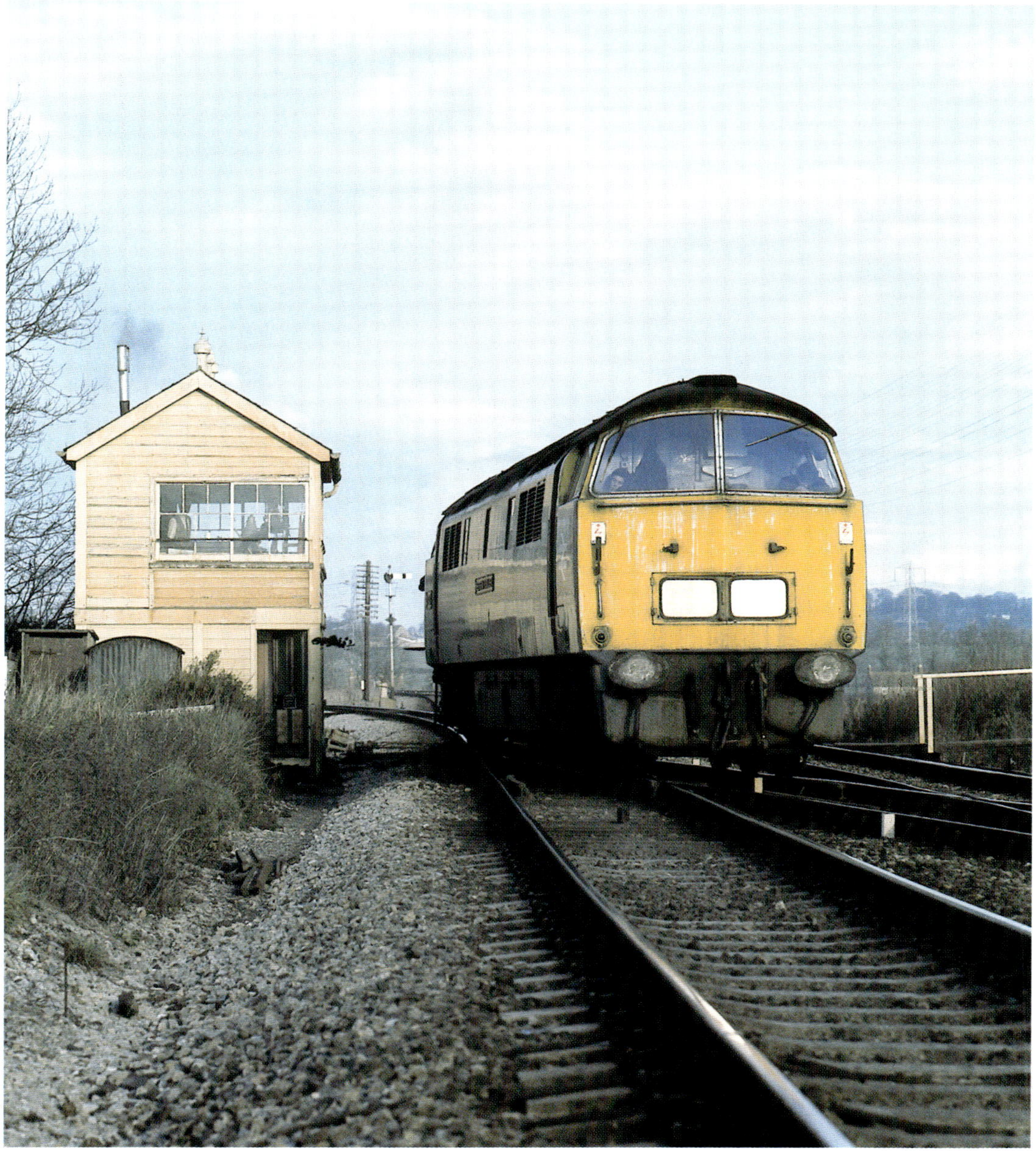

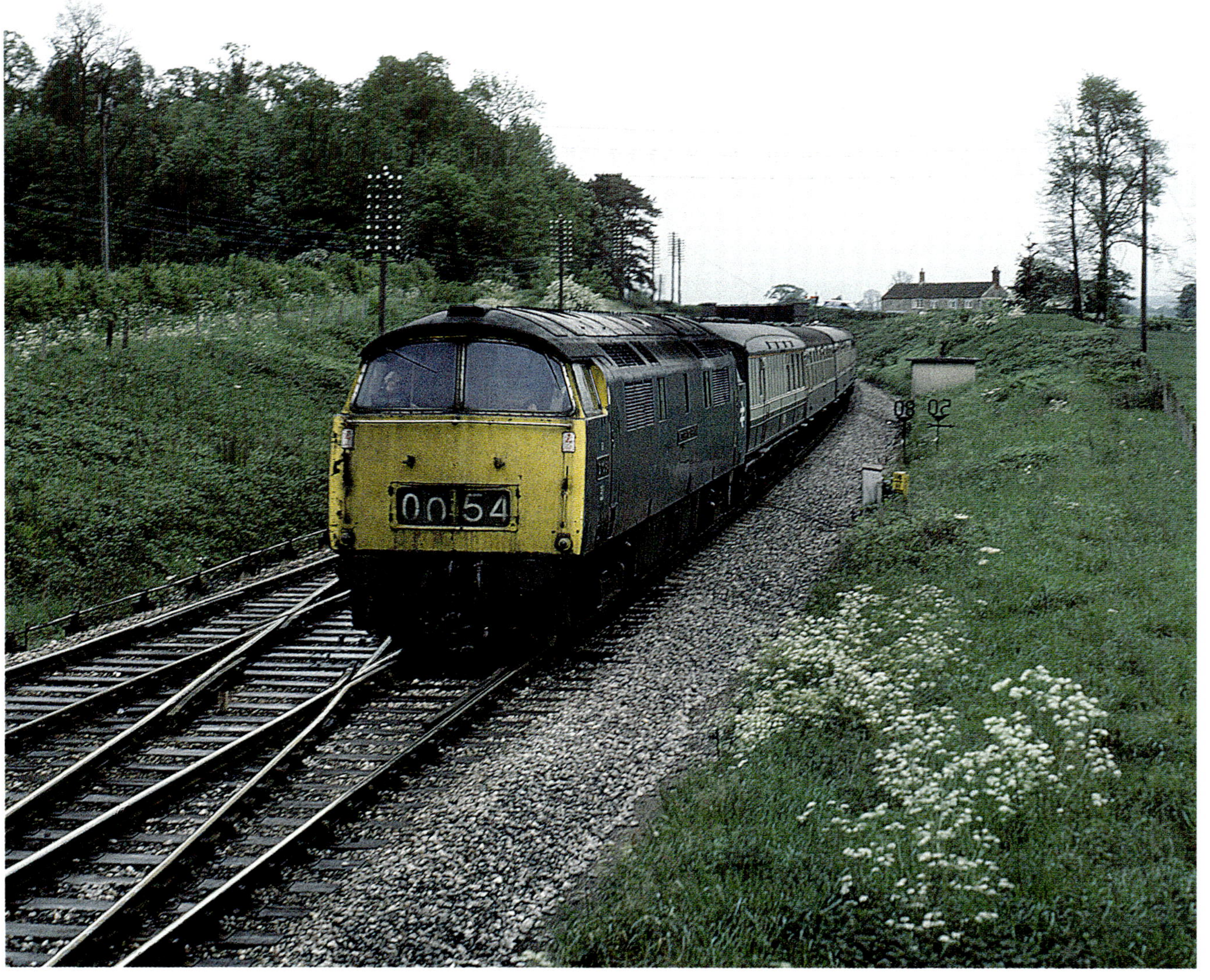

Viewed from the signalbox window at Blatchbridge Junction, D1054 *Western Governor* heads towards London in May 1976. Behind the engine is Gresley buffet car W9135E, then a regular sight on West of England expresses. Engine, coaches and signalbox are now all gone; the trees remain adjacent to the Frome by-pass, the route of which now runs parallel with the railway line all the way from Blatchbridge to Clink Road.

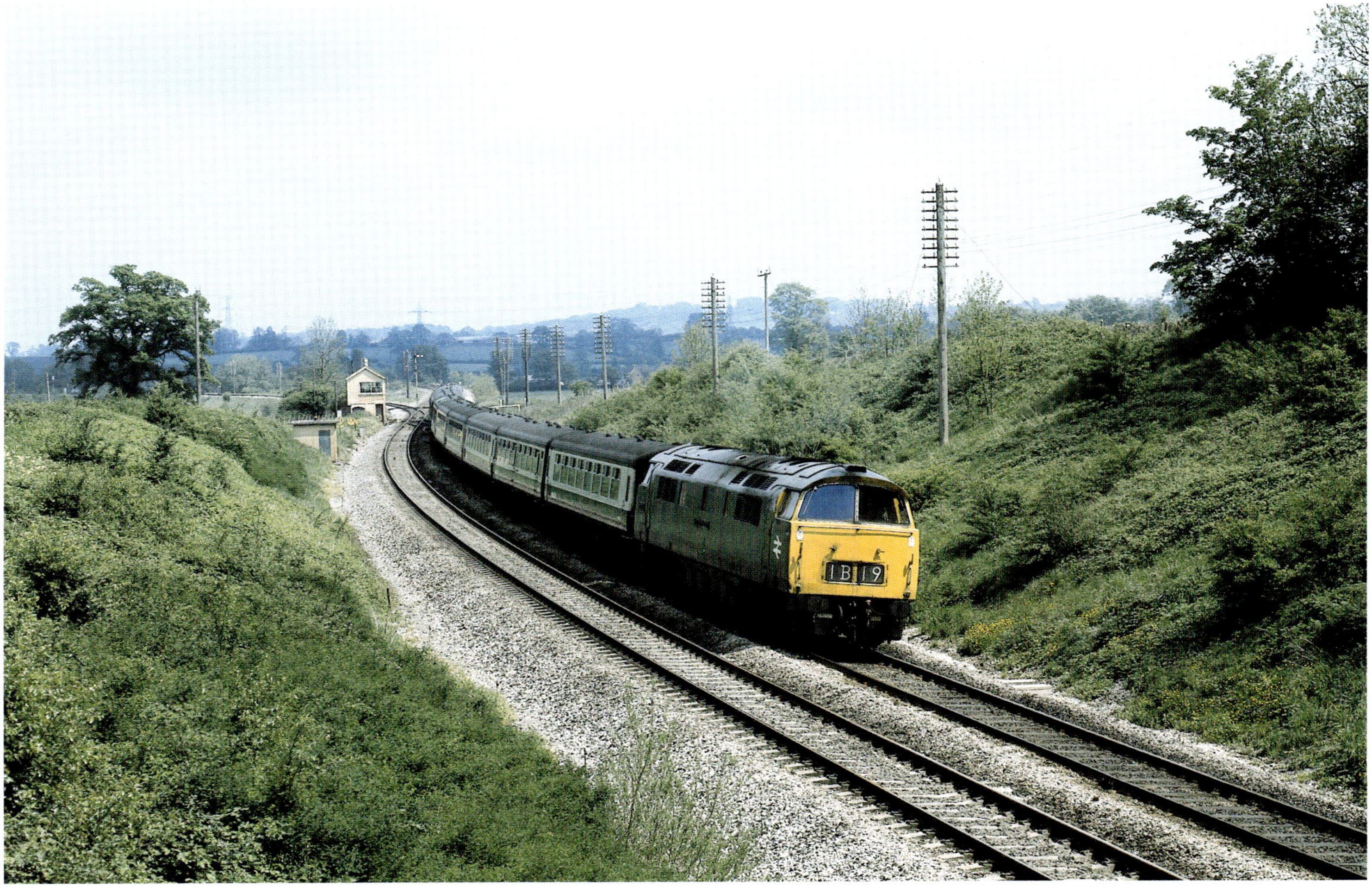

At Blatchbridge Junction on Whitsunday (18th May) 1975, D1048 *Western Lady* draws forward to the starting signal with the 10.45 Paddington to Plymouth. She was waiting for the road to Castle Cary behind the *Cornish Riviera*, which must have been running slightly late that day. On Sundays, the block section was normally from Blatchbridge to Castle Cary, which left little room for error with late running; the fourteen miles between boxes had a sectional running time of ten and a half minutes for Class 1 expresses.

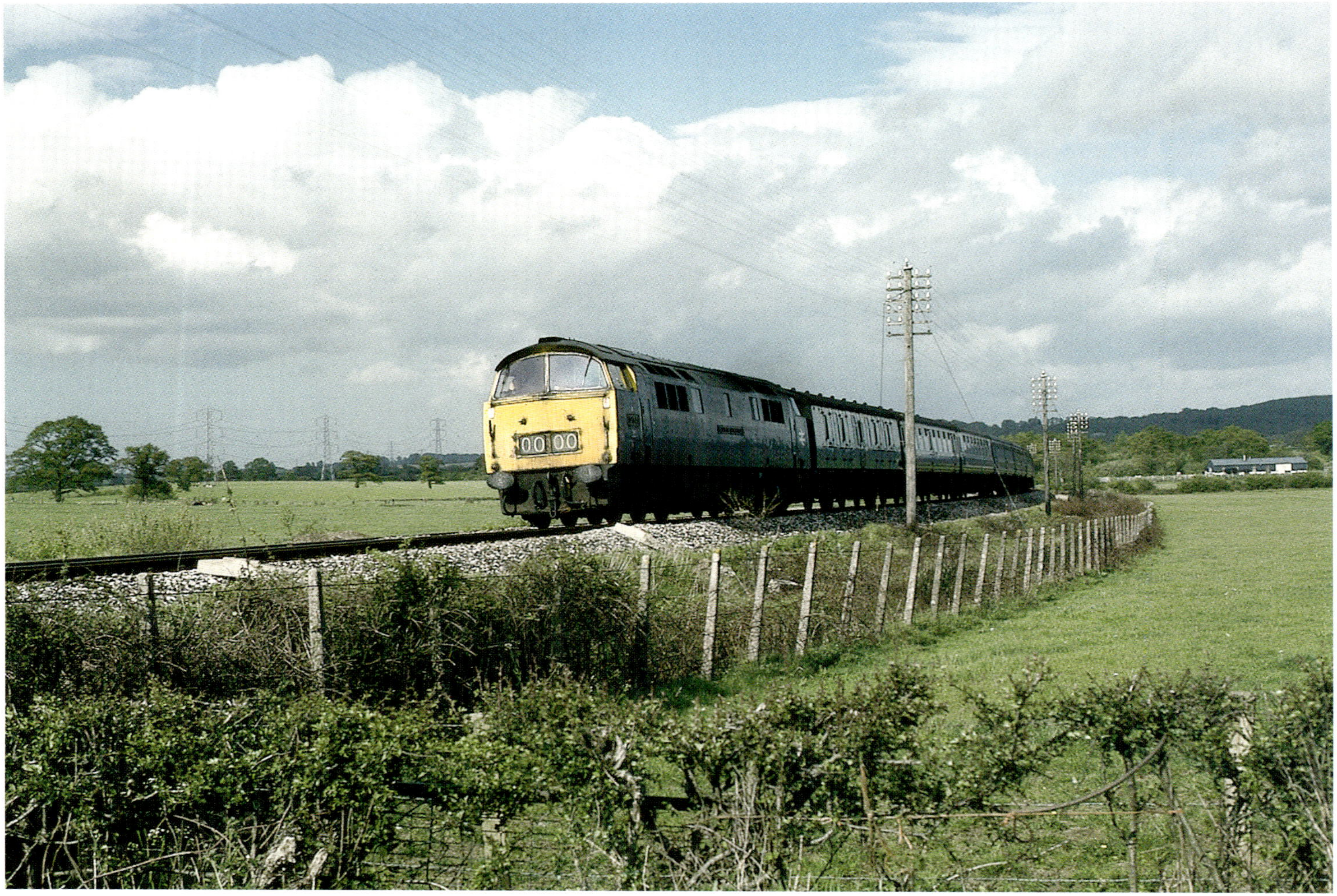

D1001 *Western Pathfinder* interrupted our Saturday tea-time picnic at Bunns Lane between Blatchbridge Junction and Witham, on 15th May 1976, whilst hauling the 15.30 Paddington to Penzance. It was well worth leaving the chocolate spread sandwiches to get this shot.

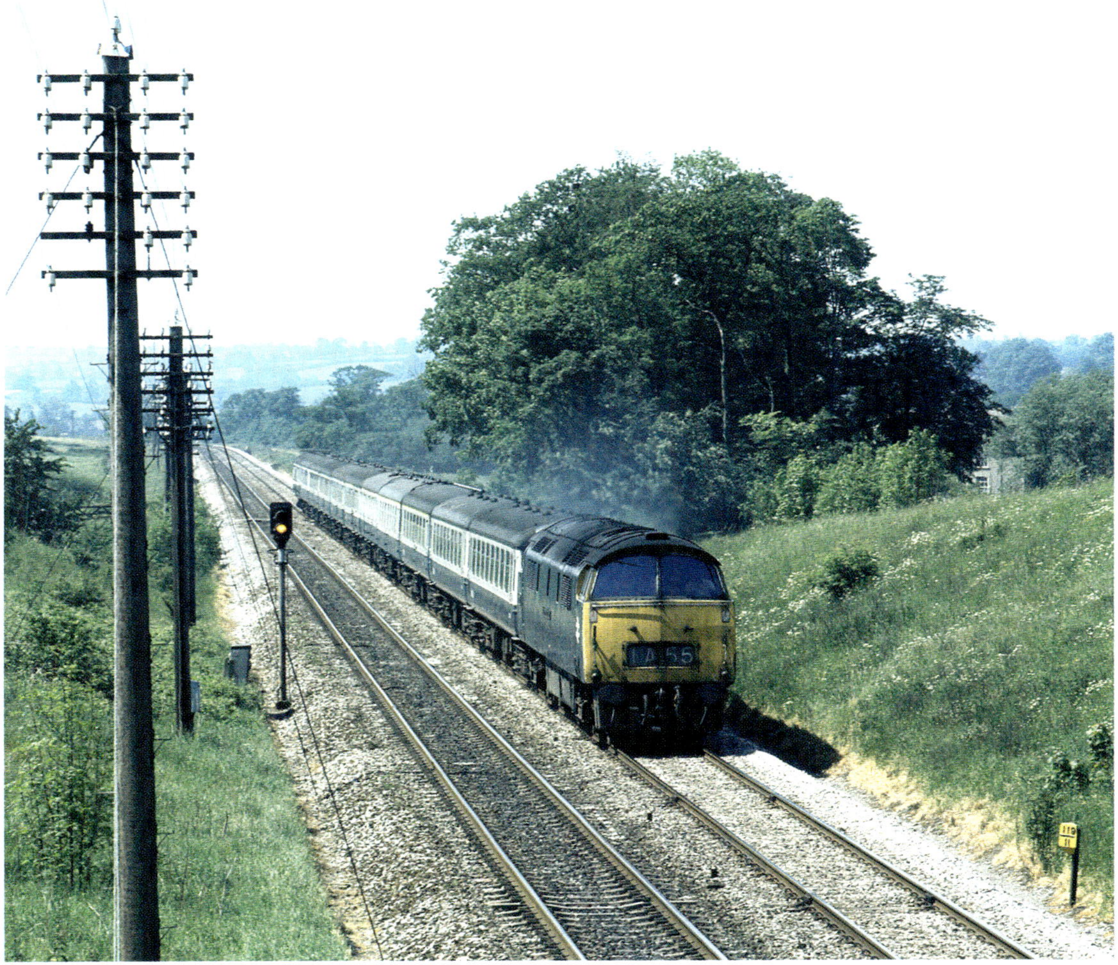

On a summer Saturday, this unidentified Western has already passed the fishponds at Witham, and approaches Bunns Lane overbridge with the 10.00 Paignton to Paddington. In 1975 it left Paignton five minutes later on Saturdays than on weekdays. The telegraph poles which were such a feature of the lineside from Westbury to Cogload were recovered in 1984 and the copper line wires sold for scrap, after the line was resignalled as part of the West of England resignalling scheme.

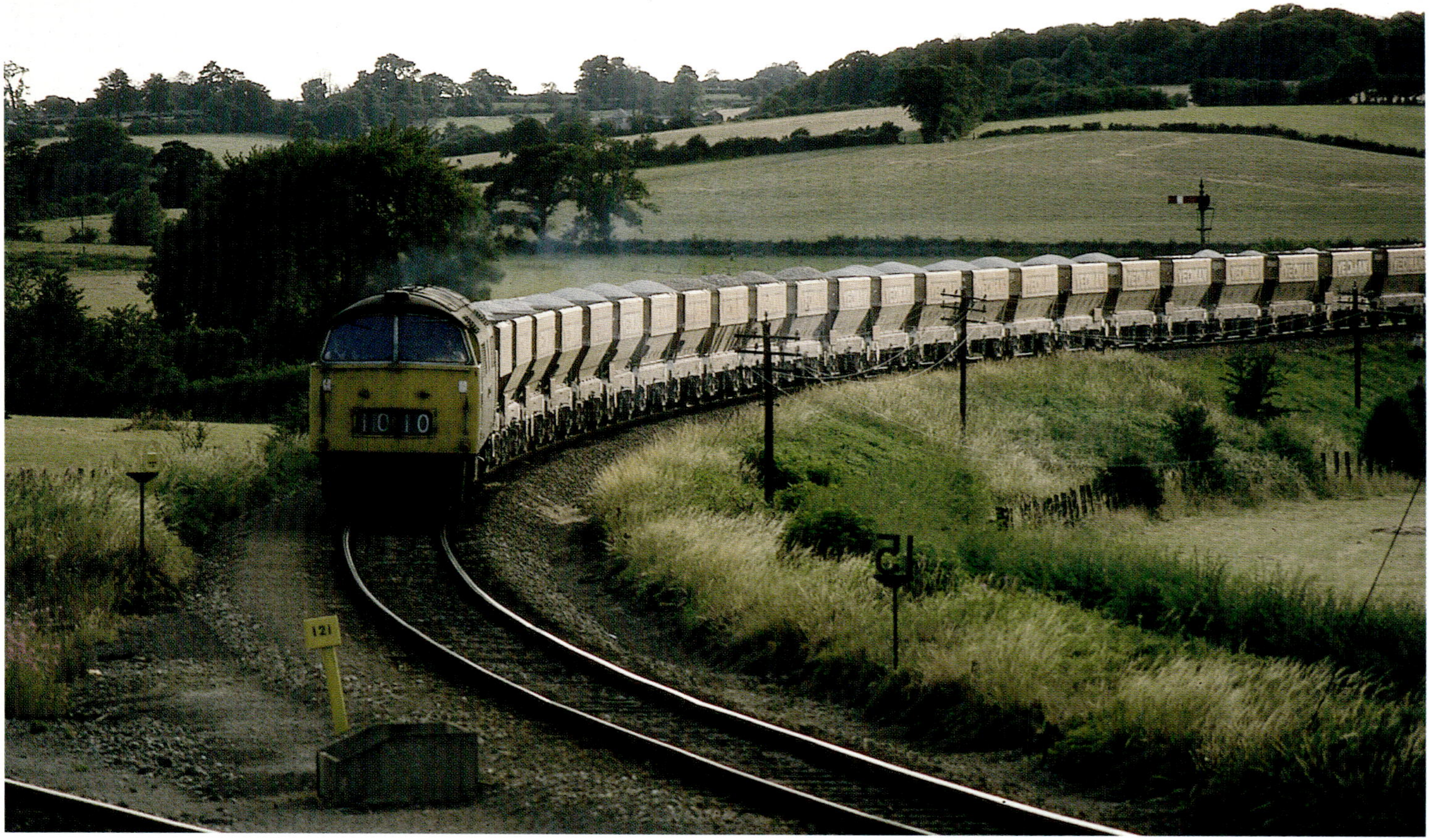

It is 27th July 1976 and the drought is beginning to show in the surrounding countryside. With brakes on and flanges squealing as the 1 in 49 gradient is descended, D1010 *Western Campaigner* approaches Witham with a train of fully laden Procor wagons on a trip working from Merehead Quarry to Westbury. Nearly at the end of the single line section from Merehead Quarry Junction, the secondman will soon be leaning out of the cab to surrender the single line token engraved 'WITHAM - MEREHEAD' to the Witham signalman. This trip would form the Wootton Bassett working from Westbury, leaving there at 04.30 the following morning. On Monday, 7th February 1977, *Campaigner* had the distinction of being the last Western ever to work a stone train from Merehead Quarry to Westbury.

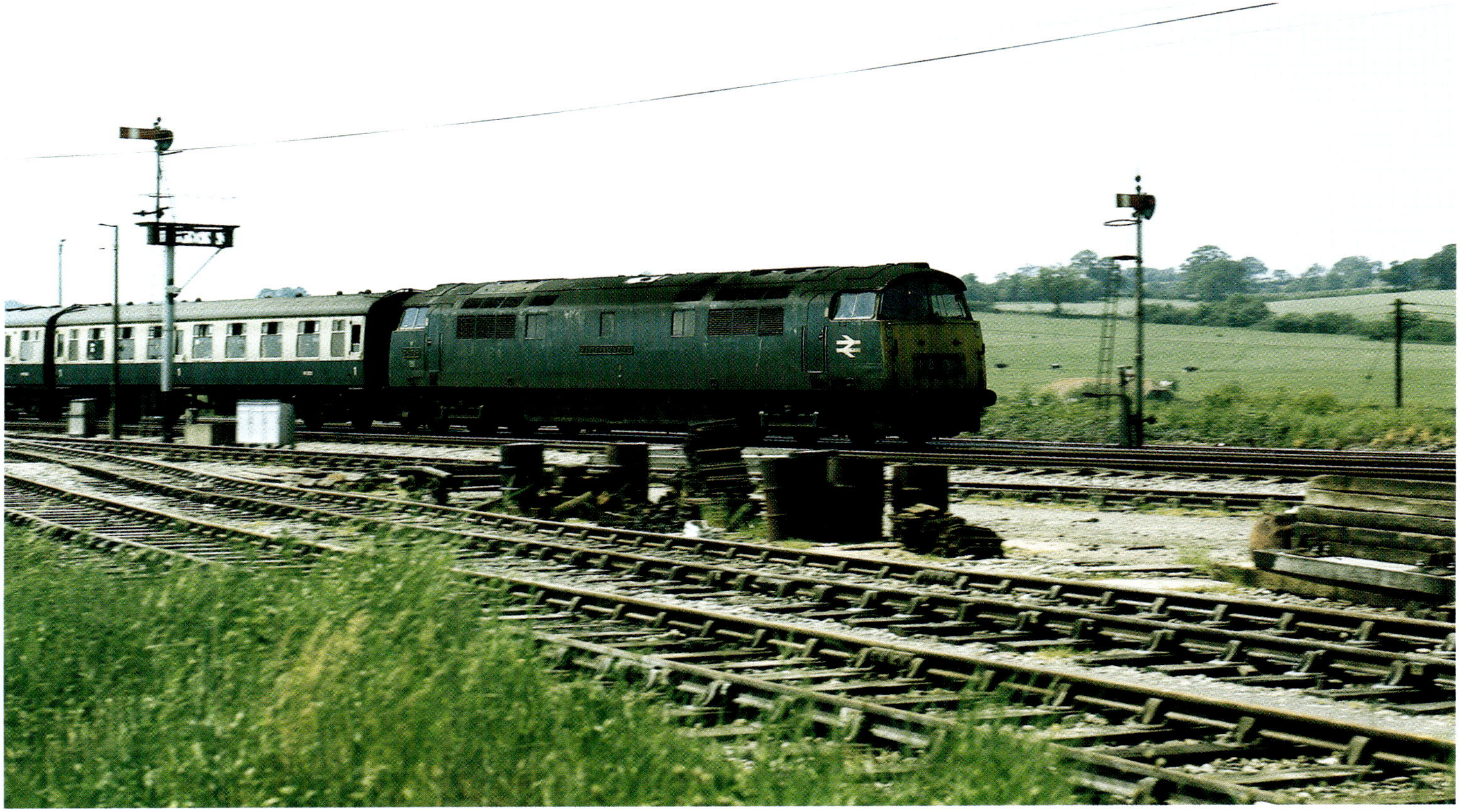

Above: Past assorted permanent way materials, D1059 *Western Empire* was rushing the 12.00 Paignton to Paddington through Witham 'right time' at 13.54 on Saturday, 7th June 1975, The Witham signalman's duties included adding the additional bell-code '1-3' to the normal Class 1 train bell-code, so that Fairwood Junction would receive it as a '4-1-3' and route the train via Westbury avoiding line - 'up the back road', as the signalmen used to say.

Overleaf left: D1033 *Western Trooper* makes a fine sight approaching Witham signalbox on a Saturday in 1975 with the 10.26 Paddington to Paignton, comprised of a set of Mk I coaches.

Overleaf right: D1013 *Western Ranger,* recessed in the down refuge siding at Witham, provided us with an unexpected treat when we arrived there on 25th May 1976. The loco was on a special light engine working, 0Z72, routed via Yeovil at Castle Cary. It had been let out of Westbury in a bit of a rush after the 16.53 Paddington to Newton Abbot and before the 17.45 Bristol to Weymouth stopper. It didn't have a margin to run to Castle Cary without delaying the *Golden Hind*, so was 'put inside' at Witham. Even so, it still managed to 'tickle' the *Hind* between Clink Road and Blatchbridge. The Weymouth followed the *Hind* down and then *Ranger* was let out in front of the Exeter cement. So we had nearly half an hour to photograph her in the evening sunshine. The traincrew didn't like the attention they were getting as I circled the light engine with the Rolleiflex, responding by blasting the horn as I was about to take a photograph! I jumped about two feet sideways, much to their amusement, but still got the shot. In the meantime, D1048 *Western Lady* passed by on the up main with the 15.00 Penzance to Paddington.

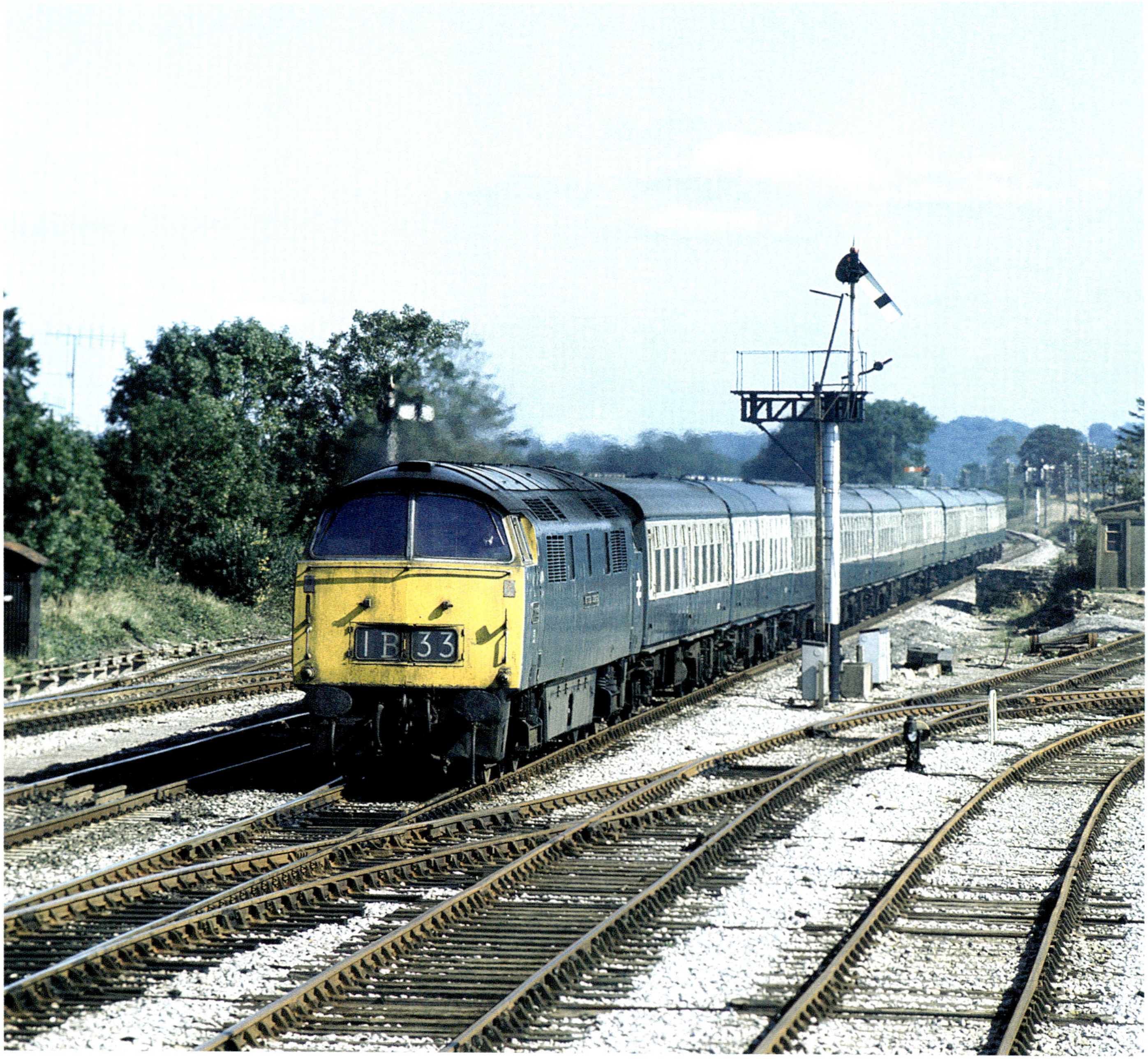
1B33

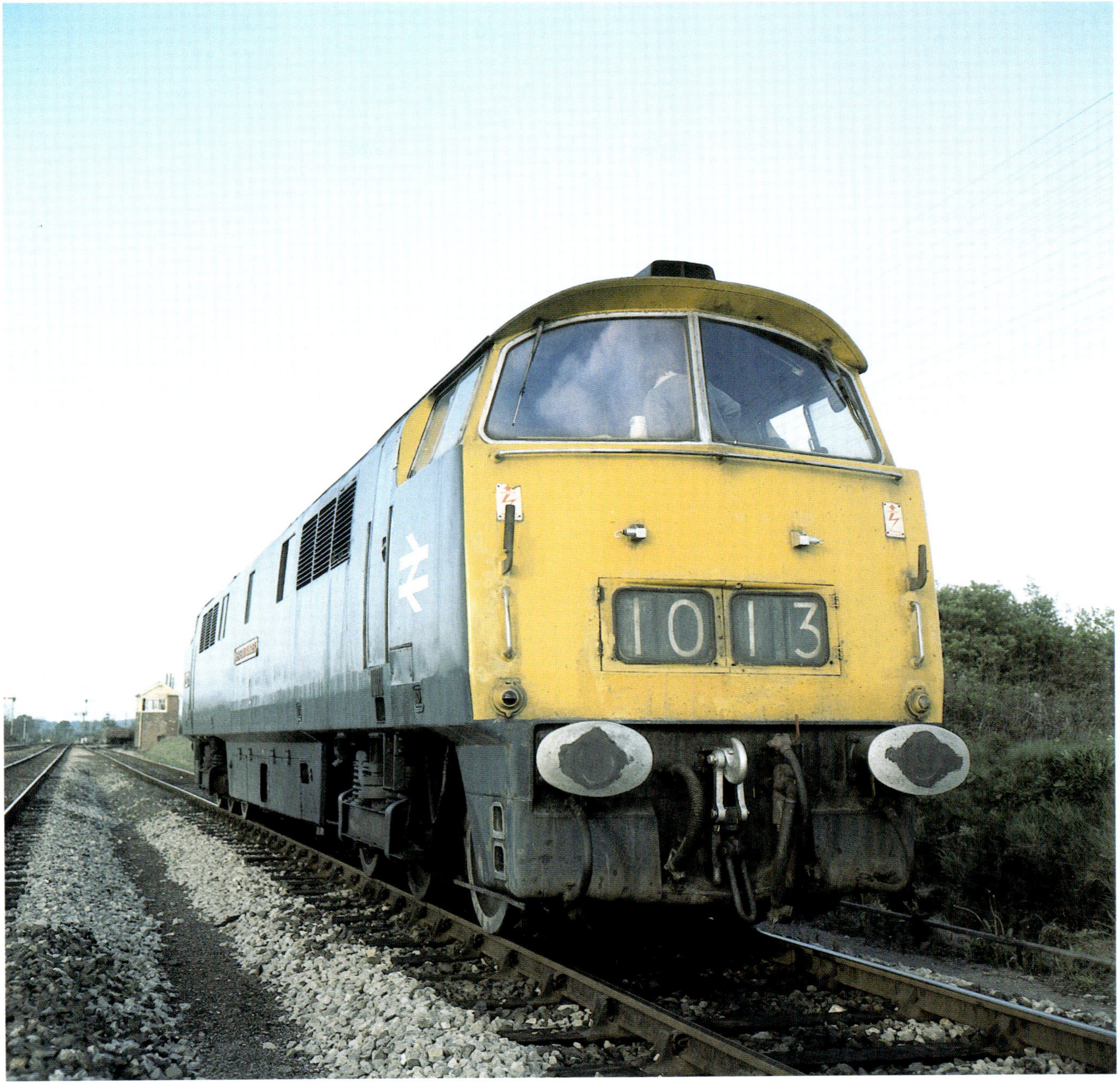
1O13

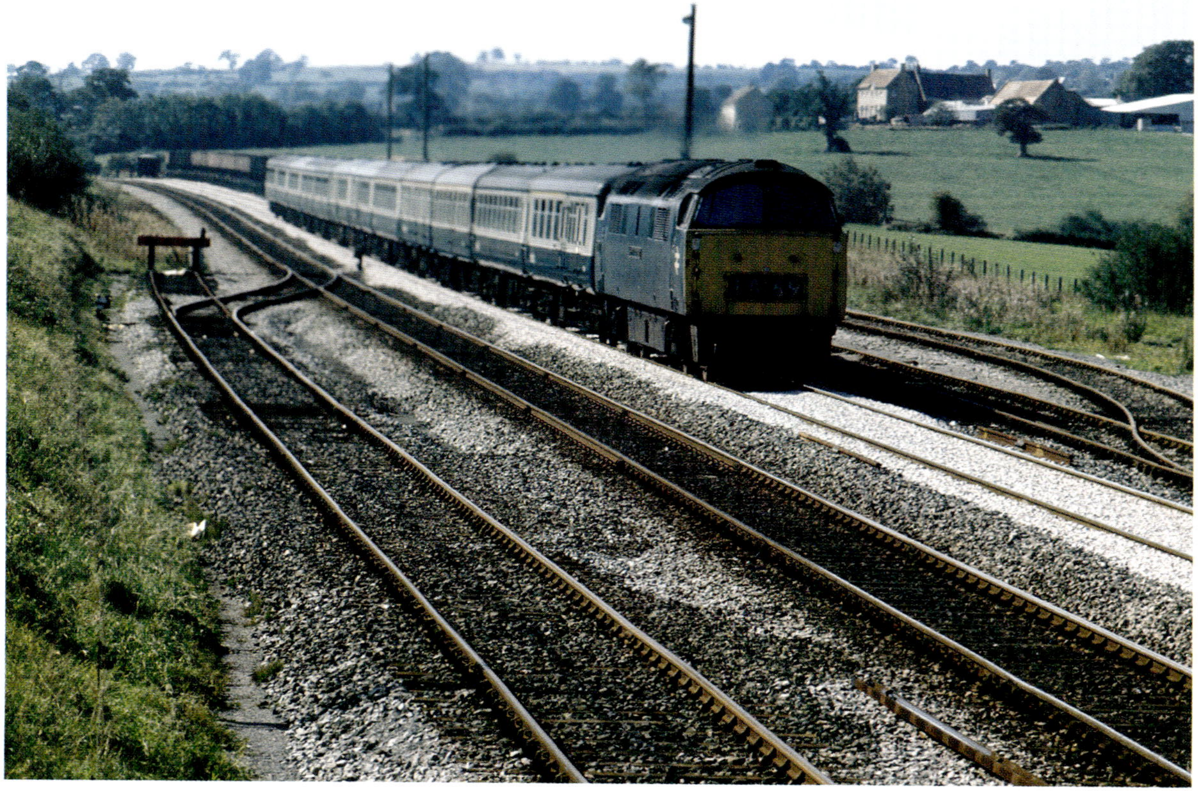

In this view from the signalbox window, an unidentified Western passes along the newly reballasted up main, hauling the 08.40 Penzance to Paddington through Witham on a summer Saturday in 1975. Empty stone hoppers are stabled in the up sidings whilst bullhead track is still in evidence on the down main.

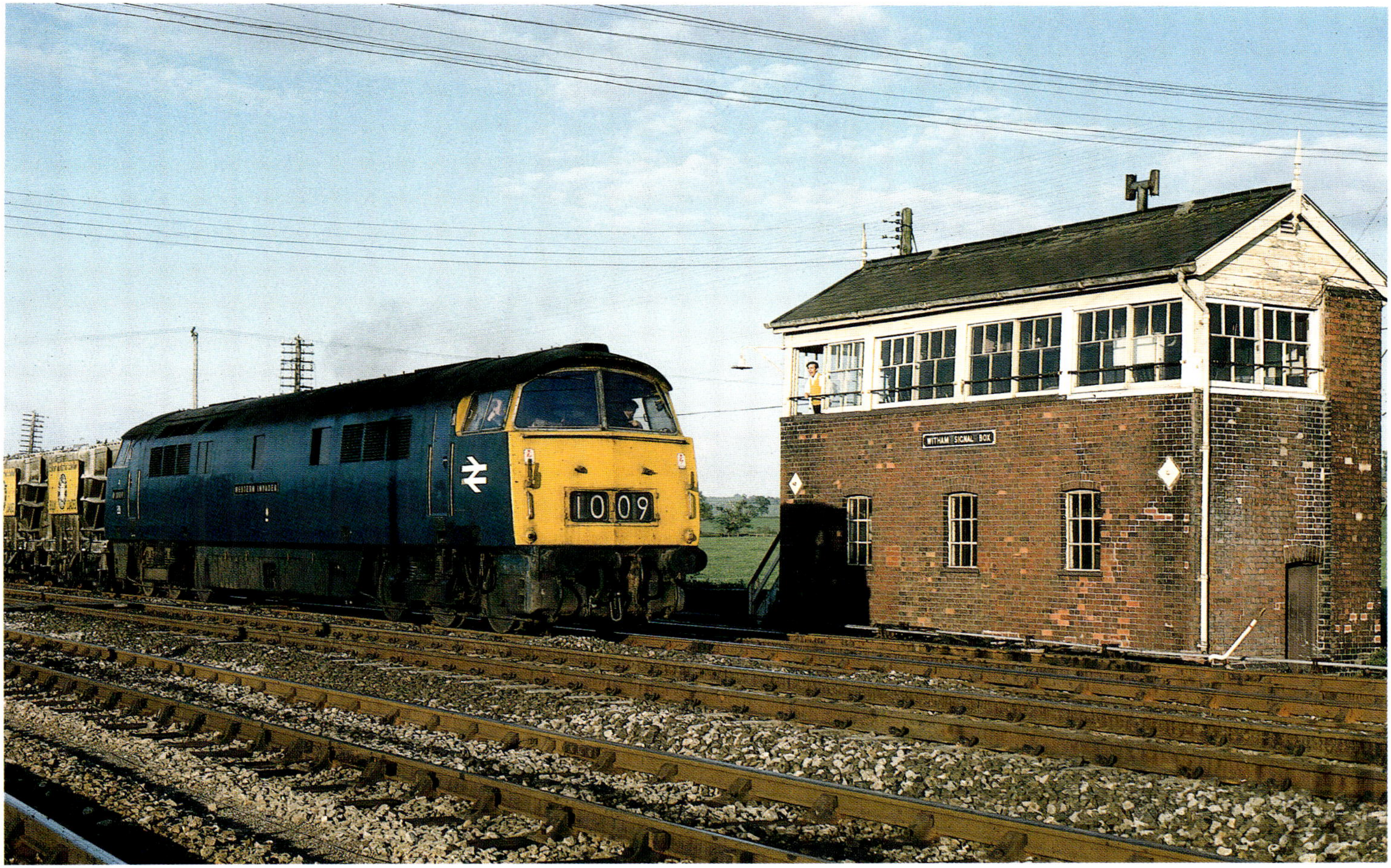

Witham was a good place to catch the 19.07 Westbury to Exeter cement. It was often checked there, waiting for the road to Castle Cary behind the 17.45 Bristol to Weymouth down stopper, which was booked to leave Bruton at 19.22 as the cement train passed Blatchbridge Junction. The stopper then departed from Castle Cary at 19.28, by which time the cement had usually passed Witham's down distant signal at 'caution', getting clear signals when approaching the signalbox. Here on 25th May 1976, D1009 *Western Invader* passes the box, the driver sharing a joke about his secondman with signalman John Francis, before opening up towards Brewham. On this occasion, the cement was checked at Blatchbridge behind the down stopper and also had to wait at Witham until light engine D1013 *Western Ranger* cleared the block section to Cary at 19.35, as described on page 39.

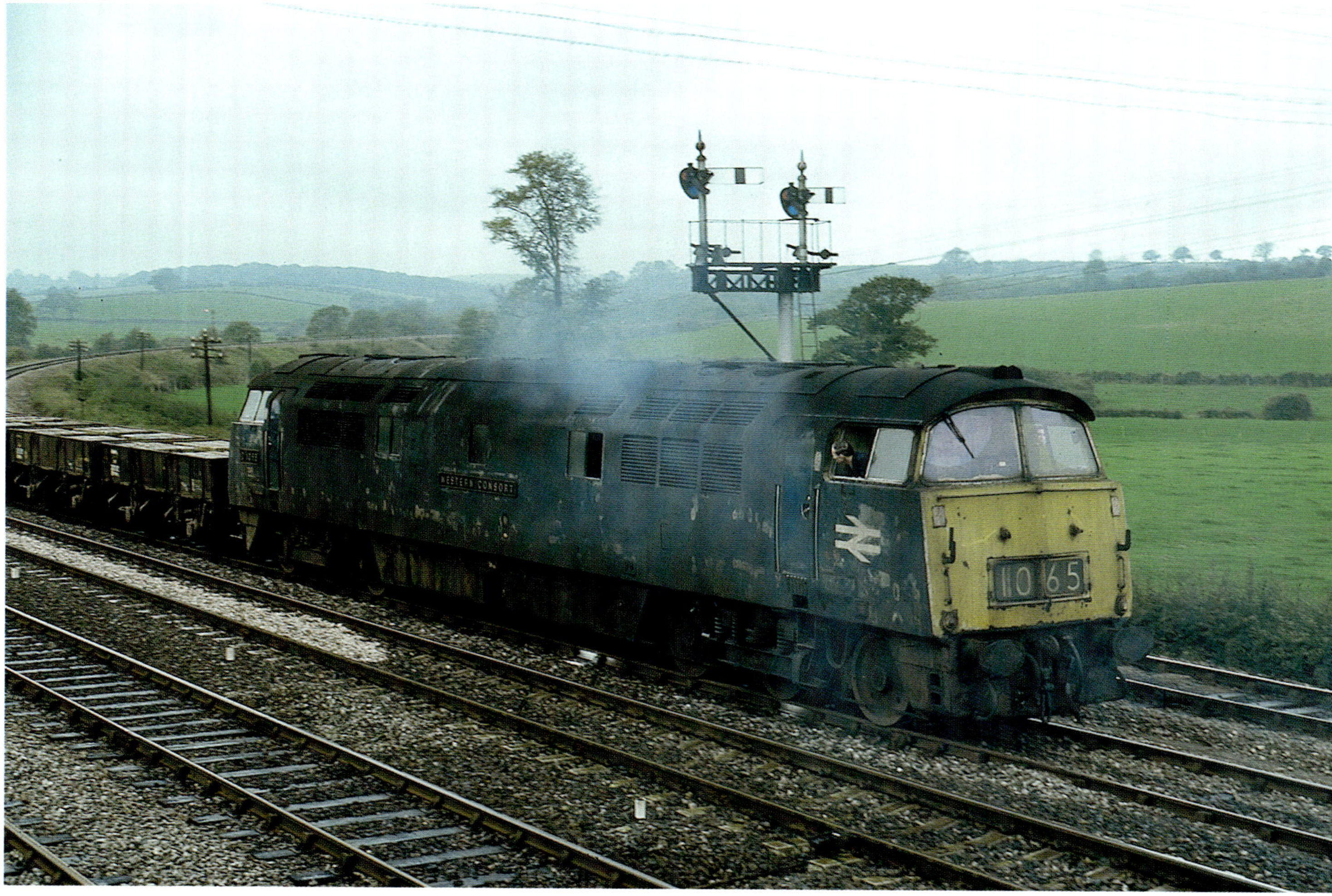

In the poor exterior condition characteristic of the last year of operations, D1065 *Western Consort* shunts wagons full of recovered sleepers into the up sidings at Witham, following Sunday engineering works in September 1976. She was withdrawn at the end of October. The driver looks a little dubious at being the subject matter of our camera, whilst the secondman is too busy looking out at the propelling move to take any notice.

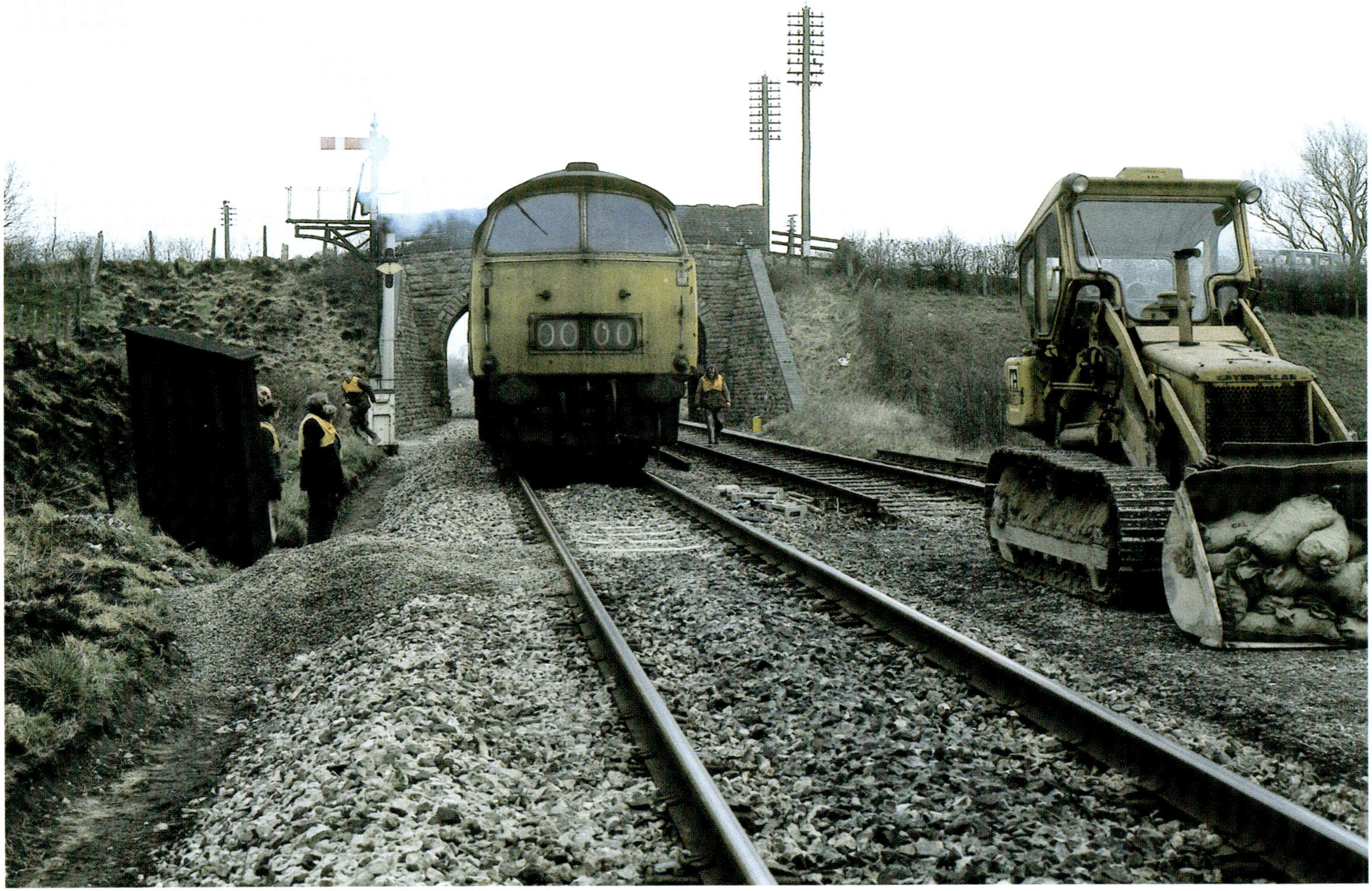

The local signalmen helped us enormously with information leading to coverage of some obscure Western workings in the Westbury area. On Sunday 7th March 1976, we saw D1058 *Western Nobleman* on a relaying job at West Barn bridge, near Witham. The down main line was being 'blanketed', a sheet of polythene being placed on the track bed and covered with stone dust and ballast before the track was relaid. *Nobleman* was just about to pass Witham's up home signal, held at danger for the duration of the occupation. The Permanent Way Supervisor, distinguished by his green coat and welllingtons, has just leapt out of the way of the loco, whilst the track workers look on and wonder what on earth we are photographing.

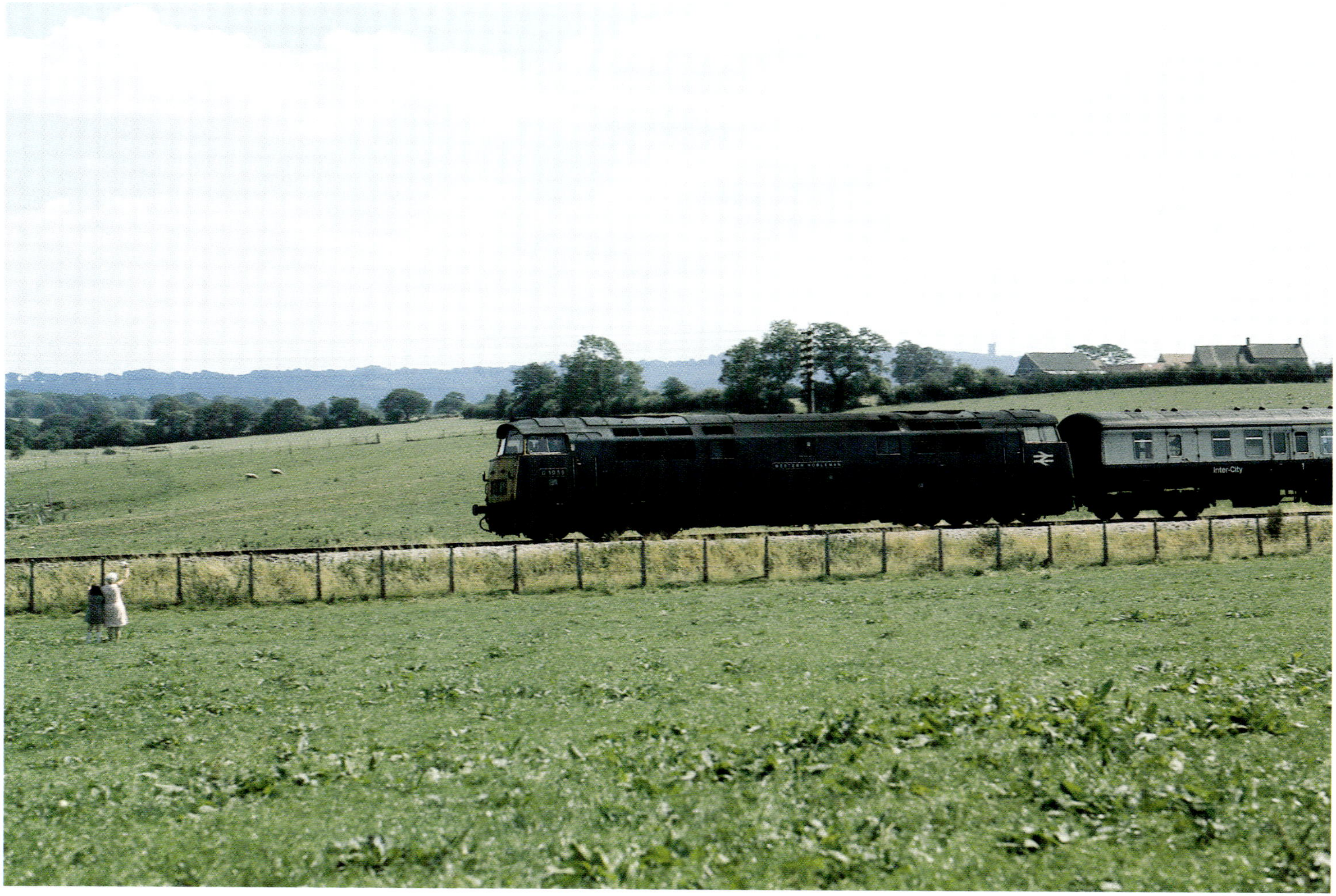

In sunnier times than the previous photograph, *Western Nobleman* has ascendedBrewham bank and is seen here on the descent into Witham vale after the short level stretch at the summit. Across the valley, Alfred's Tower can be seen on the horizon. Meanwhile, my grandmother and sister wave to the driver as he approaches the accomodation crossing for Little West Barn Farm, known as Dennings Crossing, on Sunday, 27th July, 1975.

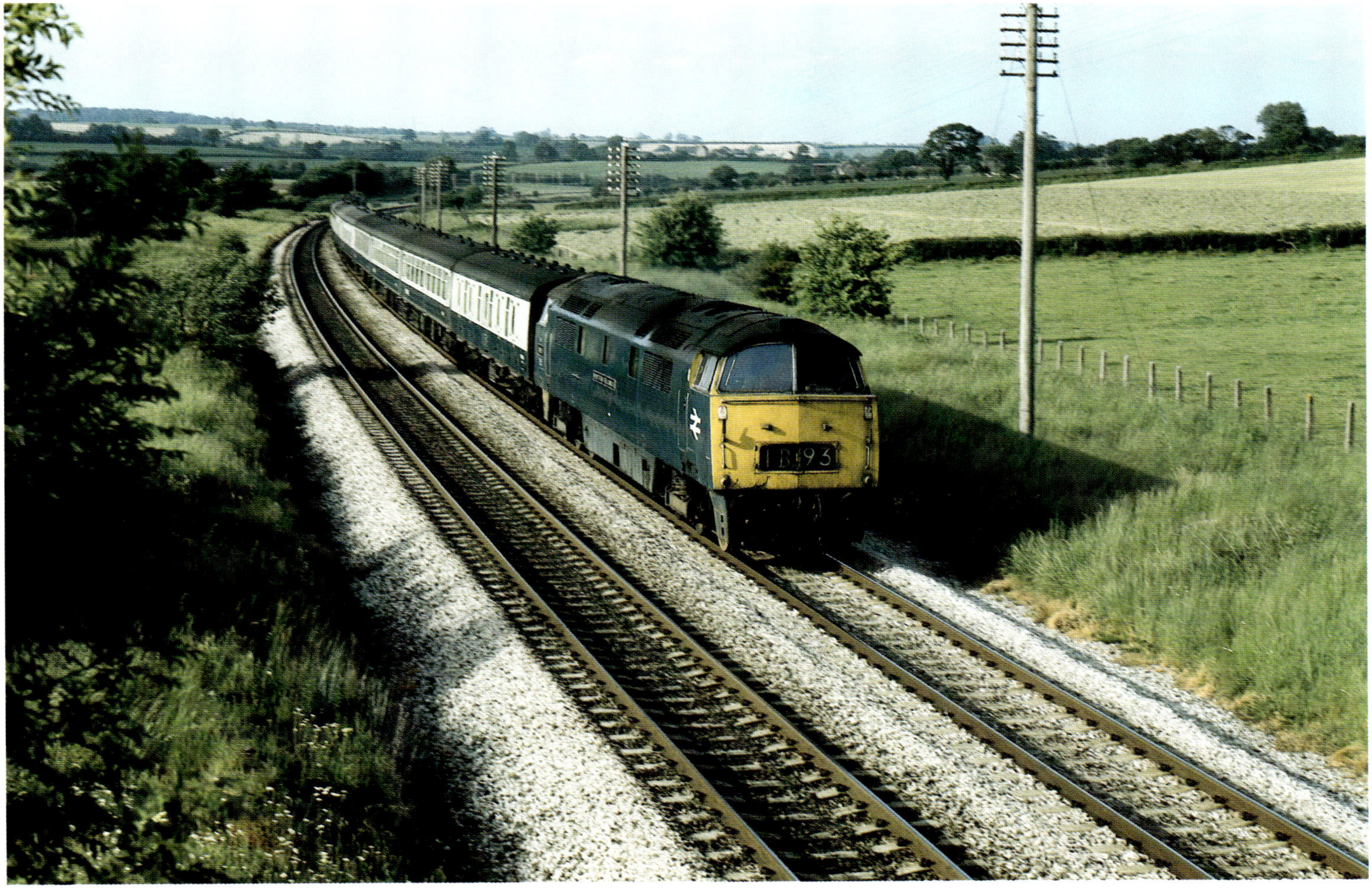

D1068 *Western Reliance* is about fifteen minutes late passing the site of Brewham signalbox with the 16.30 Paddington to Paignton on June 14th 1975 as she approaches Strap Lane overbridge, having taken exactly two hours to reach the summit of the bank after leaving London.

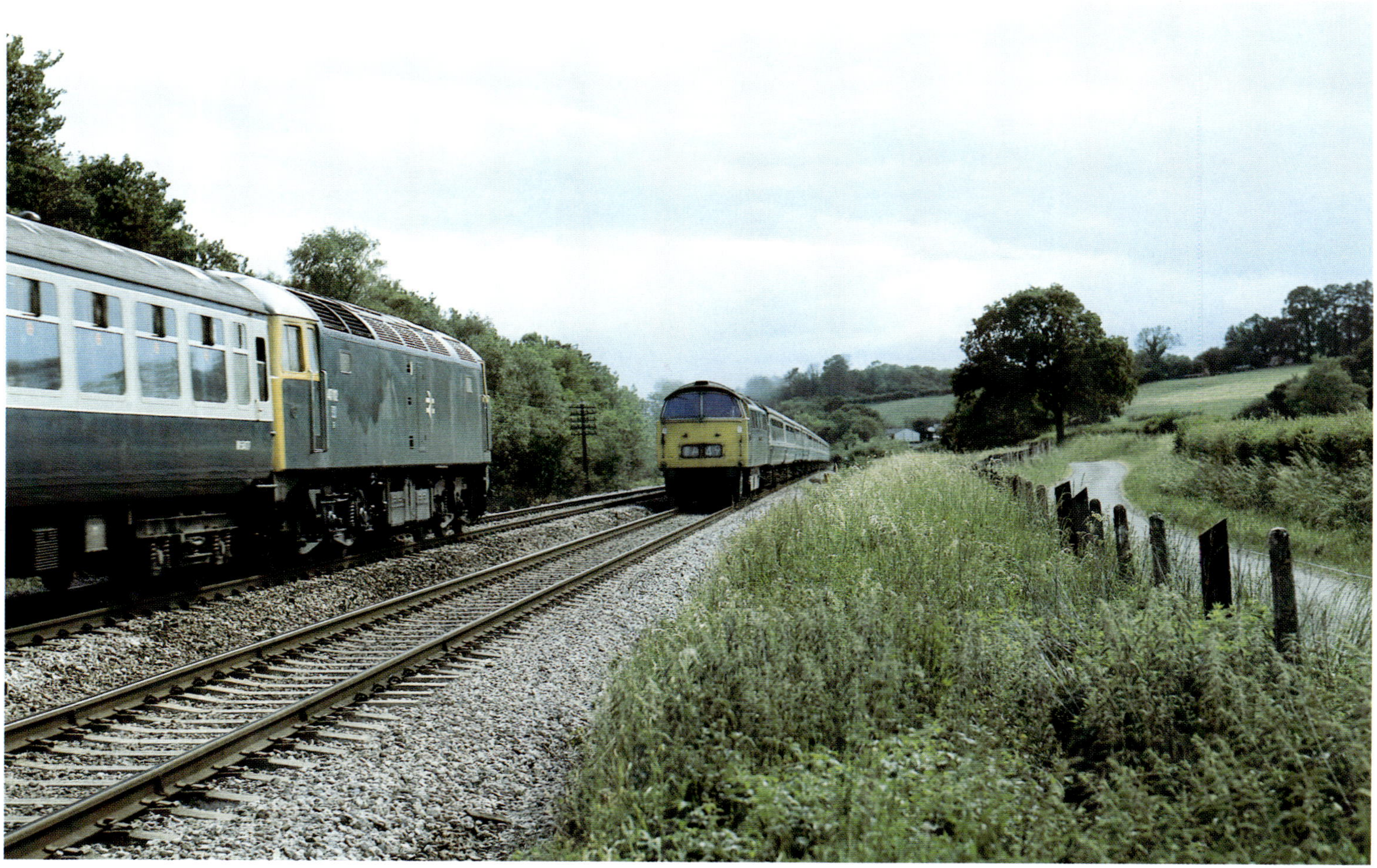

We had always been impressed by the railway photography of Ivo Peters, so it was enjoyable to seek out some of the locations where he had photographed years before. One of these was at Pinkwood near Bruton, where on a humid afternoon in June 1975 we found this spot. A Western could be heard approaching from the Bruton direction, working hard on the 1 in 93 gradient, after the short level stretch through the station. The timing couldn't have been better, for as D1011 *Western Thunderer* came into view with the incorrectly headcoded 09.00 Penzance to Paddington, 47 112 appeared from the east with the down *Cornish Riviera Limited* to complete the photograph, the bucolic lane alongside devoid of all traffic.

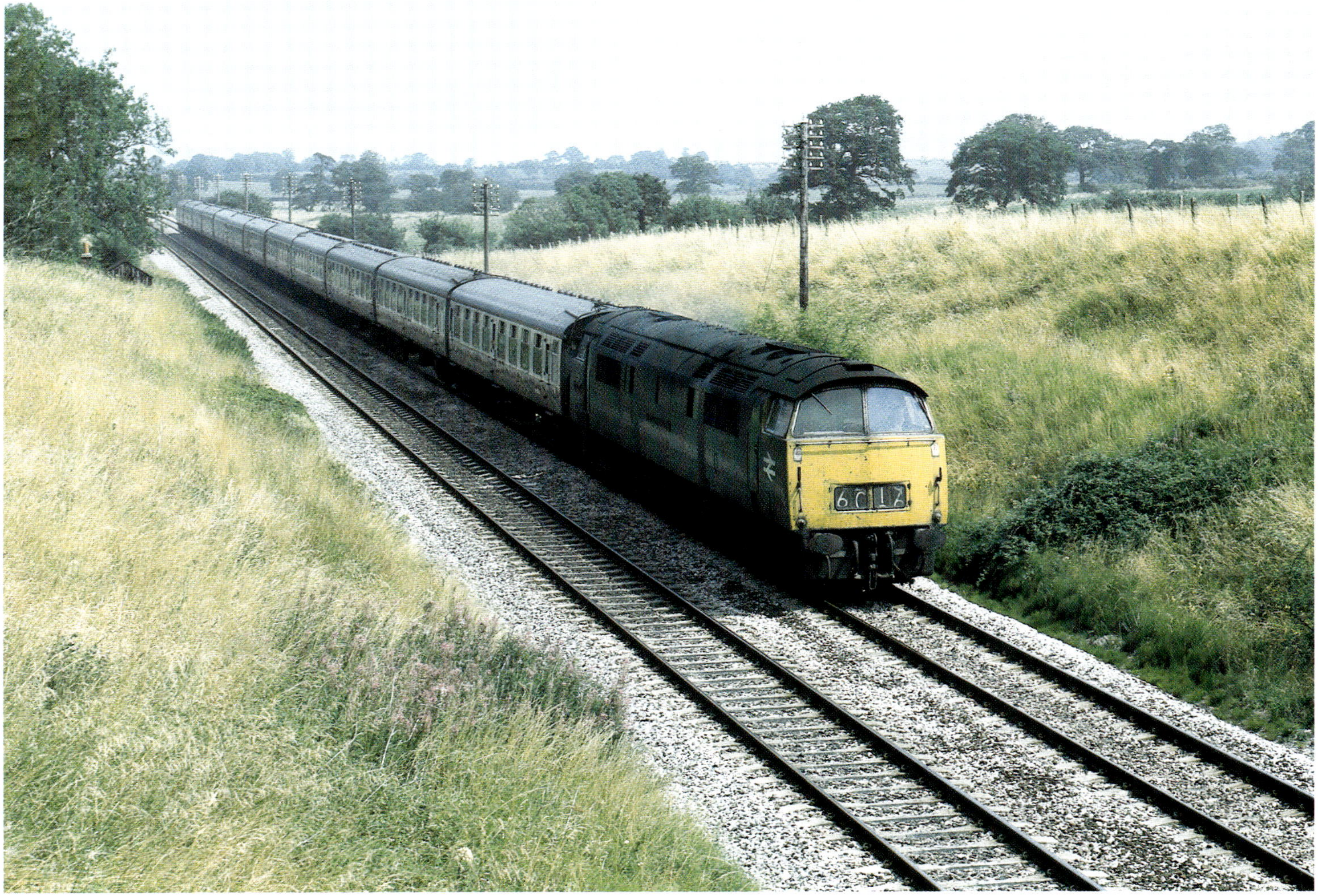

Between the curves of Brewham to the east and Pinkwood to the west lies this straight formation of about half a mile on the western side of Brewham bank. An overbridge was conveniently placed to watch Westerns on up trains tackle the final ascent, or see trains to the West Country coast downhill after ten miles of being 'in the collar' from Westbury. Here is D1027 *Western Lancer* on 2nd August 1975 with the 10.56 Paddington to Penzance, a Saturday train which ran non-stop to Exeter.

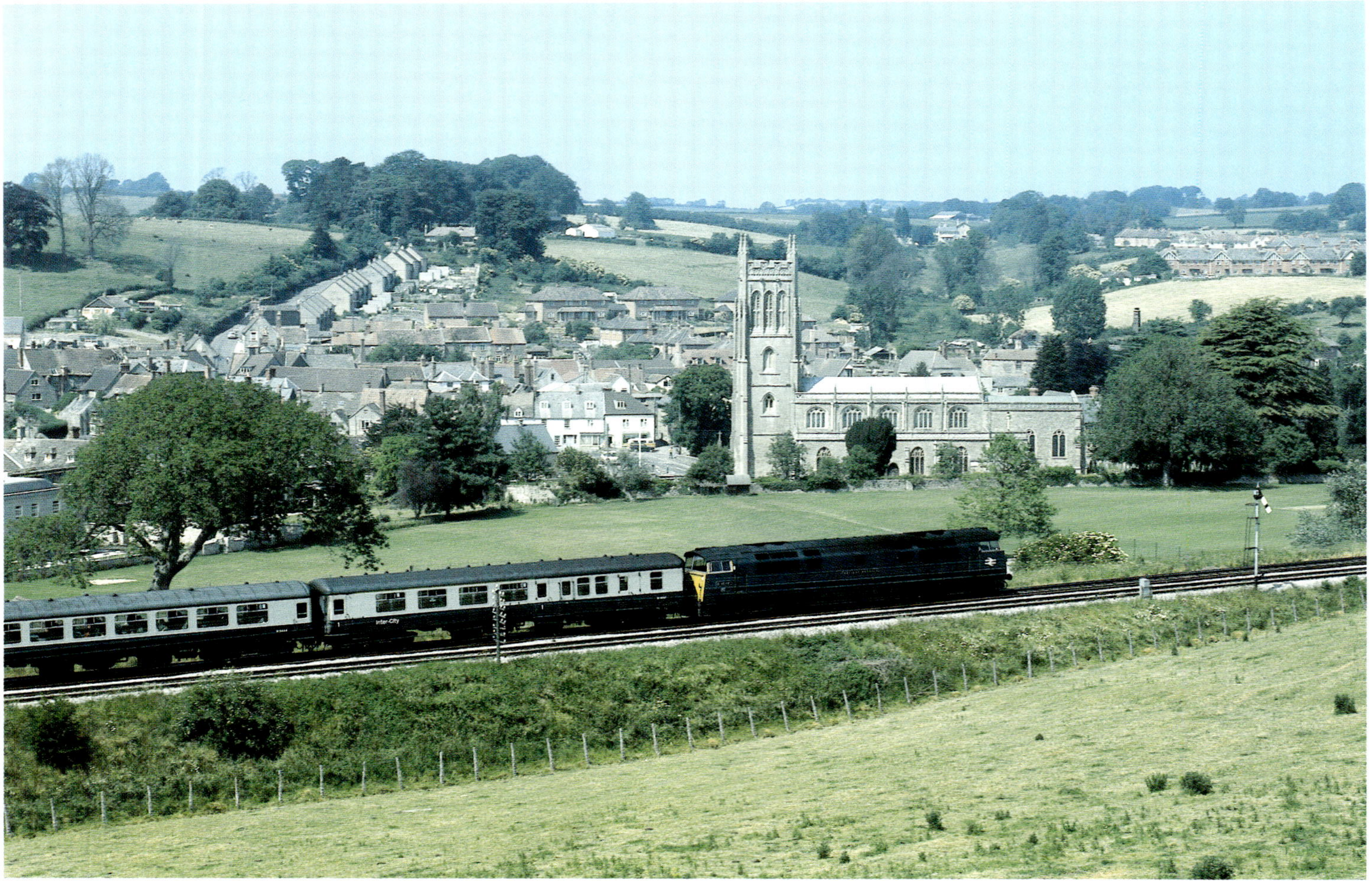

D1046 *Western Marquis* thunders up the last of the 1 in 98 bank towards Bruton station with the up *Cornish Riviera* on Sunday 22nd June 1975. Both of my parents were keen bell-ringers so perhaps it is no surprise that the fine Somerset tower of Bruton parish church vies for attention with *Western Marquis* in this photograph! Leafless Dutch elm trees can be seen on the hill in the distance, the disease removing the trees as surely as the Western Region removed the last of the diesel hydraulics.

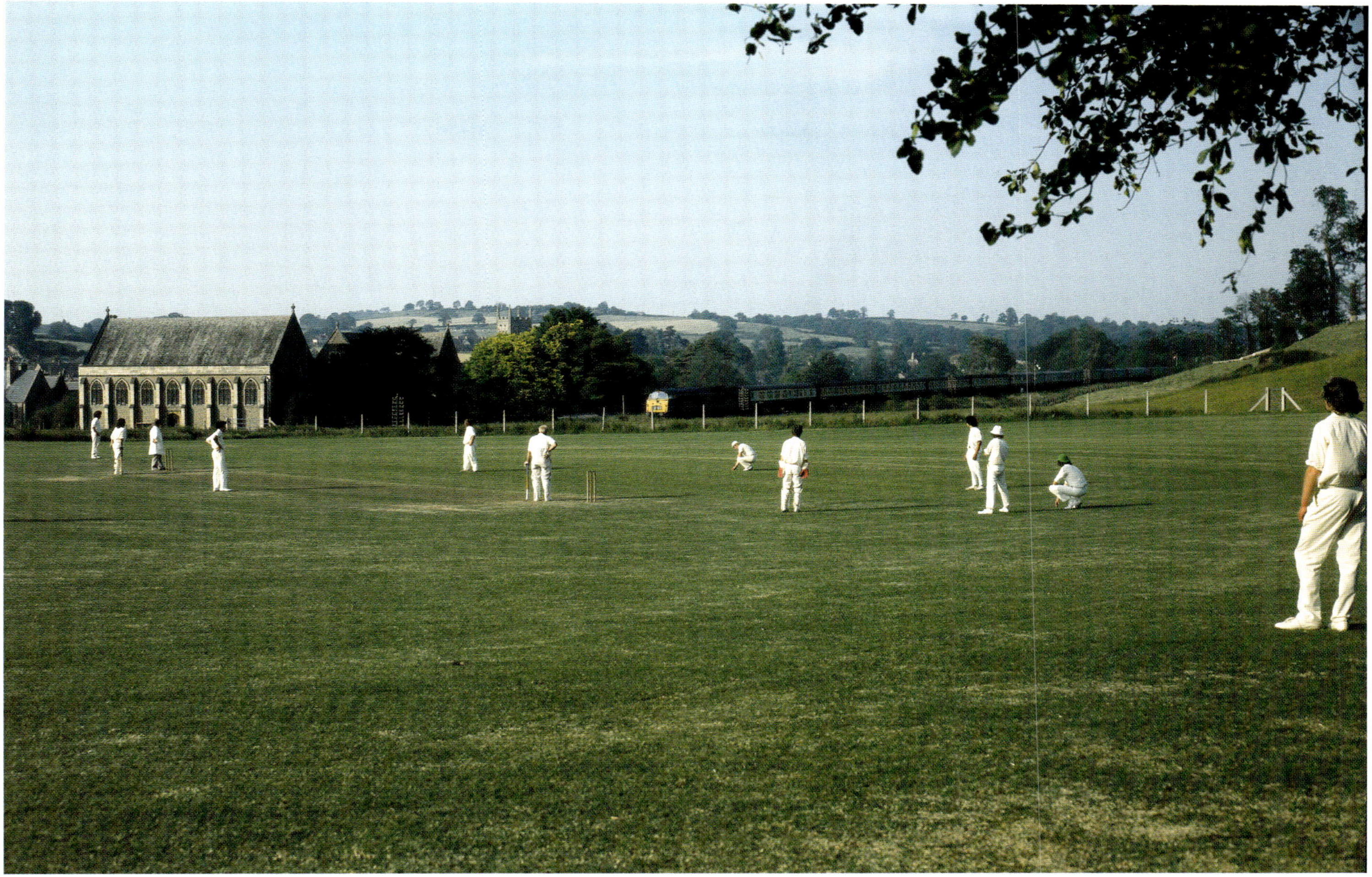

Later the same day, and the Sunday cricketers seem more interested in watching D1056 *Western Sultan* leave Bruton and descend the bank towards Castle Cary than in starting the next over. The weather in the summer of 1975 was pretty good although it wasn't as stupendously hot as the following year turned out to be. The train was the 16.30 Paddington to Penzance, seen at 18.33.

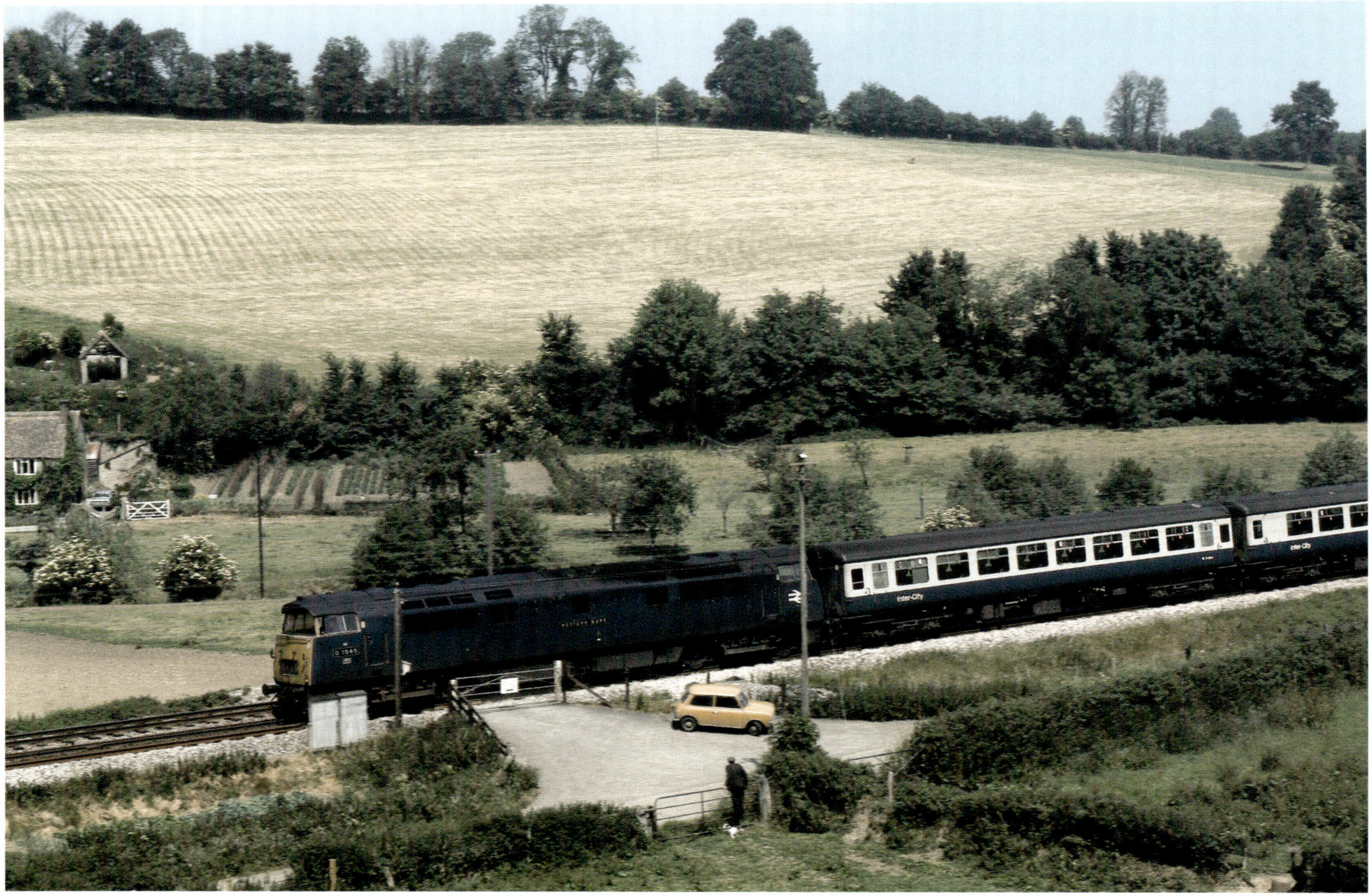

Above: D1043 *Western Duke* glides down Bruton bank past Gants Mill crossing on the glorious afternoon of Sunday, 22nd June 1975. The old chap leans on the field gate to get a better look at the diesel-hydraulic whilst his dog remains distinctly uninterested. At this time, railway allotments were still tendedon the Castle Cary side of the crossing - the sort of activity I thought had died out with steam traction until I started research for this book. The train was the 10.45 Paddington to Plymouth, only three minutes late when photographed here at 12.52 and with recovery time after Castle Cary, likely to be on time at Taunton.

Opposite: One of our starting points for lineside photography was the Bradford Barton book, 'Great Western Steam South of the Severn', which included many shots taken in our locality and it proved very useful as we began to explore the area. One such location was at Cole, where the Somerset & Dorset had passed over the West of England route. By 1975 the overbridge had been demolished but the bridge abutments were still there and provided the same fine vista of the Western line. It was also the spot where the gradient steepened in earnest for up trains - D1040 *Western Queen* hauling the 13.30 Paignton to Paddington was certainly doing 90 mph in readiness for the climb in this view on Sunday 15th June 1975.

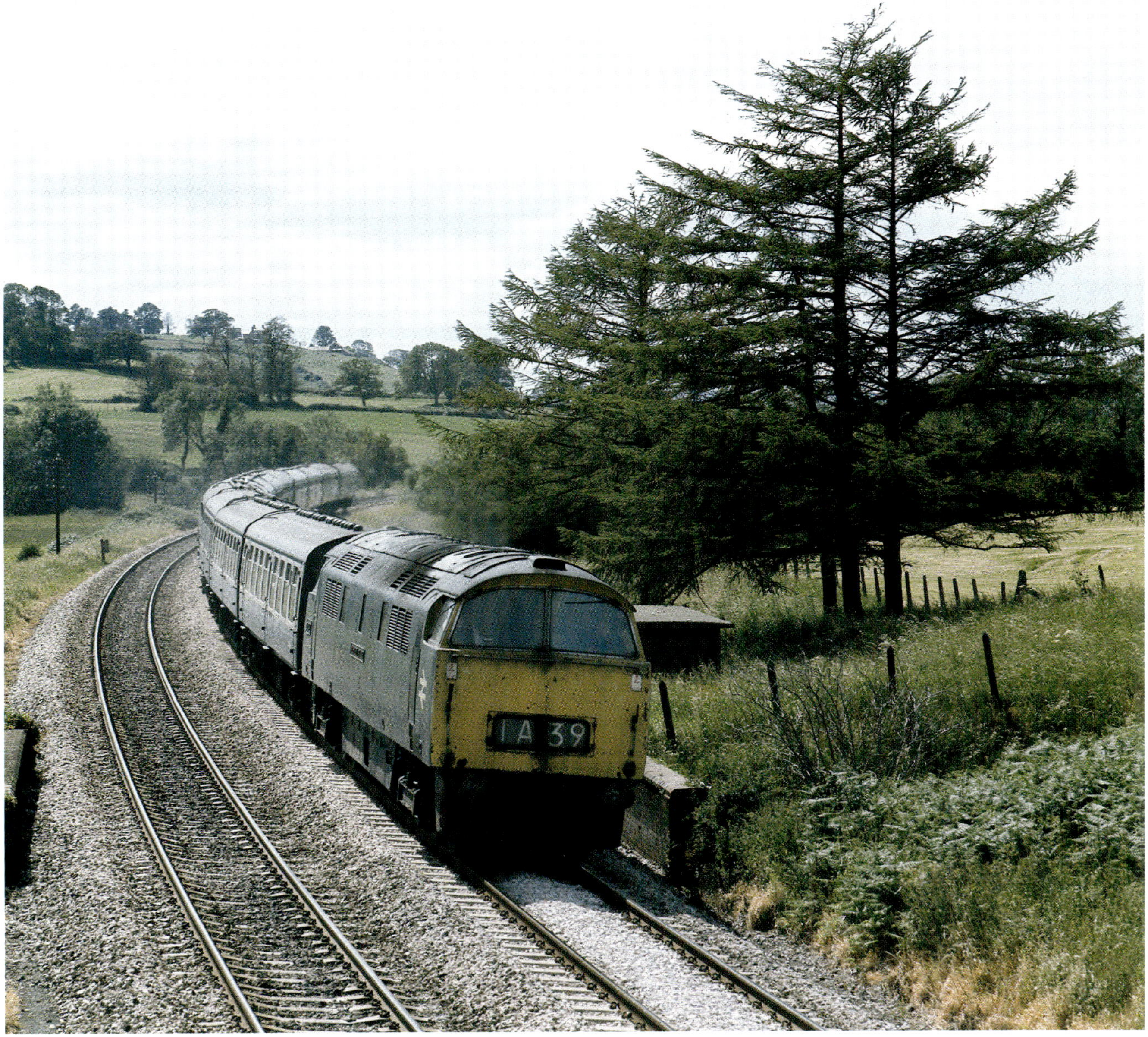
1A39

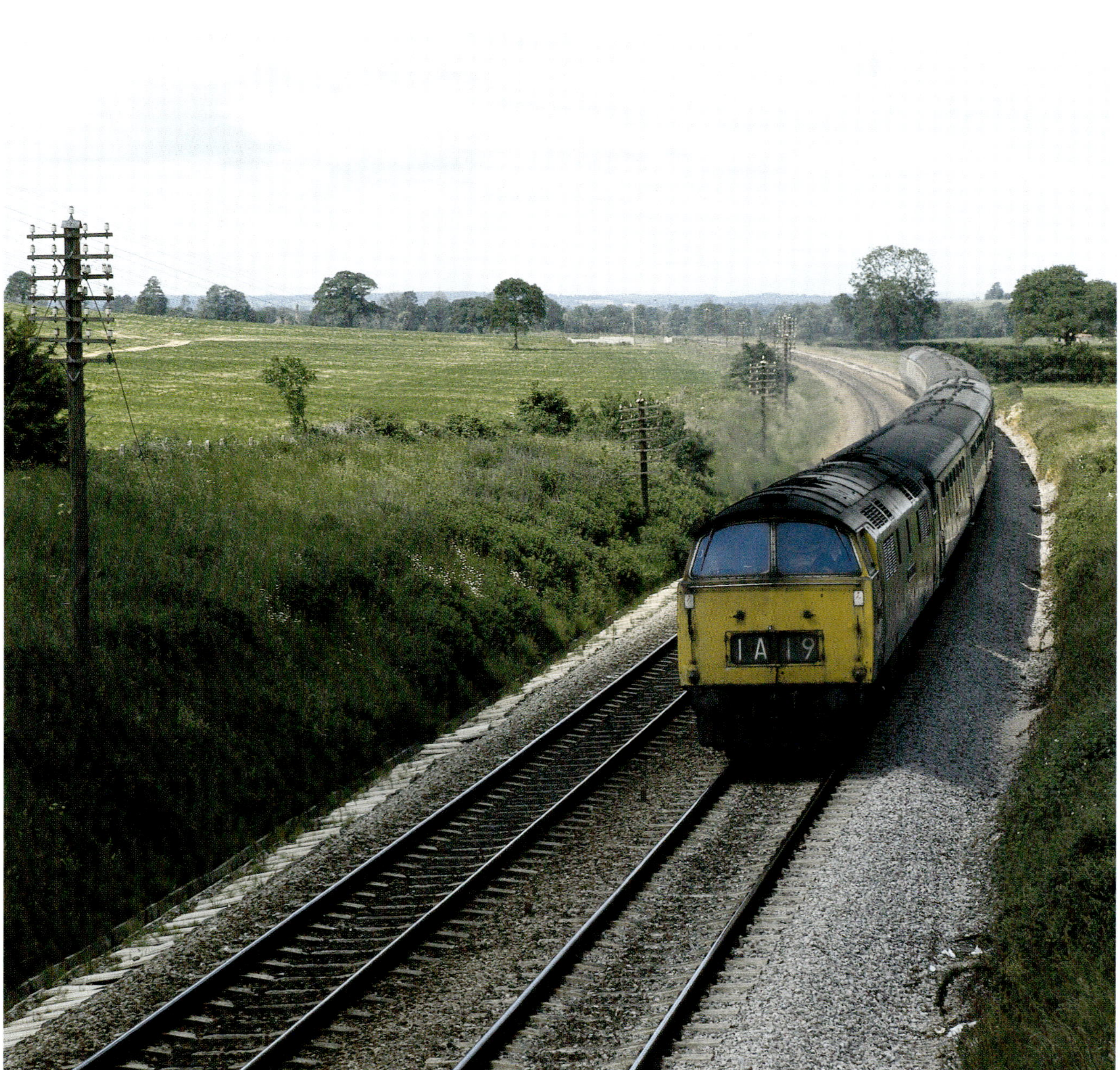
1A19

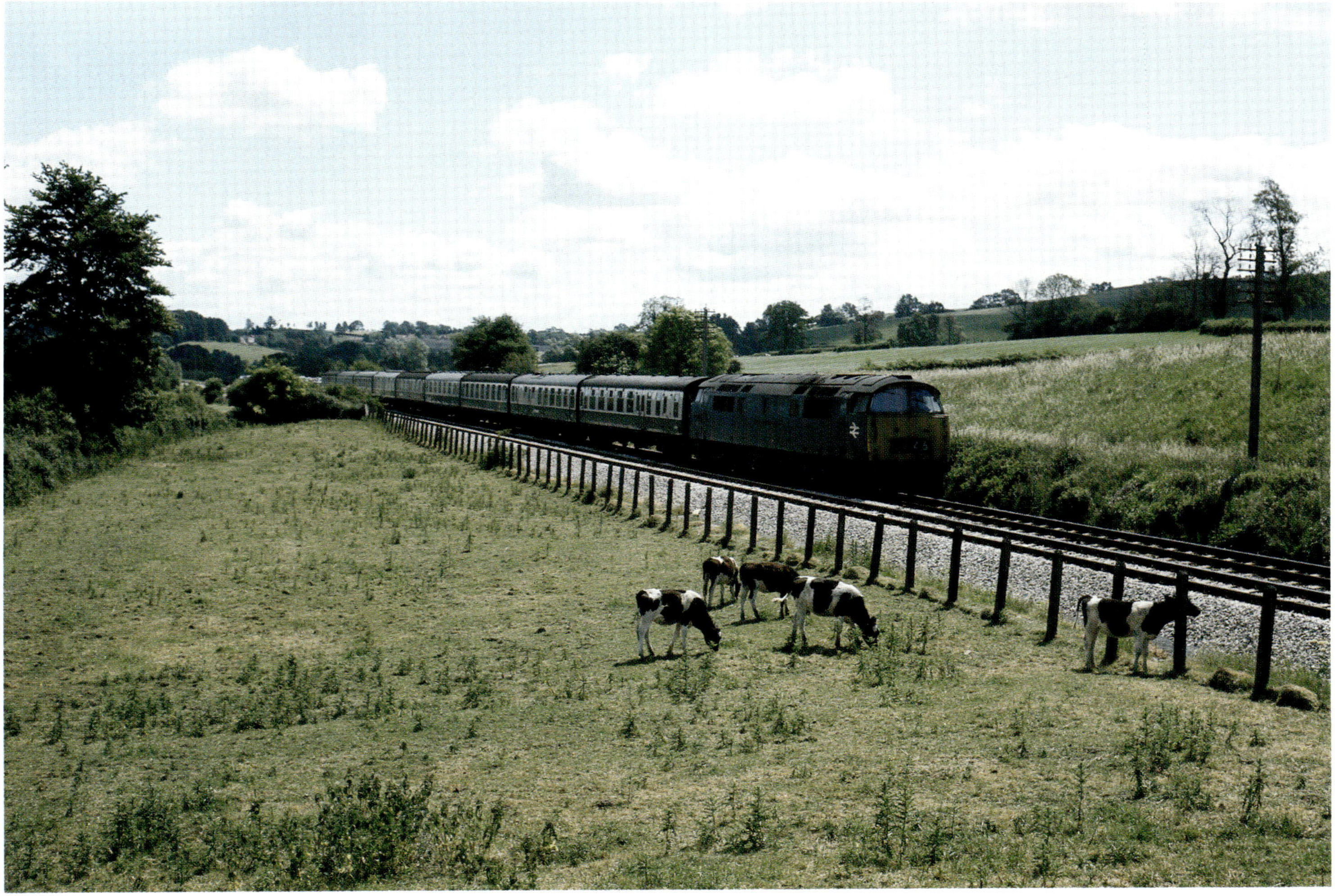

Above: With a few curious Friesians in the field opposite, D1069 *Western Vanguard* heads the 06.45 Dover to Newton Abbot Motorail at Wyke Champflower on Sunday 15th June 1975. Whilst Sunday's Motorail came from Dover, the Saturday service left Kensington at 08.40, running to Paignton but detaching the Motorail portion at Newton Abbot. On weekdays the train ran from Kensington to St Austell, unloading some carflats at Totnes. *Western Vanguard* was one of the locomotives culled in the planned withdrawal at the end of the 1975 summer timetable.

Opposite: From the same bridge at Wyke Champflower but heading towards Bruton, came D1052 *Western Viceroy* with the 08.30 Plymouth to Paddington. It was the sort of cloudy bright weather which had us reaching for the light meter as the train was approaching, frantically opening the apertures of our cameras by a stop as the sun went in. She was over twenty minutes late at this juncture - even with recovery time there would have been no chance of a right time arrival at Paddington. Like *Western Vanguard, Viceroy* was also withdrawn at the end of that summer.

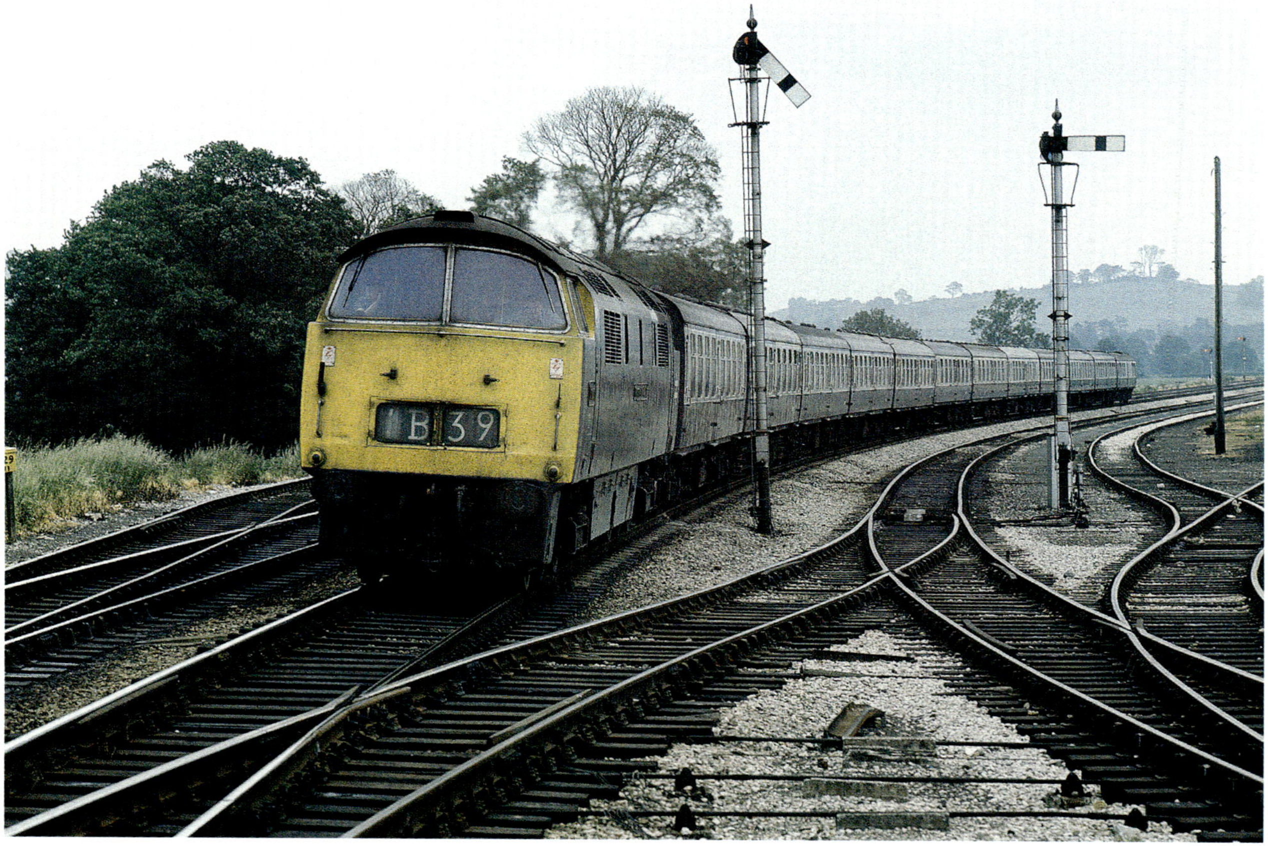

It is easy to forget that twelve coach trains were commonplace in the seventies. Without a rusty rail in sight, not even in the sidings, the Saturdays only 10.56 Paddington to Penzance passes Castle Cary down main intermediate home with a rake of vacuum braked stock hauled by D1011 *Western Thunderer* on Saturday, 14th June 1975. Note the buffet car at the London end of the train, marshalled in readiness for detaching at Plymouth. The latter half of this train would return from there to London, being attached to the Cornish coaches from a up through working at North Road, the buffet ending up in the middle of the train for the run back to Paddington. There were no through buffet facilities for Cornish travellers, except on the *Cornish Riviera* and the *Golden Hind*.

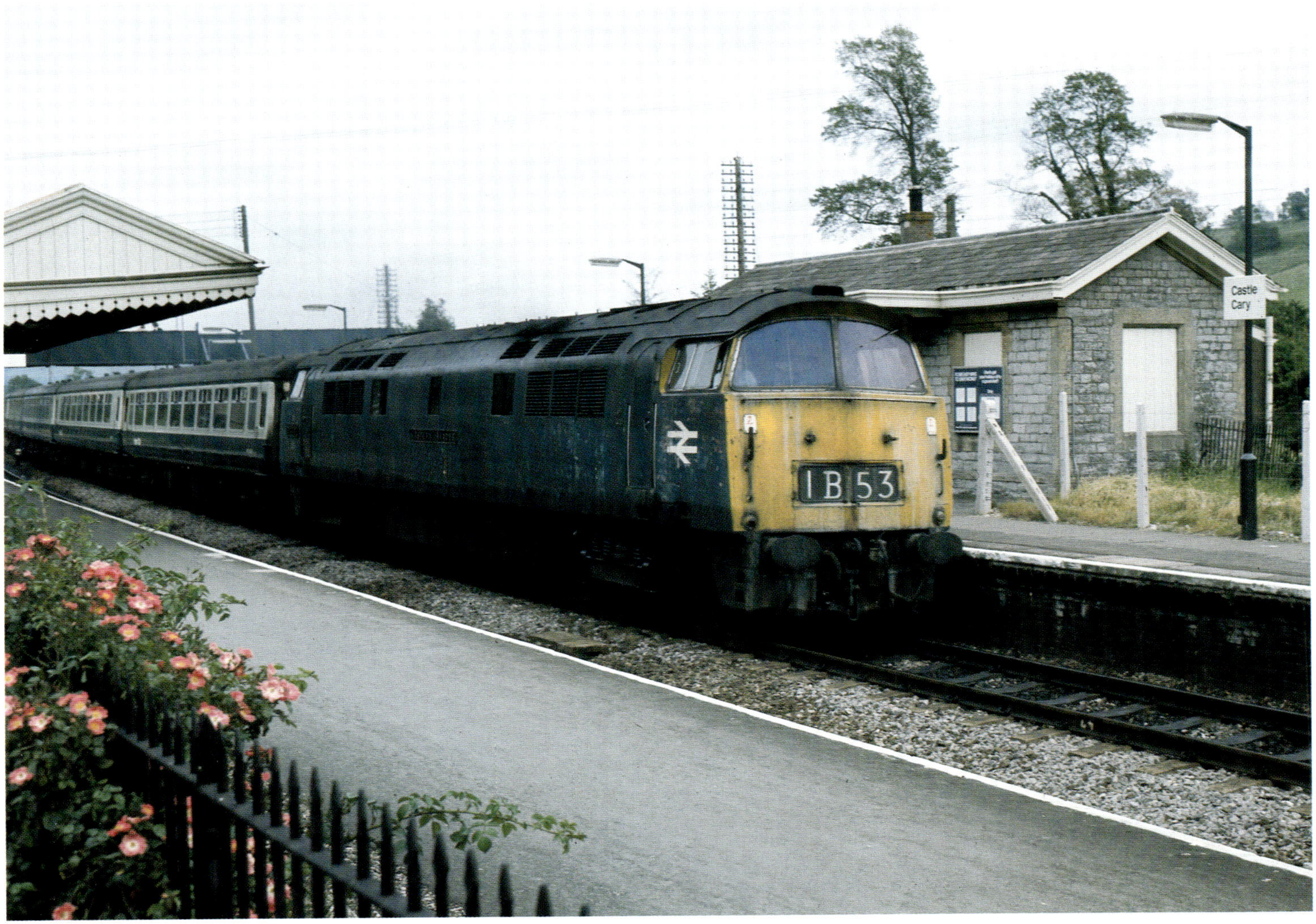

From the start of the summer timetable in 1974, Castle Cary station boasted a direct service to London and the West Country, a mere 118 years after the station opened! Initially this was limited to a couple of Class 1 trains in each direction on weekdays and Saturdays, the 05.05 (06.50 SO) Plymouth and 07.53 Paignton in the mornings and the 16.30 and 18.30 departures from Paddington in the evenings. Sunday passengers had no choice: they could only catch the 17.30 Plymouth back to town after a weekend in Somerset. The roses complete the picture whilst on the same day as the previous photograph D1009 *Western Invader* still creates an enormous impression of speed with the 12.26 Paddington to Paignton, despite having braked for the 75 mph curves through the station. Western availability was very high on that day in June 1975; in addition to the photographs reproduced here we also saw D1052 *Western Viceroy* on the 08.40 Penzance, D1027 *Western Lancer* on the 09.00 Penzance, D1043 *Western Duke* on the down *Cornish Riviera*, D1047 *Western Lord* on the up *Cornish Riviera* and D1040 *Western Queen* on the 12.30 Paddington.

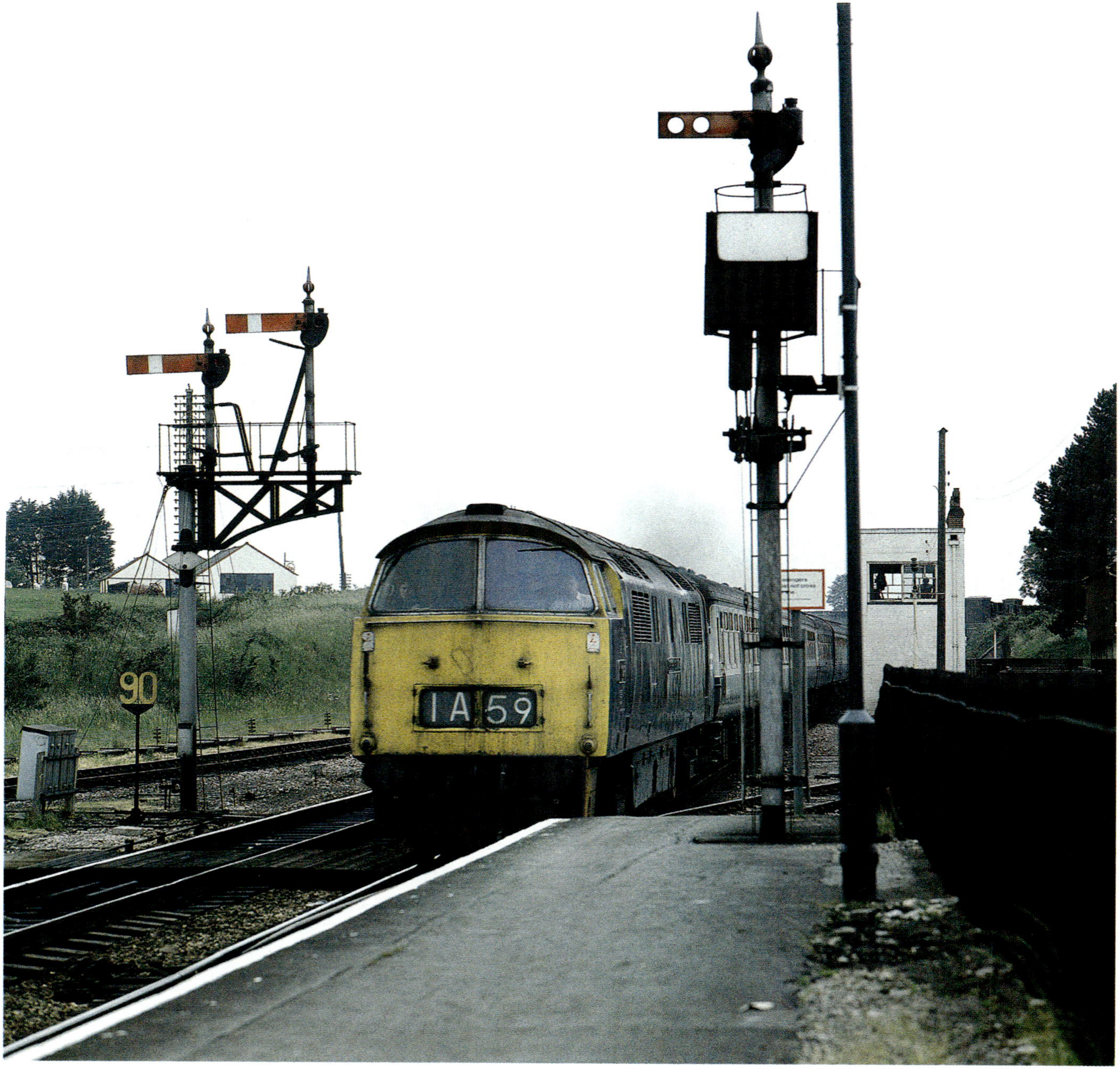
90
1A59

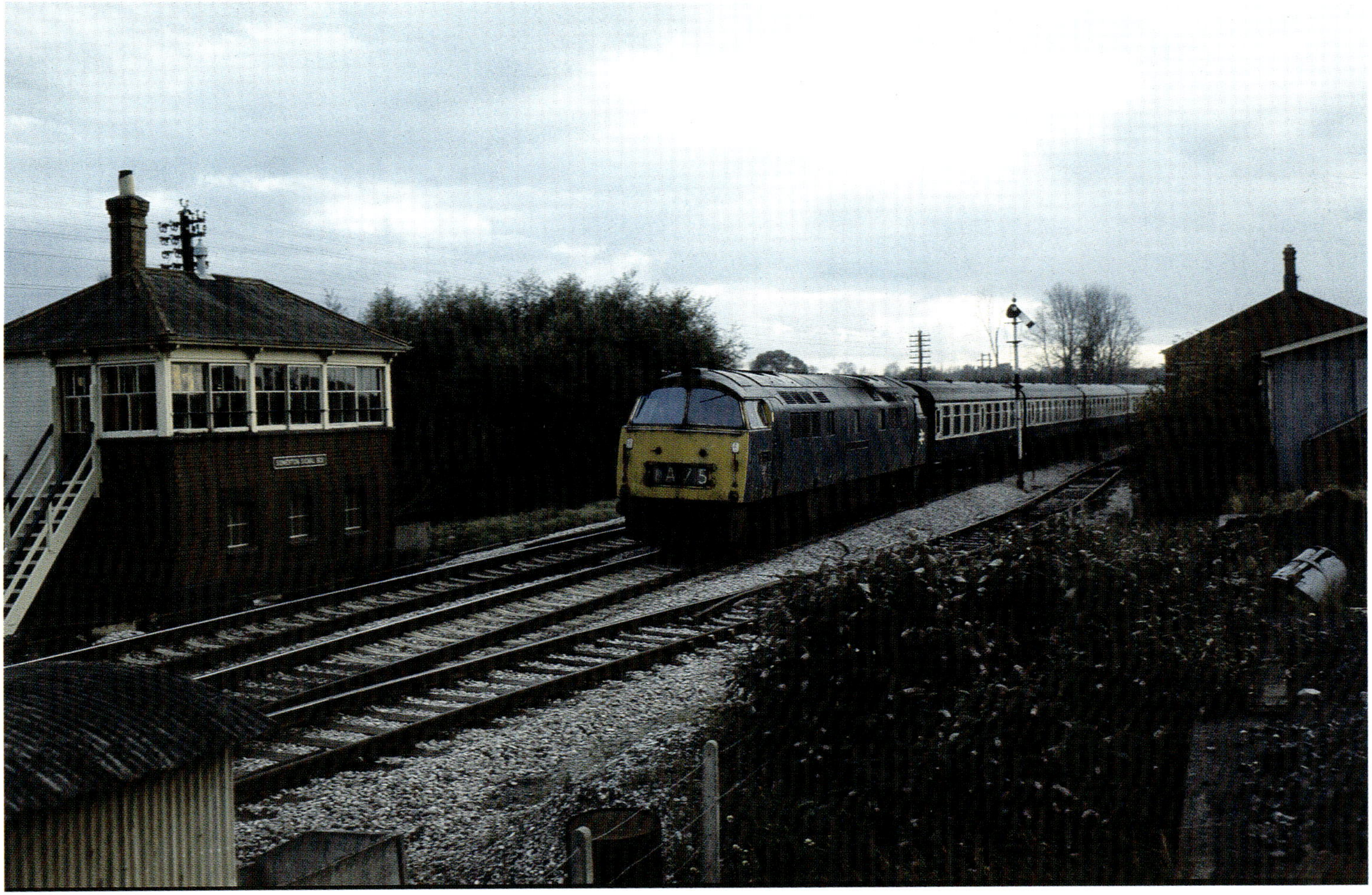

Above: on Sunday, 21st September 1975, D1016 *Western Gladiator* passes Somerton signalbox with the 13.50 Penzance to Paddington. The day was memorable for me as we visited Athelney and Somerton, starting our cunning ruse to illicitly gain entry to signalboxes. Clutching my copy of Adrian Vaughan's *Great Western Signalling*, I would walk up the signalbox stairs and ask the signalman if he could sign my copy of the book. The signalman at Athelney said yes, and later at Somerton I asked the same question to which the signalman there replied, 'But I'm not Adrian Vaughan!' It was one of the first occasions when I realised how close-knit the railway community was. It turned out that his name was John Cornelius and he was a church bell-ringer who already knew my parents, both avid campanologists.

Opposite: D1068 *Western Reliance* rushes through Castle Cary on Saturday, 14th June 1975 with the 09.50 Plymouth to Paddington, flanked by Great Western signals provided after enemy action flattened the original junction on 3rd September 1942. The backing signal with the characteristic holes in the arm was the last of its type to remain in use on the Western Region, finally succumbing to modernisation in February 1985.

PART 2: SOMERTON to PENZANCE

Not far from the long defunct station of Long Sutton and Pitney lies the western portal of Somerton Tunnel. We spent some time exploring the area on Sunday, 21st September 1975 and saw D1068 *Western Reliance* dashing past with the 15.15 Paignton to Paddington at 17.28.

Having photographed *Reliance* approaching the tunnel portal, we only had to wait another fifteen minutes for a down train, being rewarded with the sight of D1047 *Western Lord* exiting the tunnel mouth on the 15.30 Paddington to Plymouth. Timings over the section from Castle Cary to Taunton had recovery for both trains; two minutes on the up and a generous five minutes on the down. It was a great temptation but I resisted montaging these two photographs together!

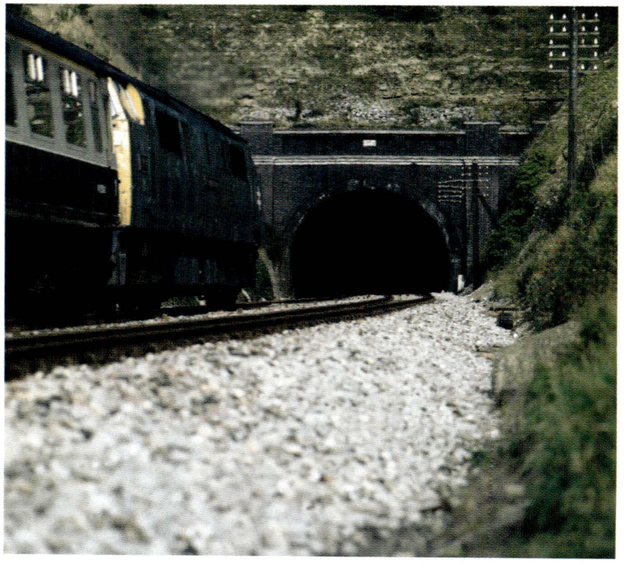

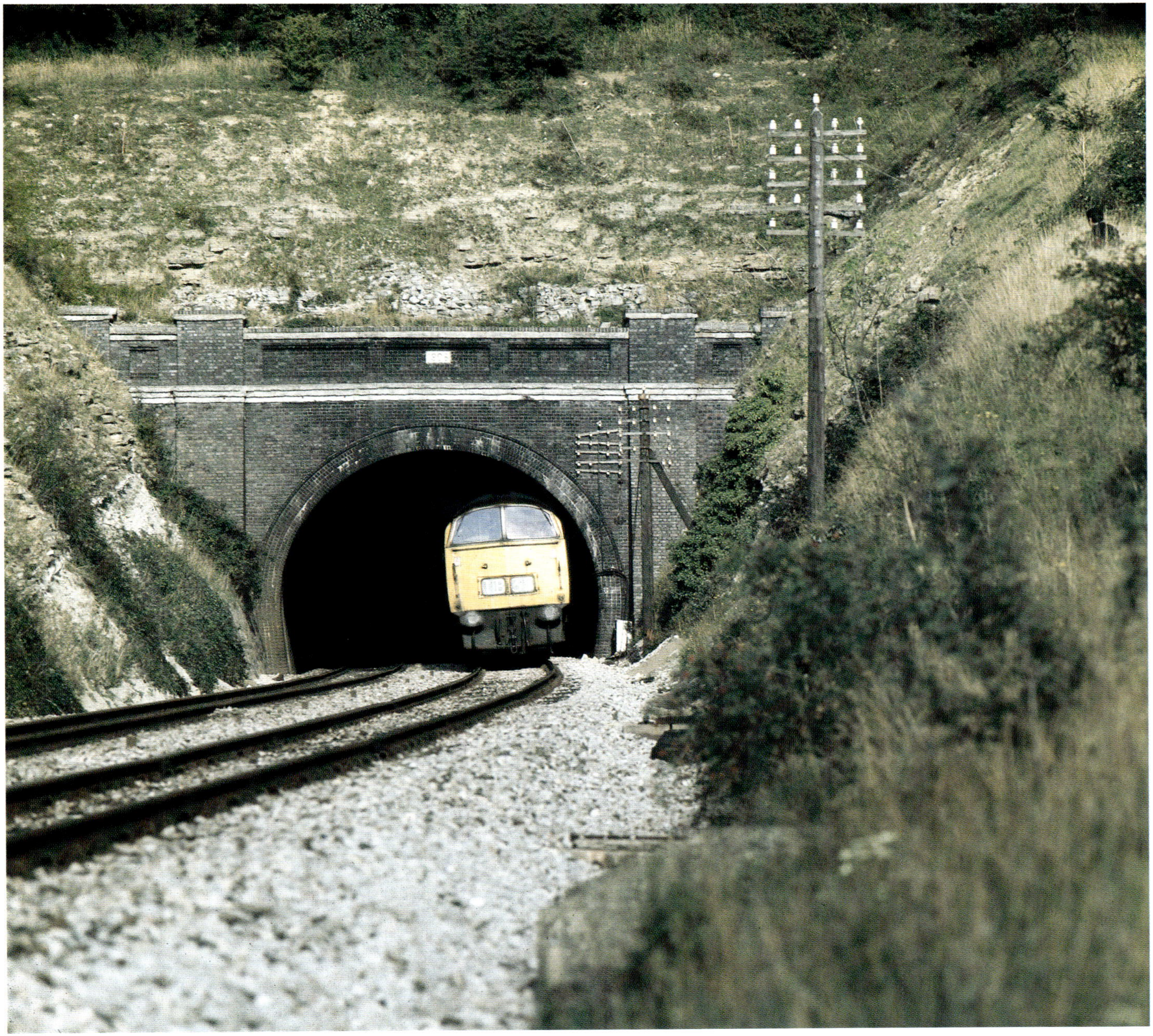

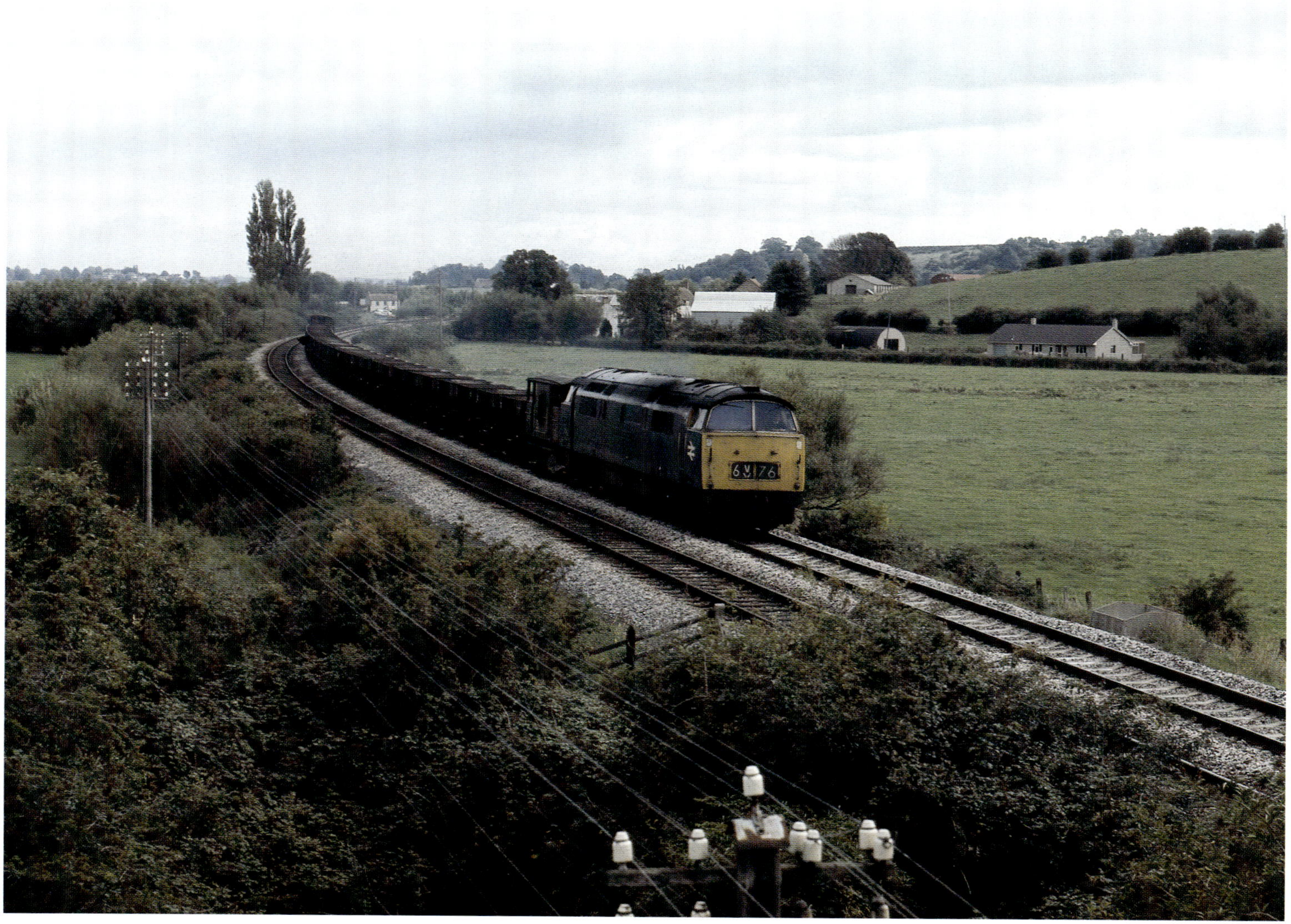

On a lazy summer afternoon in 1975, D1051 *Western Ambassador* rolls into the Somerset Levels at Oath Bridge, between Langport and Athelney, with a ballast working to Taunton Fairwater. The headcode is a remnant from a Botley to Westbury stone working.

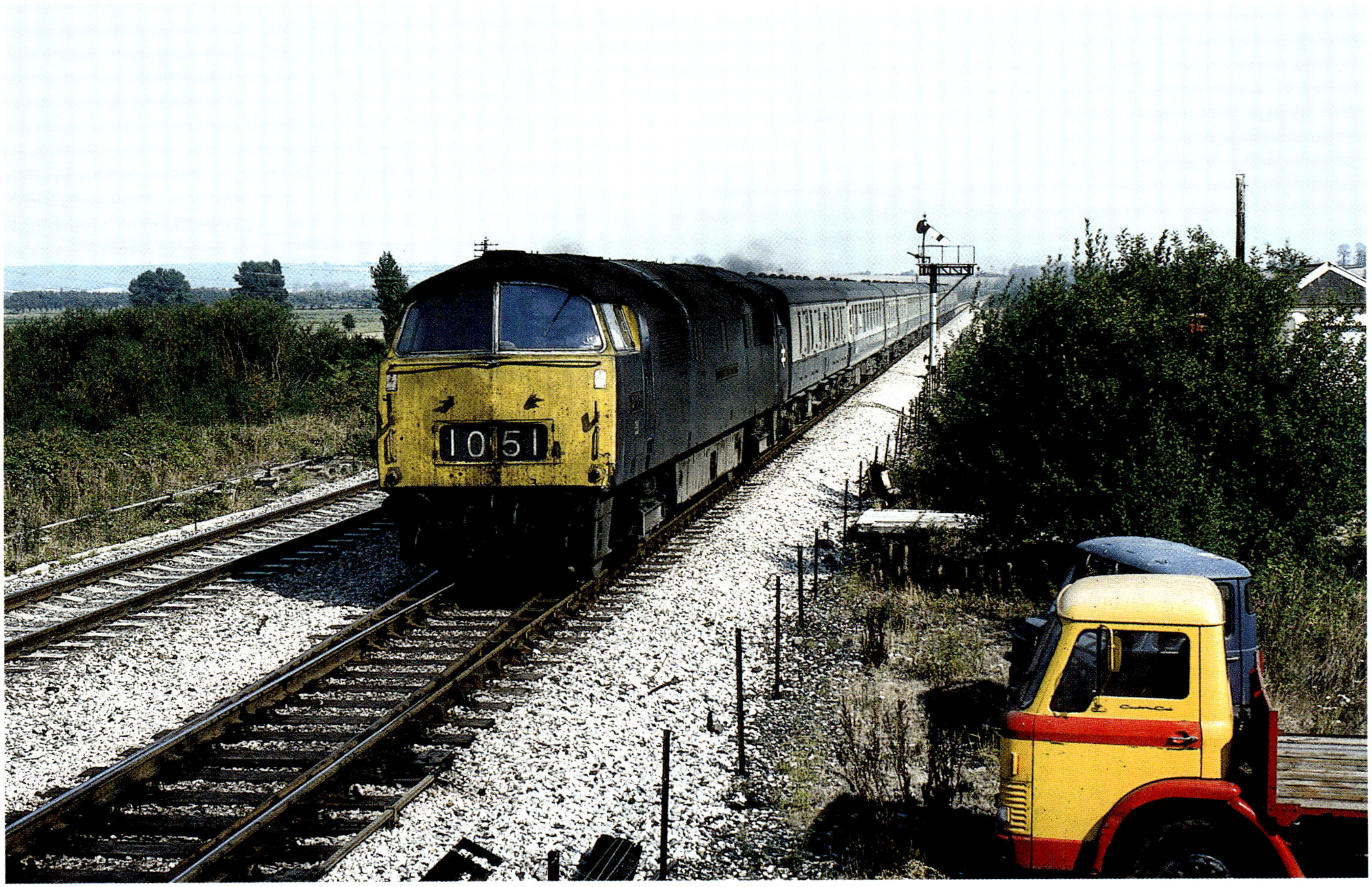

The end was nigh for *Western Ambassador* by the time this photograph was taken on Thursday, 26th August 1976. Seen at Athelney hauling the 13.30 Paddington to Penzance, she had previously worked up to Old Oak Common that morning from Plymouth with the empty vans from the overnight paper train. The following Wednesday, whilst on the 08.30 Paddington to Plymouth, she hit ballast at Cogload Junction, the next block post west of Athelney. Subsequent assessment lead to withdrawal of an otherwise perfectly serviceable locomotive, ending the longest allocation of a Western to Laira; continuously from January 1964.

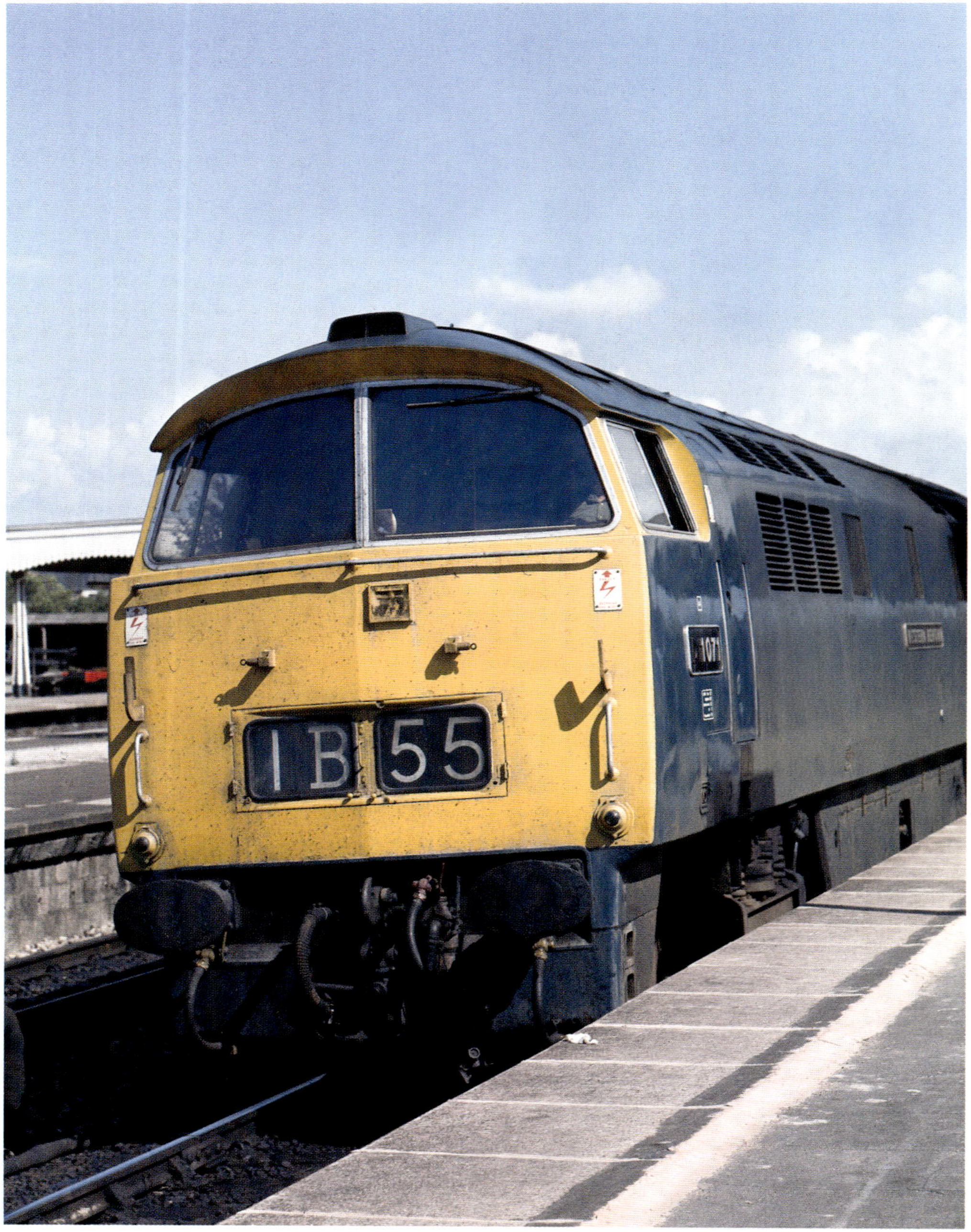

Still quite dapper from a repaint three months earlier, D1071 *Western Renown* is seen here during a station stop at Taunton with the 12.30 Paddington to Paignton on 25th August 1975. The vent provided in the cab end attempted to improve cab air circulation, but was not particularly successful and only a handful of the class received this modification. The numberplate had the 'D' painted out in accordance with the new numerical classification introduced in 1972 in readiness for TOPS, which made the distinction between diesel and electric locomotives unnecessary. However, this practice was abandoned for the repaint of *Western Ranger's* numberplates in red for the last year of operation.

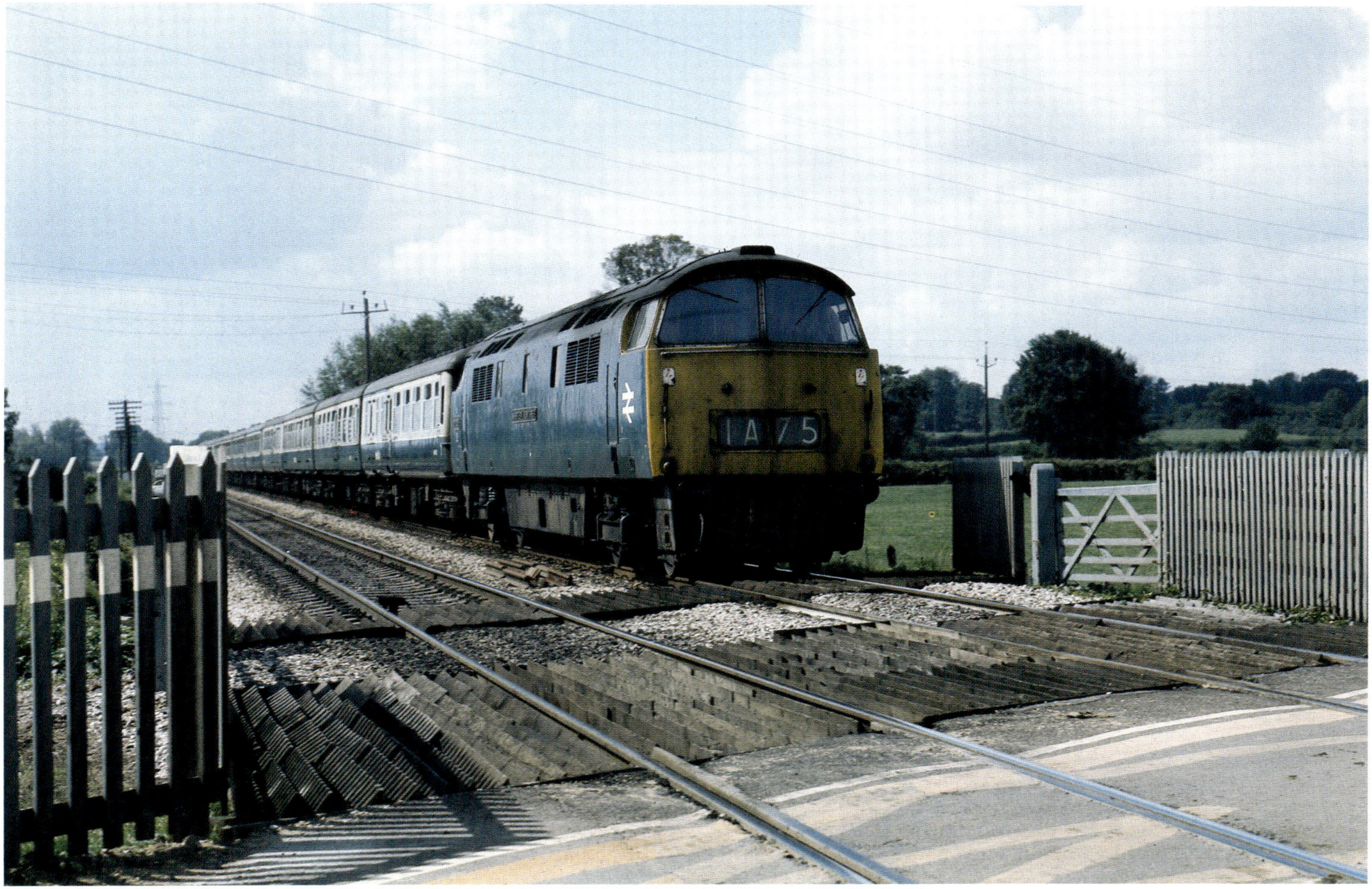

It is quite an experience to stand at Victory Crossing and see a train rushing down the bank from Wellington. The automatic barriers lowering and the din of the audible warning only seem to accentuate the speed of the oncoming train. Minutes after seeing *Western Chieftain* on a down special (shown overleaf), we were rewarded with the sight of D1005 *Western Venturer* on the 11.00 Plymouth to Paddington, easily matching the permissible line speed of 90 mph.

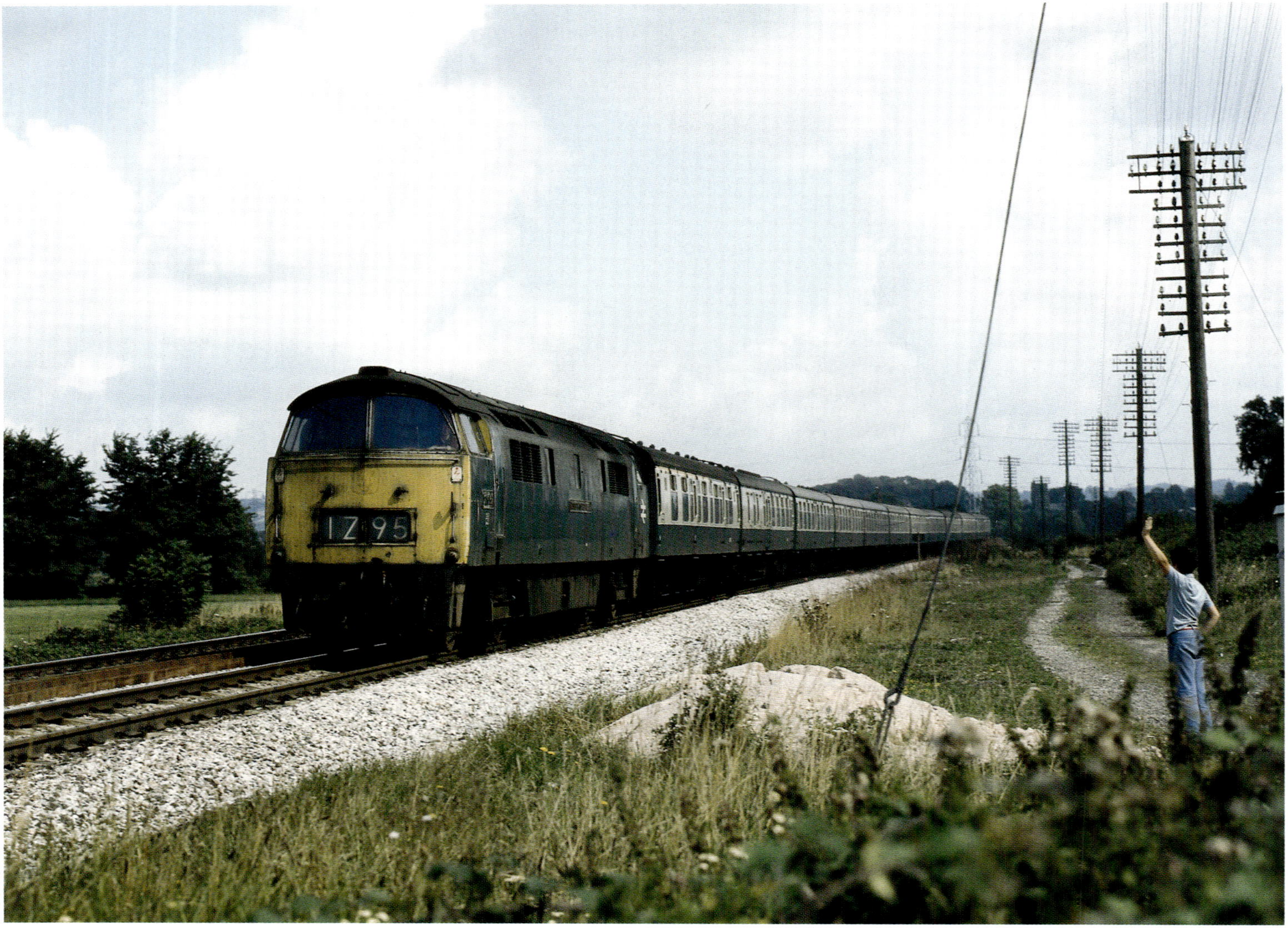

Fresh from a crew change at Taunton, D1057 *Western Chieftain* accelerates towards Victory Crossing, eleven on with the 09.13 Adex Paddington to Paignton on August Bank Holiday Monday 1975. I can be seen waving to the driver for photographic effect; most of them waved back.

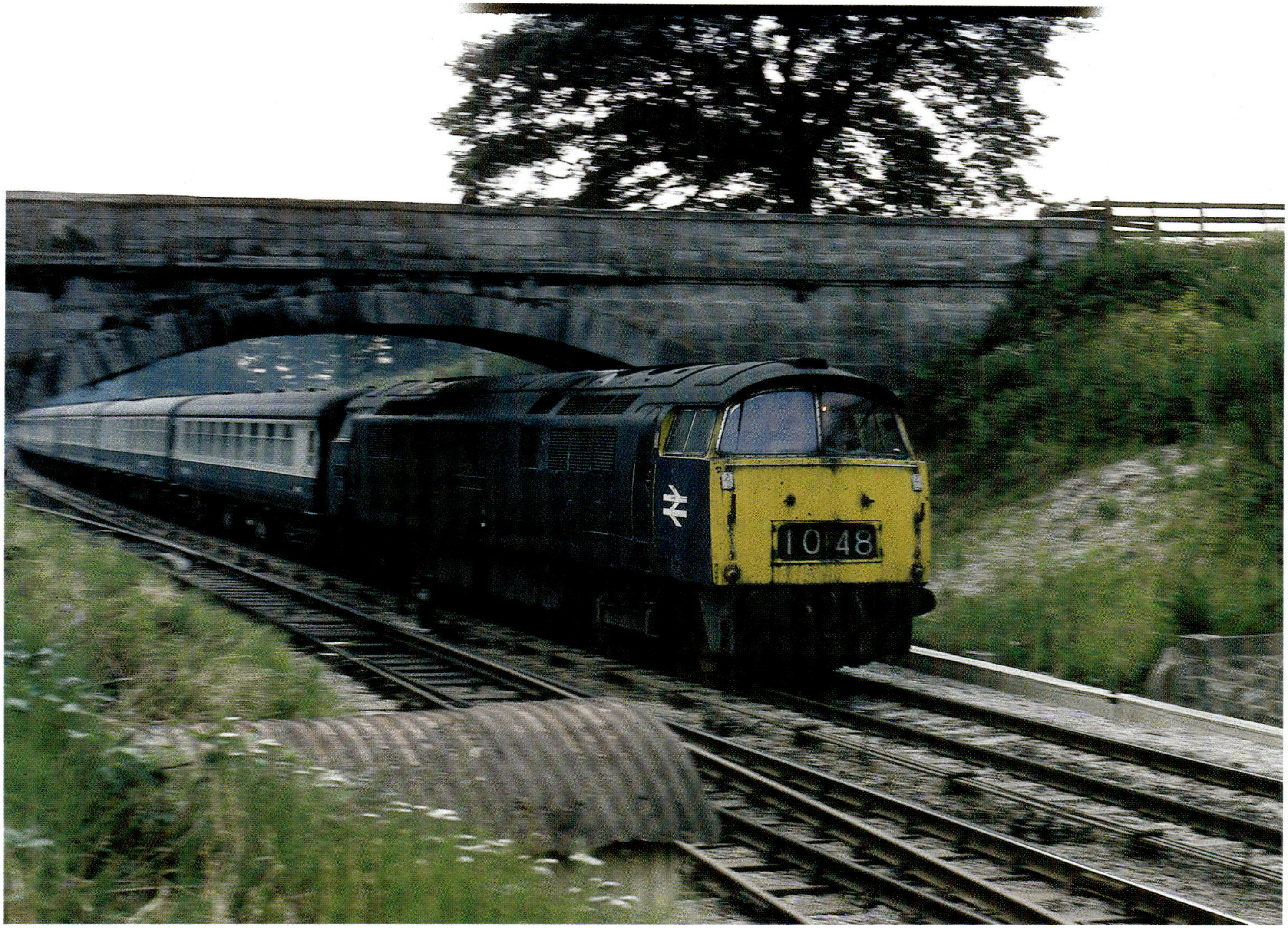

Crossing from Somerset into Devon by rail is evident by passage through the 1092 yards of Whiteball Tunnel. The A38 road straddles the tunnel and we found our way through the lanes to the signalbox at Whiteball Siding using our Ordnance Survey one-inch map of pre-motorway vintage. It was nice to be in the cosy little signalbox looking towards the Devon end tunnel portal, a well known view in many railway photographs. In the opposite direction, the sun had fallen behind the cutting but there was still enough light to photograph D1048 *Western Lady* with the 15.55 Plymouth to Paddington, on Thursday, 12th August 1976.

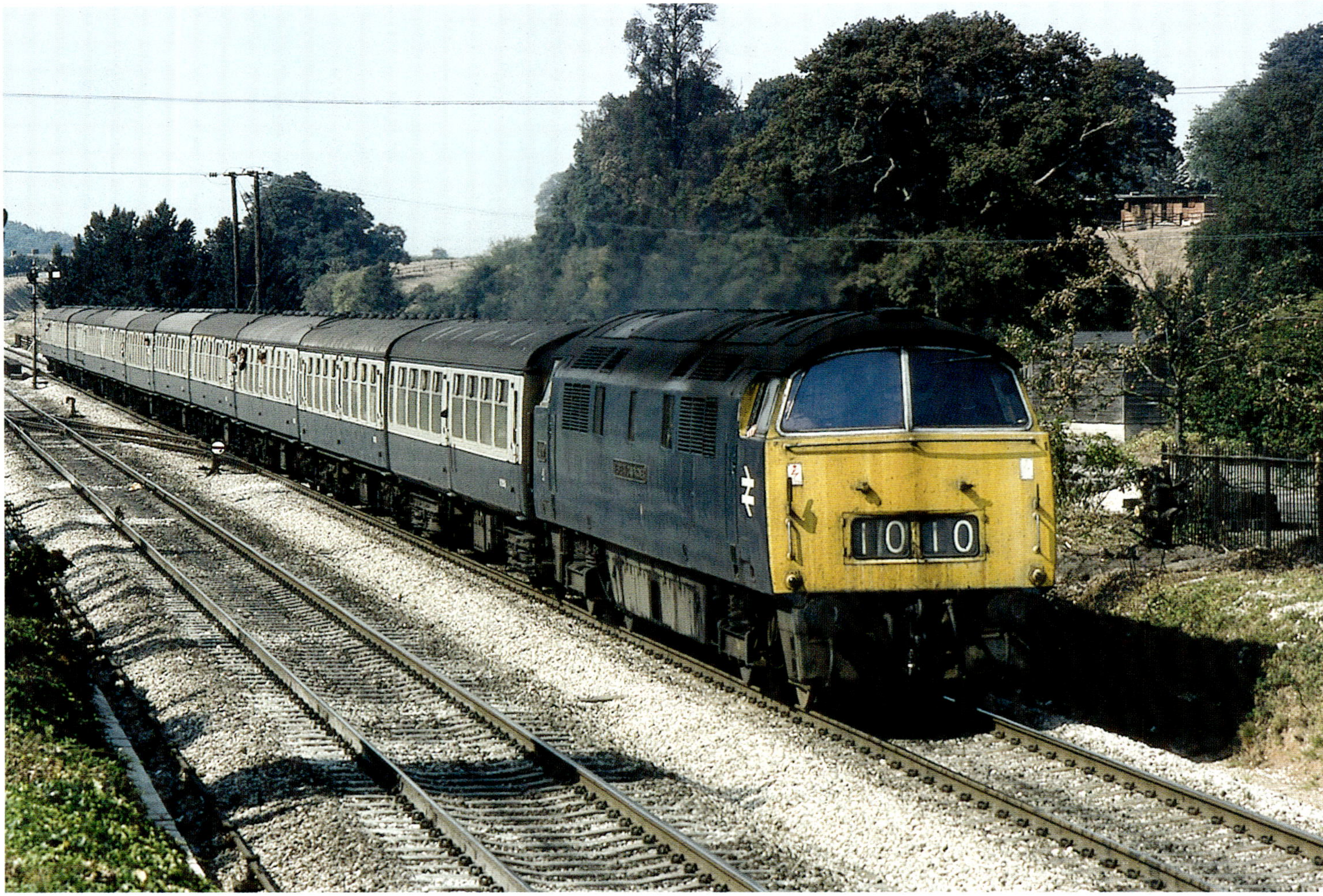

Our journey westwards continued the following morning with Hele & Bradninch as the first stop. D1010 *Western Campaigner* is hauling a rake of eleven coaches, Mark Is at the back with a B4 bogie vehicle leading. Not accounted for in the TOPS records, it is likely that this working was the 09.15 (Charter) from Okehampton to Bristol Temple Meads, running in the path of the Thursdays only 07.38 Newquay to Paddington SAGA. The signalman has already returned the home signal to danger before the whole train has passed the signal - a common practice in the West Country.

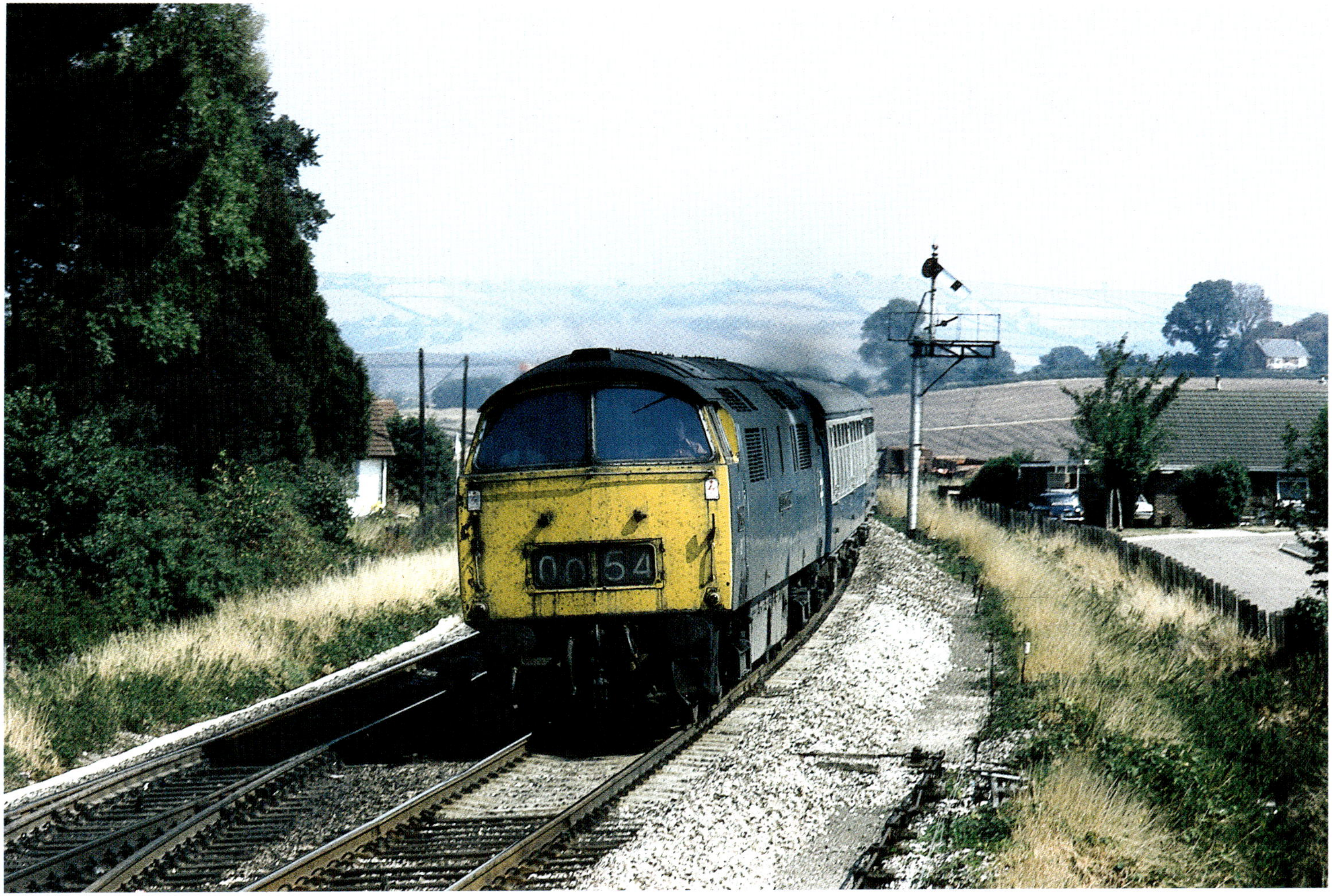

In this striking telephoto shot, D1054 *Western Governor* approaches Stoke Canon Crossing with the 08.36 Paddington to Paignton, a summer timetable train that only ran in peak season from 5th July to 3rd September. It is nearly noon on 13th August 1976, temperatures in the eighties, and the traincrew looking forward to arriving at Paignton, four hours and three minutes after departure from the capital.

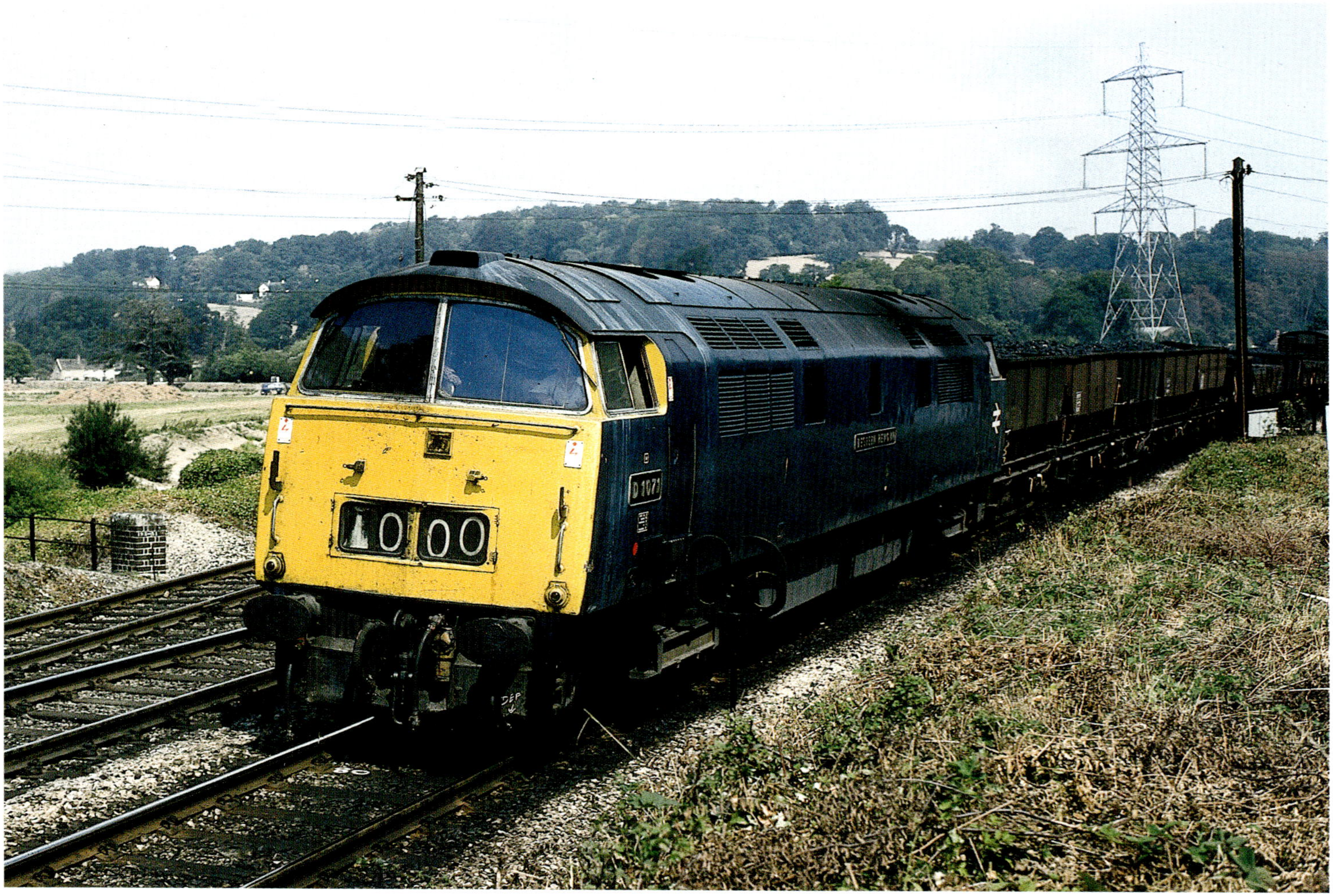

On Friday, 13th August 1976 at Cowley Bridge Junction, D1071 *Western Renown* hauls the 23.45 Warrington to Exeter Riverside class 7 freight, about to crossover from the main line to the down reception on the final leg of the journey to Riverside Yard. Note the right hand side vacuum brake hose marked as defective. The train had left Warrington late on Thursday, with *Renown* working it down from Severn Tunnel Junction to Riverside. Friday departures recessed on Saturday mornings at Severn Tunnel Junction until the following Monday.

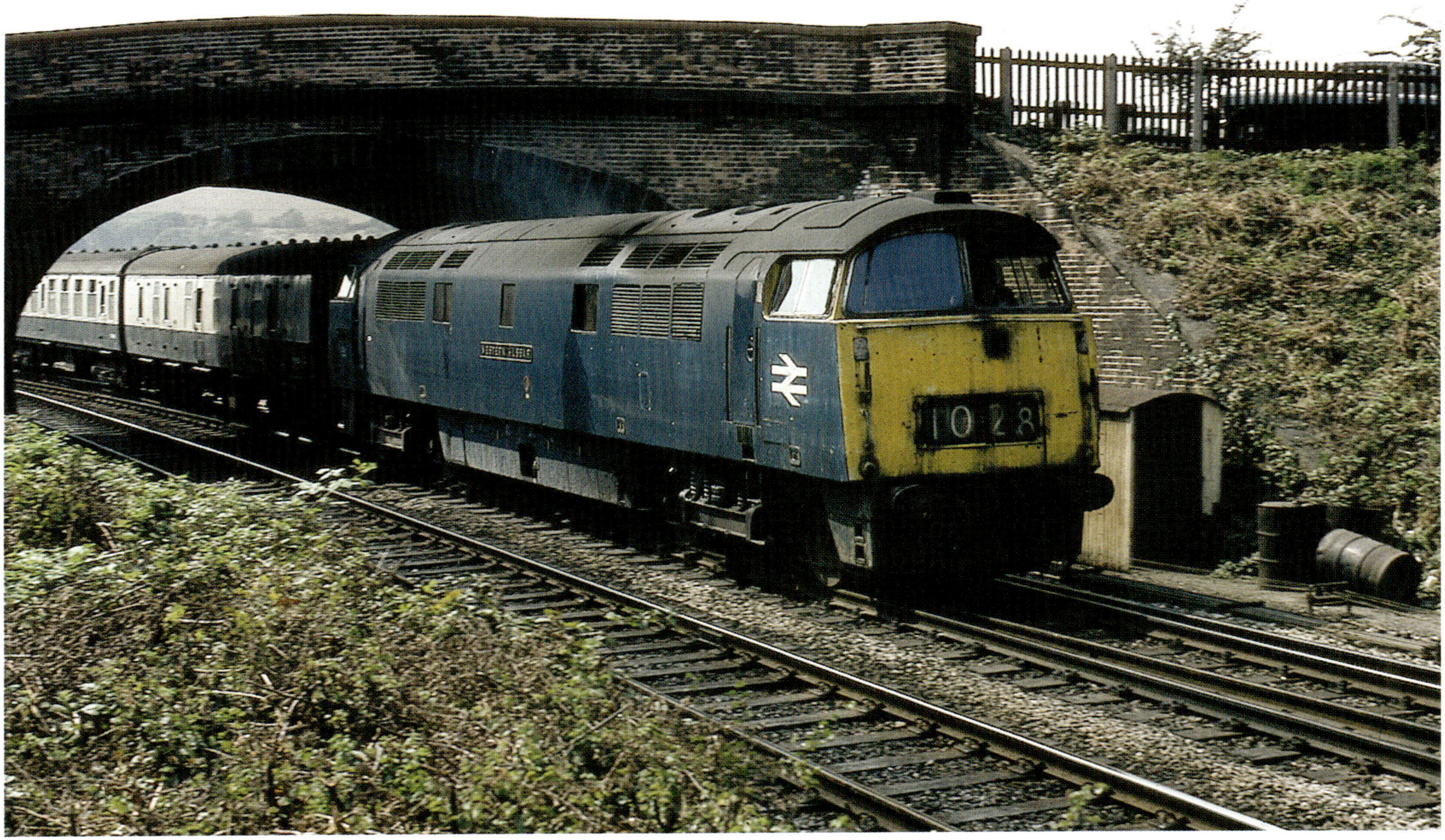

D1028 *Western Hussar* roars under the A377 overbridge at Cowley Bridge Junction with an up passenger working on Friday, 13th August 1976. Although Western availability was satisfactory in this month, they tended to be diagrammed on the additional trains which only ran in the peak of the summer period. It was therefore likely that this train was the 11.00 Plymouth to Paddington.

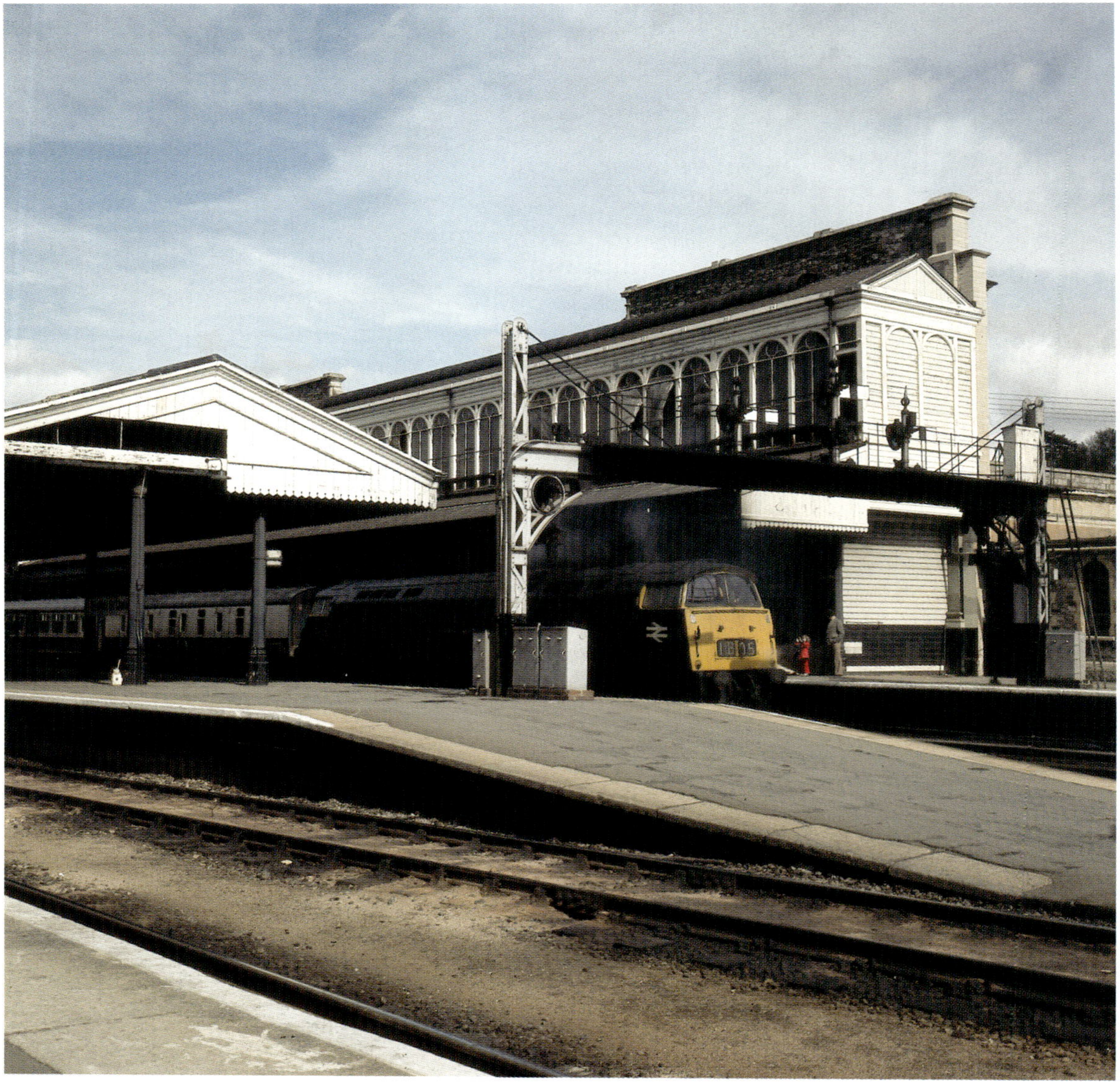

Framed by the magnificent gantry of Exeter West's down home signals, D1070 *Western Gauntlet* waits in the down main platform at Exeter St. Davids with the 08.35 Paddington to Plymouth on Sunday, 14th September 1975. With station stops at Dawlish, Teignmouth and Newton Abbot, eighty eight minutes were timetabled for the fifty two mile journey past the sea wall and over the South Devon banks. Non-stop trains such as the *Cornish Riviera* had a tighter diagram of seventy six minutes from Exeter to Plymouth.

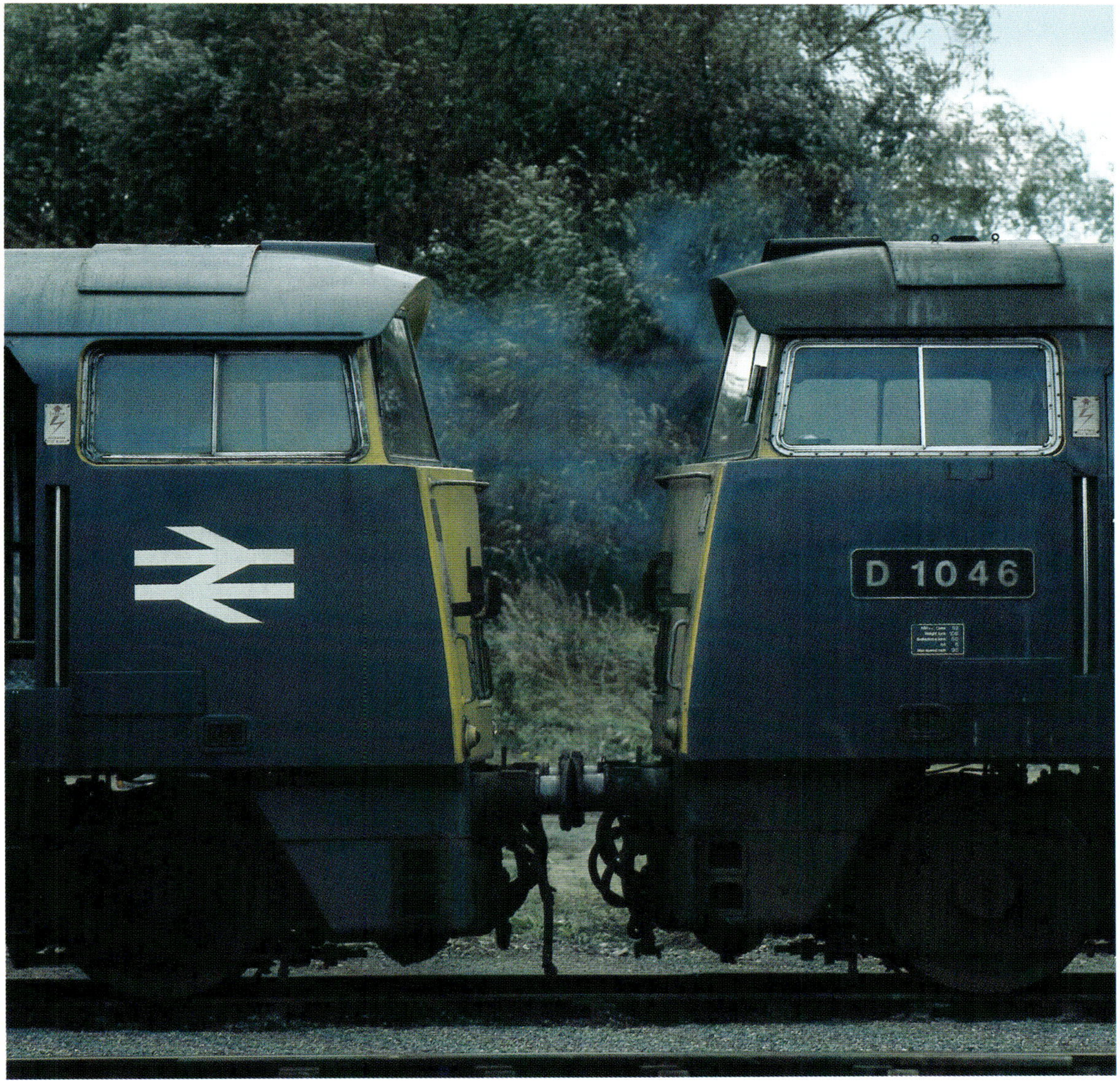

This study shows *Western Centurion* and *Western Marquis* in repose at Exeter St. Davids on 14th September 1975. Research undertaken by Adrian Curtis has clearly established that the design of the Westerns was largely the work of one man, Sir Misha Black. As a consultant to the British Transport Commission, he produced the most aesthetically pleasing diesel locomotive design this country has ever seen.

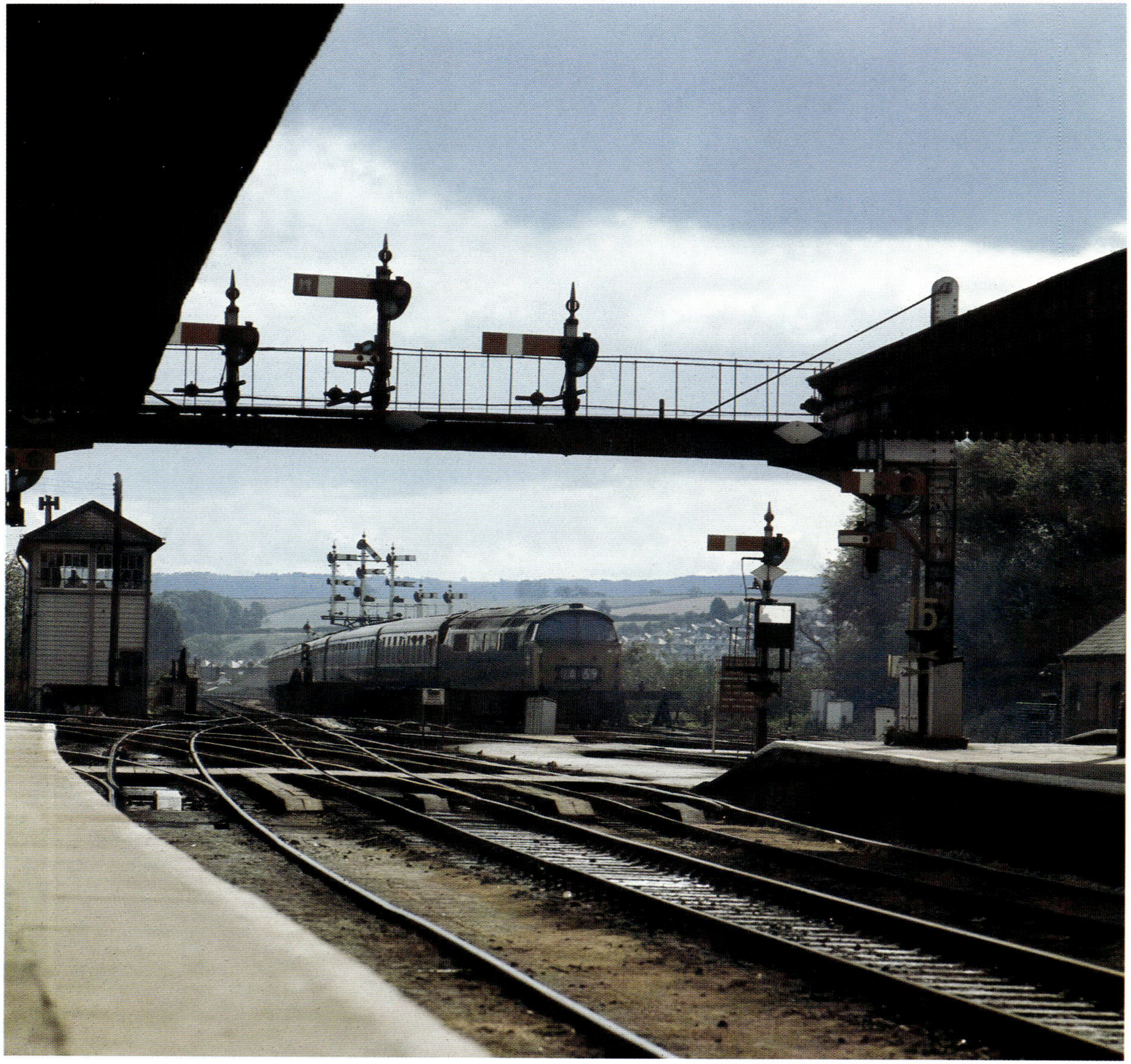

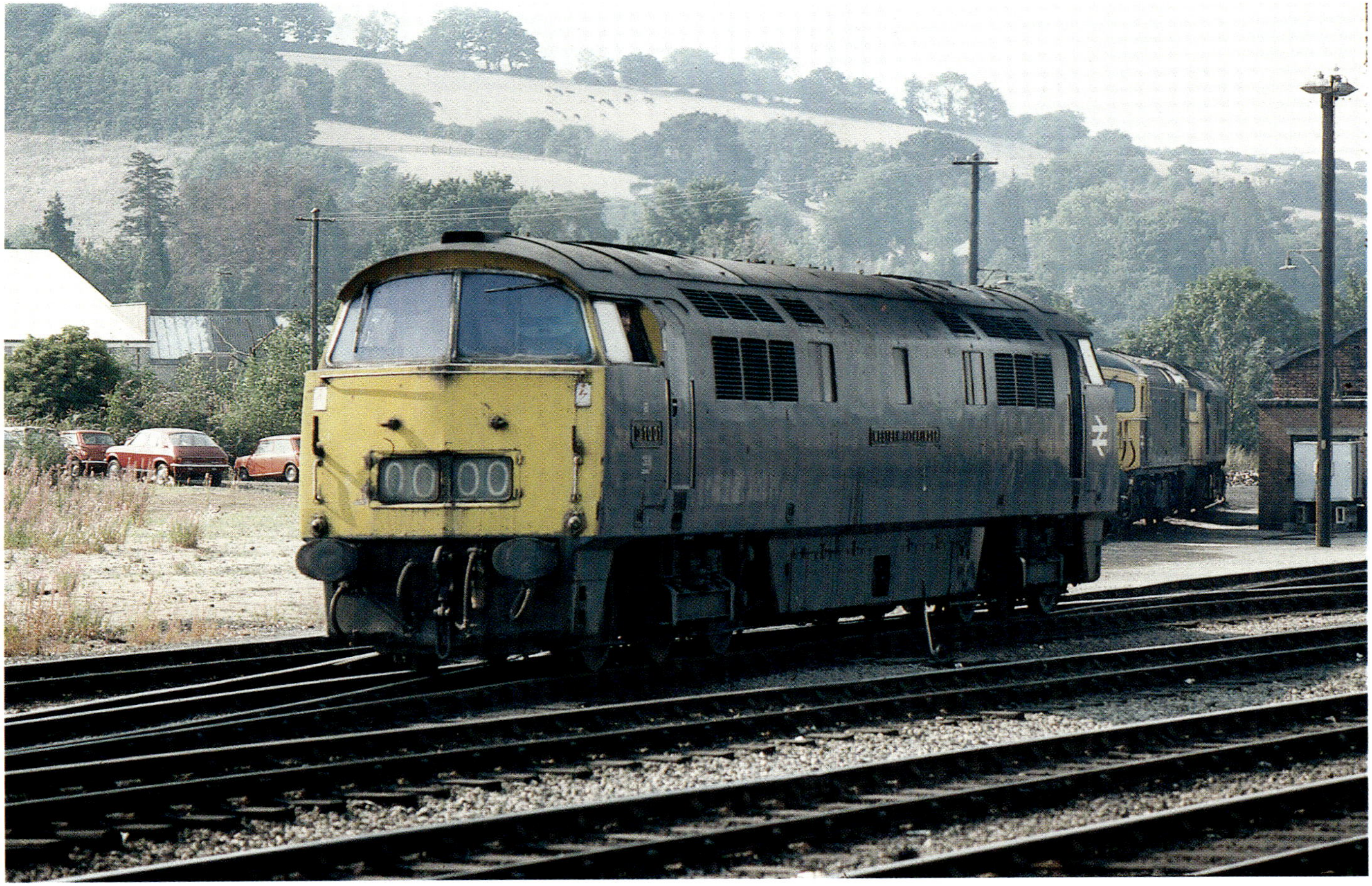

Above: Though much reduced from steam days, Exeter St. Davids remained a stabling point after dieselisation. Here on Friday, 13th August 1976 is D1001 *Western Pathfinder*, stabling from the engine spur after coming in on the goods lines. Already stabled are a Class 33/1 and a Class 25. We had decided it would be too difficult to gain access to Exeter Middle and West Boxes, so between visiting Cowley Bridge Junction in the morning and Exeter City Basin later that afternoon, we spent a few hours on the platform at St. Davids, enjoying the sunshine and also seeing *Western Trooper* roll in with an up passenger working.

Opposite: On Sunday, 14th September 1975, an unidentified Western enters Exeter St. Davids hauling the 13.30 Paignton to Paddington. Apart from the station platforms and the distant view of the Haldon Hills, nothing remains of this scene today. The wooden post home signal directing the train into the station was replaced by a tubular steel structure in 1976; the semaphore signals were replaced by colour lights in 1985 with the first stage of the Exeter MAS scheme. Colour light signals are not as photogenic as semaphores but they provided me with a promotion when I moved to Exeter Panel as a Technician Officer in 1987.

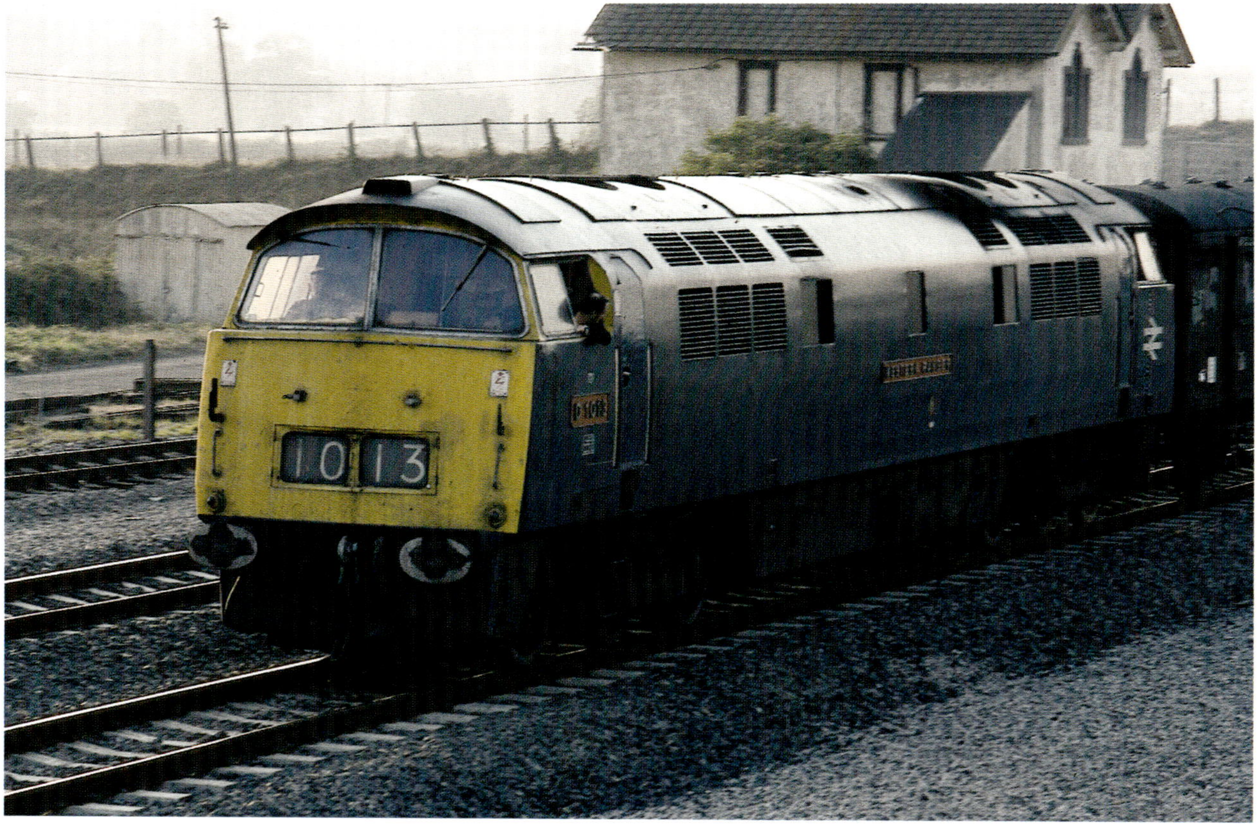

The driver of D1013 *Western Ranger* looks back out of the cab window, to check for signs of trouble on his train. He wouldn't have bothered but he saw our camera poking out from the window of Exminster signalbox and concluded something must be amiss! The train was the 15.57 Bristol Temple Meads to Plymouth Parcels, on Friday 13th August 1976. *Ranger* had her nameplates and numberplates painted red in early 1976.

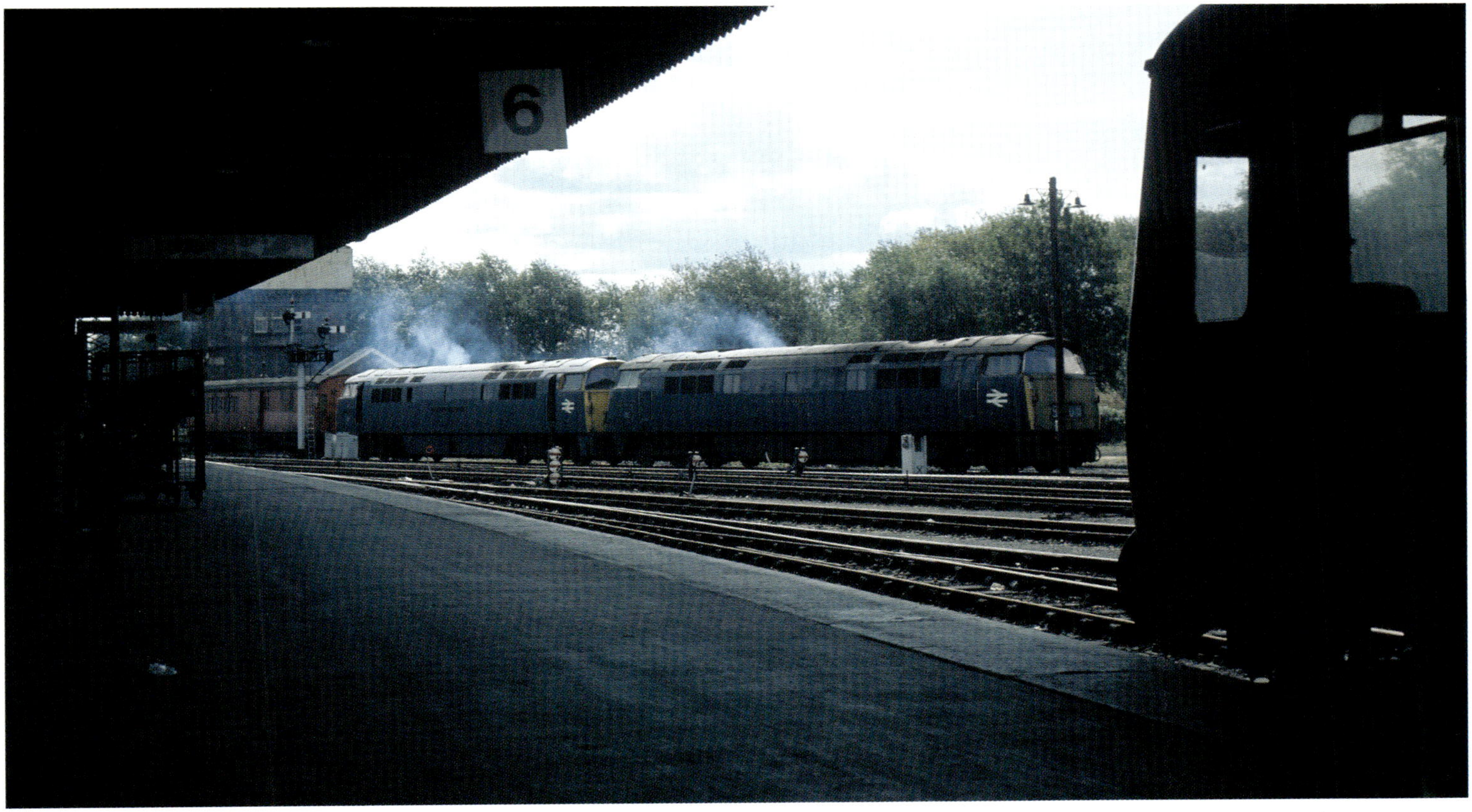

Above: Engines idling, this is a more distant view of D1046 *Western Marquis* and sister locomotive D1026 *Western Centurion* between duties at Exeter St. Davids on 14th September 1975. Although *Marquis* survived until a collision with *Western Regent* at Laira in December that year caused both locmotives to be scrapped, *Centurion* was withdrawn at the end of the 1975 summer timetable, three weeks after this photograph was taken.

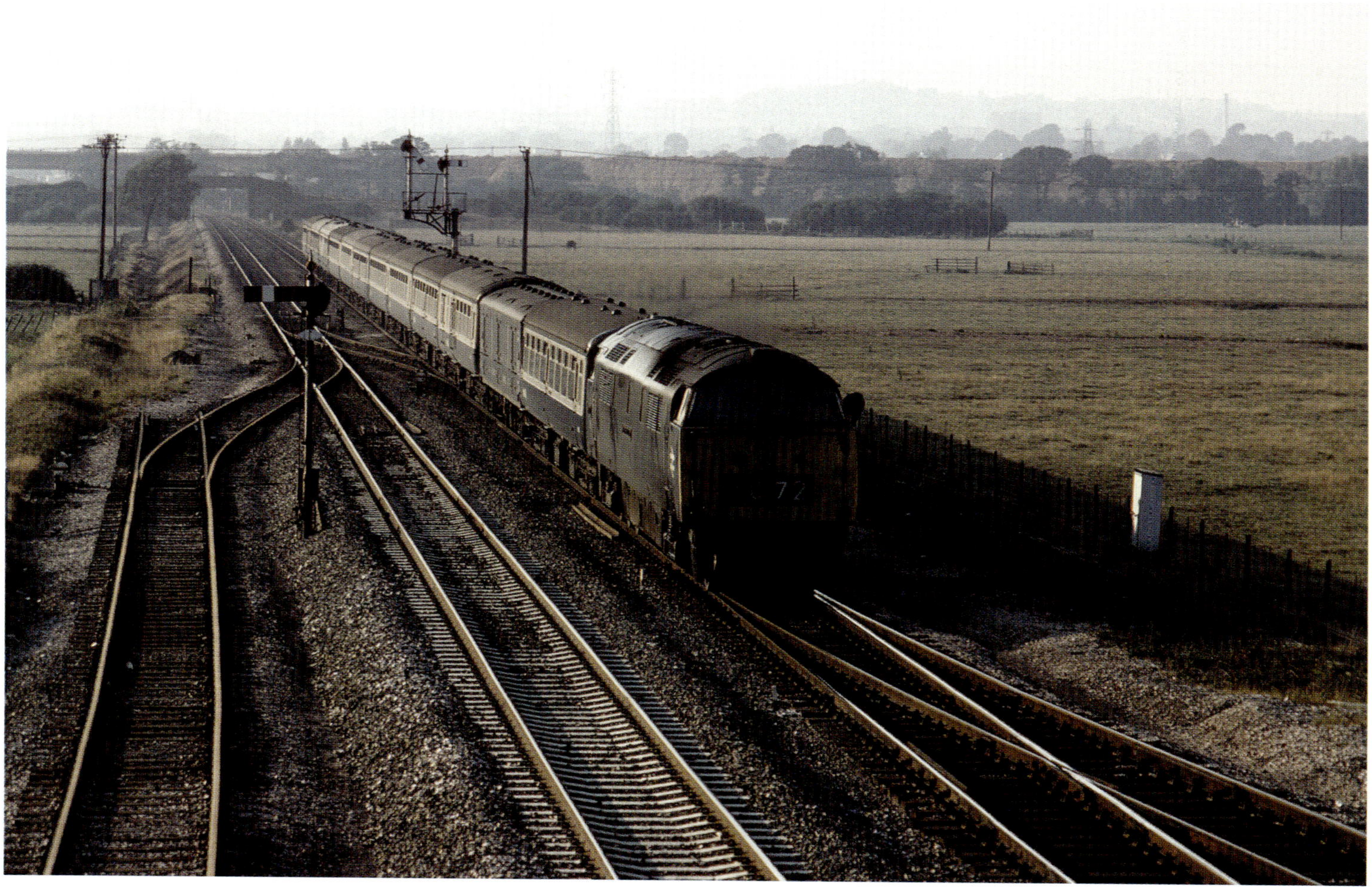

In the soft evening light of Friday, 13th August 1976, D1072 *Western Glory* passes Exminster hauling the 15.30 Paddington to Penzance before heading out alongside the Exe estuary and around the sea wall. In the background the M5 motorway embankment was still in construction but the motorway was soon to rival the railway across the river Exe.

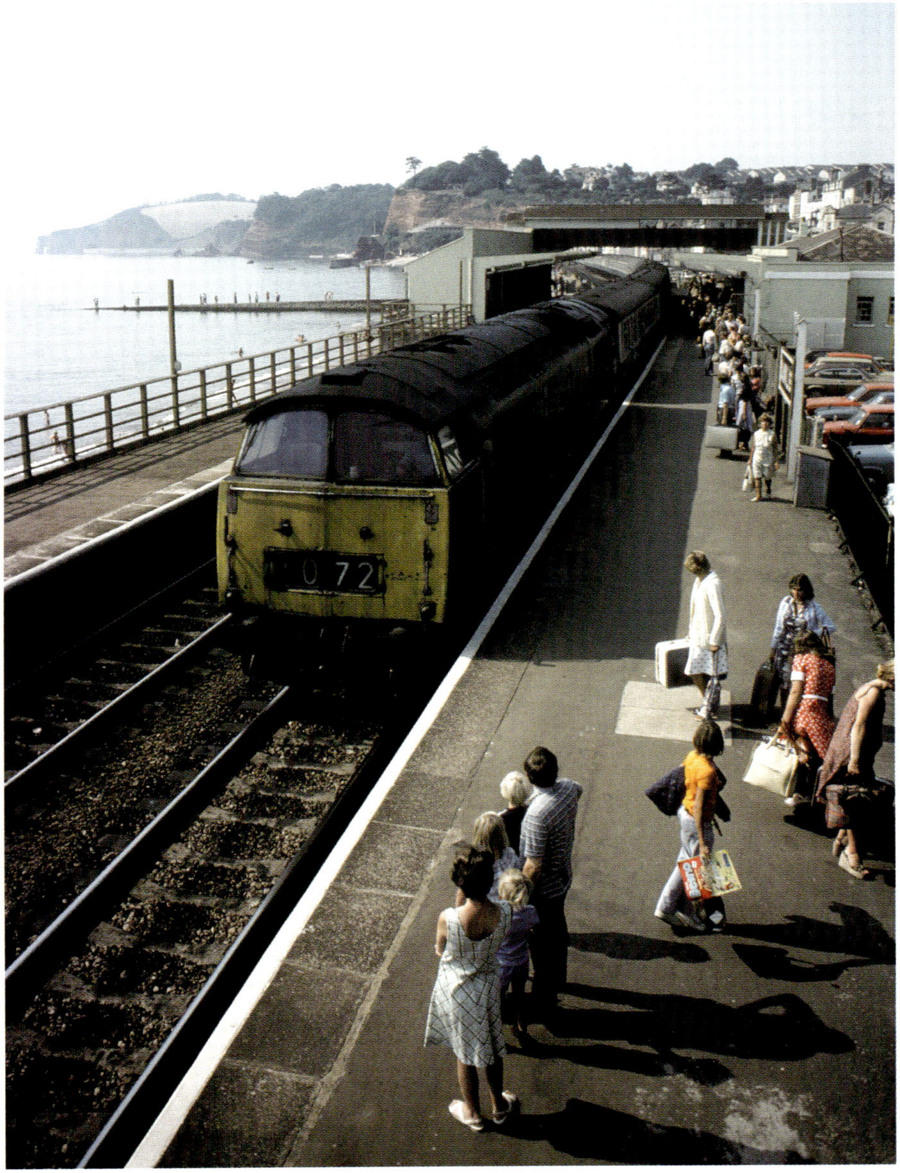

Left: On the next day, we saw D1072 *Western Glory* again, stopping at Dawlish station with the 09.50 Plymouth to Paddington. Fortunately our visit coincided with the summer Saturday opening of Dawlish signalbox, and both this view and the one overleaf are from that now redundant but listed structure. The girl in the orange top clutches her copy of the Beano Summer Special, ready for the long journey back to town.

Overleaf: The guard waits impatiently for carriage doors to be slammed shut before giving 'right away' to the driver of *Glory*. It was unusually for holidaymakers to alight at Dawlish in the up direction. Perhaps the couple walking towards the camera were Devonians returning from holiday in the Scilly Isles?

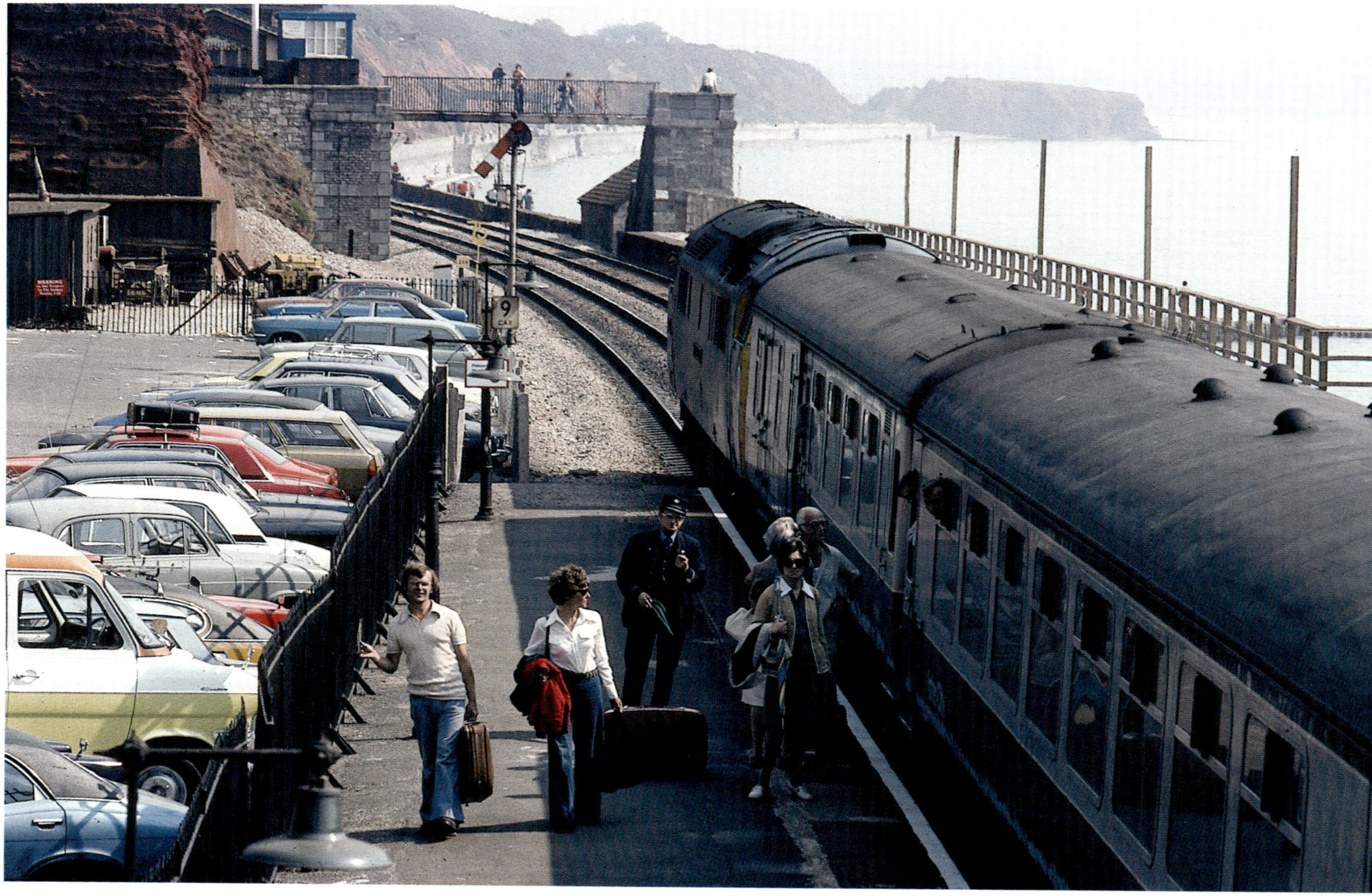
9

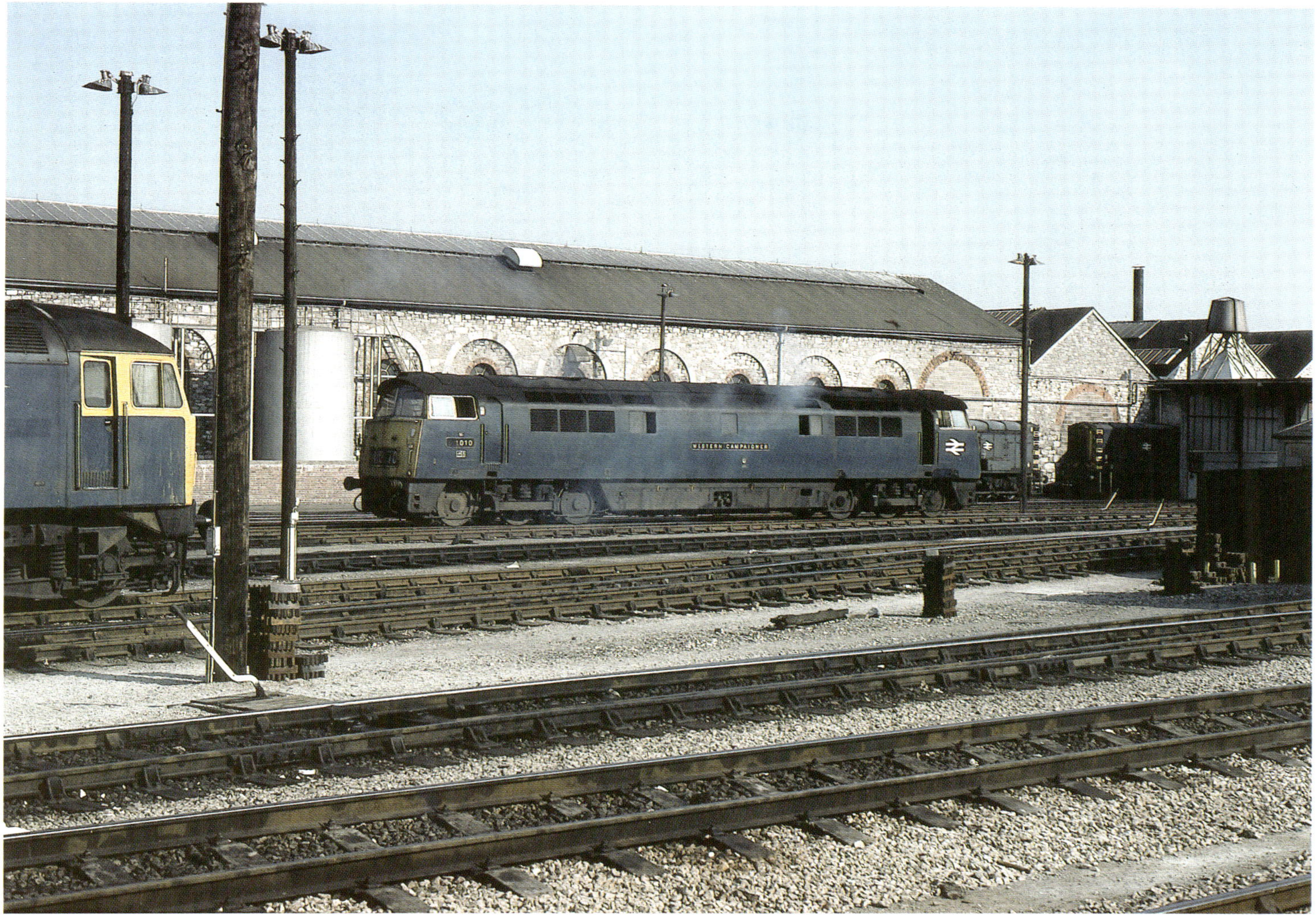

D1010 *Western Campaigner* at rest outside the shed at Newton Abbot, before marshalling the 19.30 Newton Abbot to Stirling Motorail on Saturday, 14th August 1976. It was barely more than six months later when *Western Ranger* towed her here from Laira on the day after withdrawal from service. The two class 08 shunters were allocated to the east and west ends of the layout, one shunting the carriage sidings and the other shunting at Hackney and working trips on the Heathfield branch.

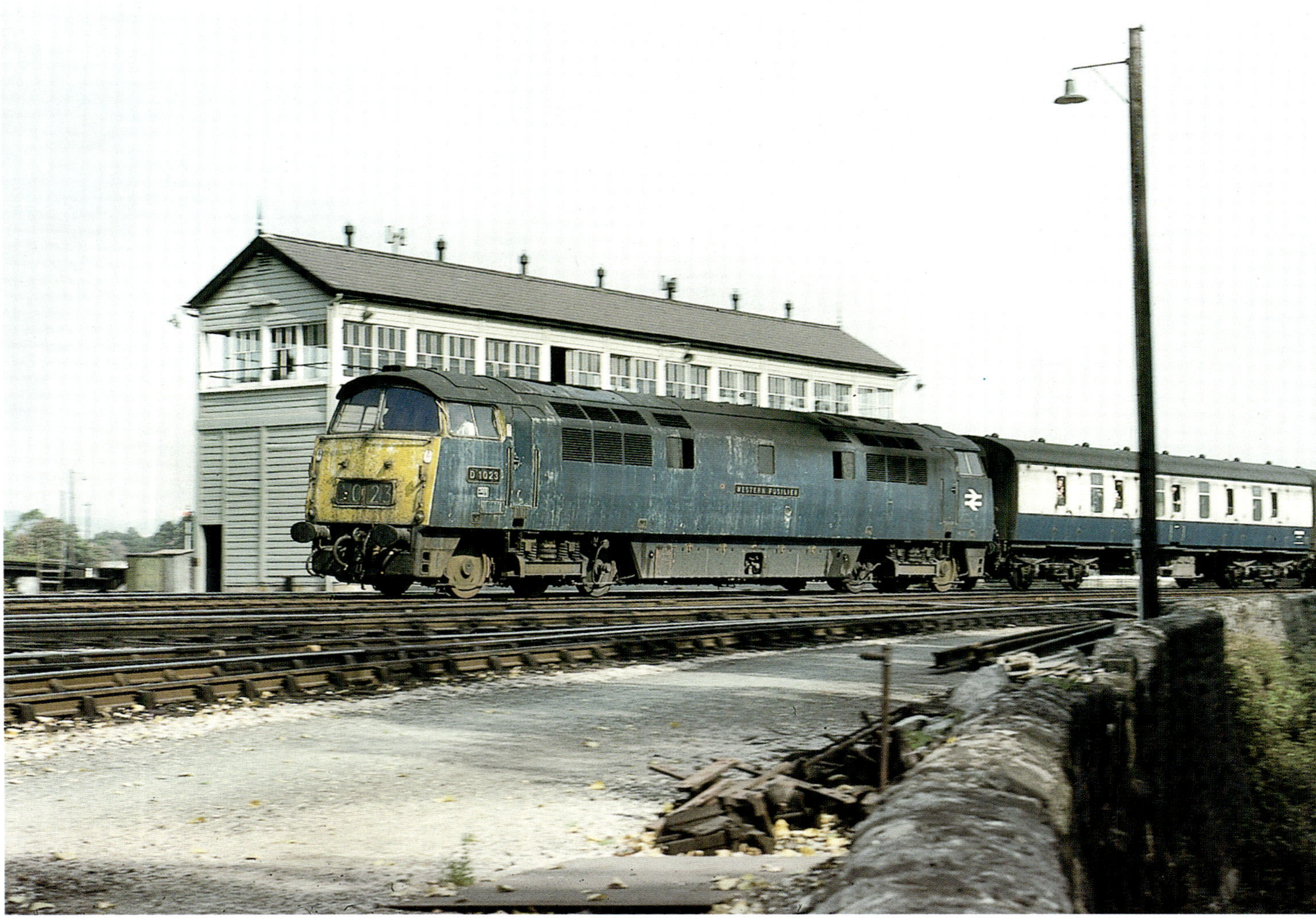

D1023 *Western Fusilier* runs past Newton Abbot East box with a morning train in August 1976. There are several enthusiasts in the leading van listening to the loco as it negotiates the point work into Newton station. The double manned signalbox was the largest ex-Great Western box in existence at the time, and until closure in 1987 had the largest operational lever frame on BR, with 206 levers. It was an impressive place which controlled the west end of Hackney yard, the east end of Newton Abbot station, carriage sidings, loco shed, goods yard connections and the Heathfield branch. Like many before him, Dave Richards (our friend at Fairwood Junction) started his railway career here as a booking boy.

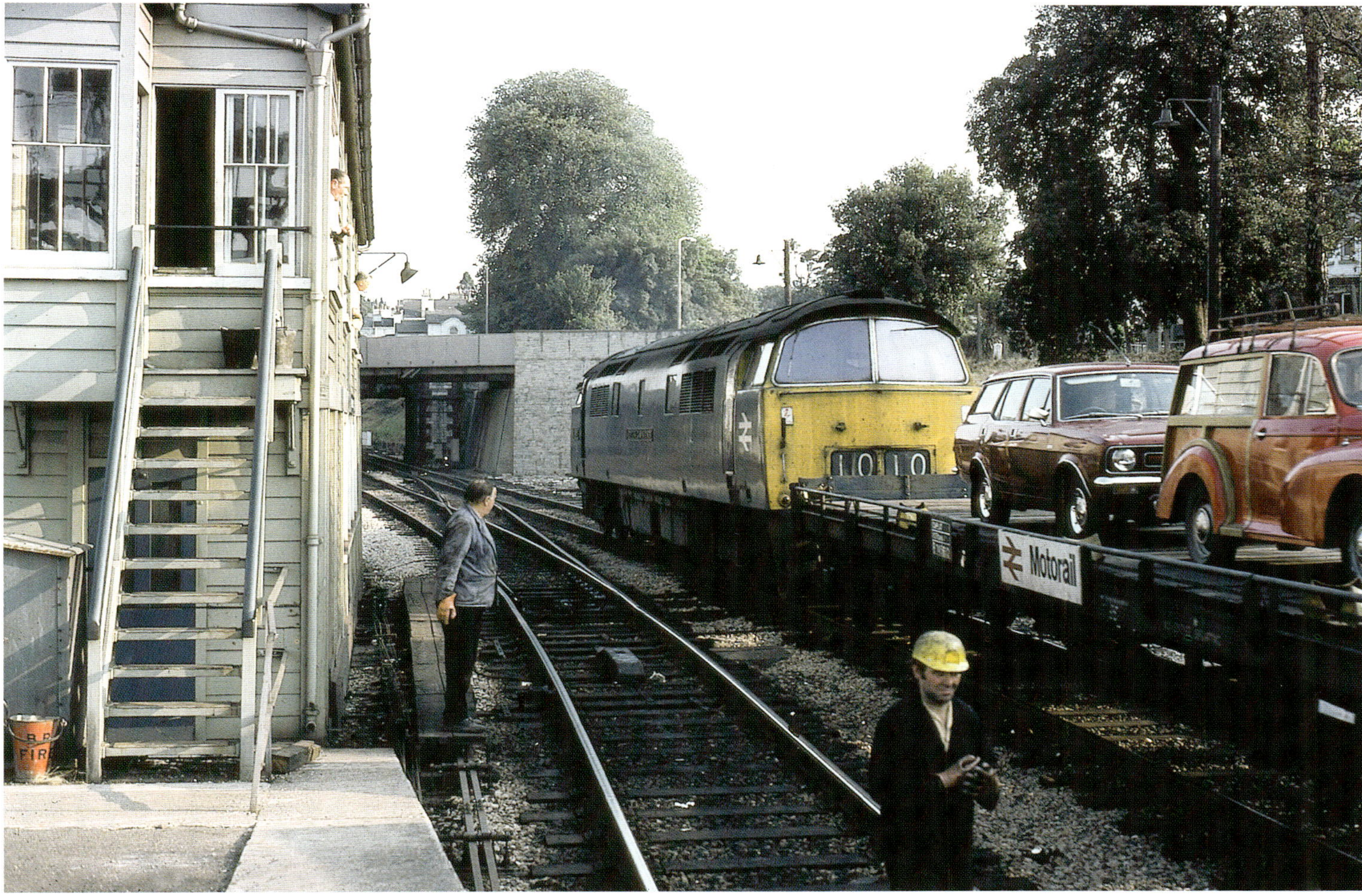

The Stirling Motorail was marshalled at great length in Newton Abbot as well as the other West Country Motorail workings which attached or detached there. Outside Newton Abbot West box on Saturday 14th August 1976, D1010 *Western Campaigner* is about to pull the train off the up through line, whilst signalman Charlie Hammacott and his telephonist Charlie Lloyd look enviously at the cars (which they couldn't afford on signalman's wages) from the rear of the 153 lever box. Telephonists were usually referred to as booking boys, the traditional name for the signalman's assistant who recorded train register entries and answered telephones in the busier boxes. In this case the 'boy' was closer to retirement than school leaving age! The fire bucket, Marina estate and Morris Traveller complete the period scene.

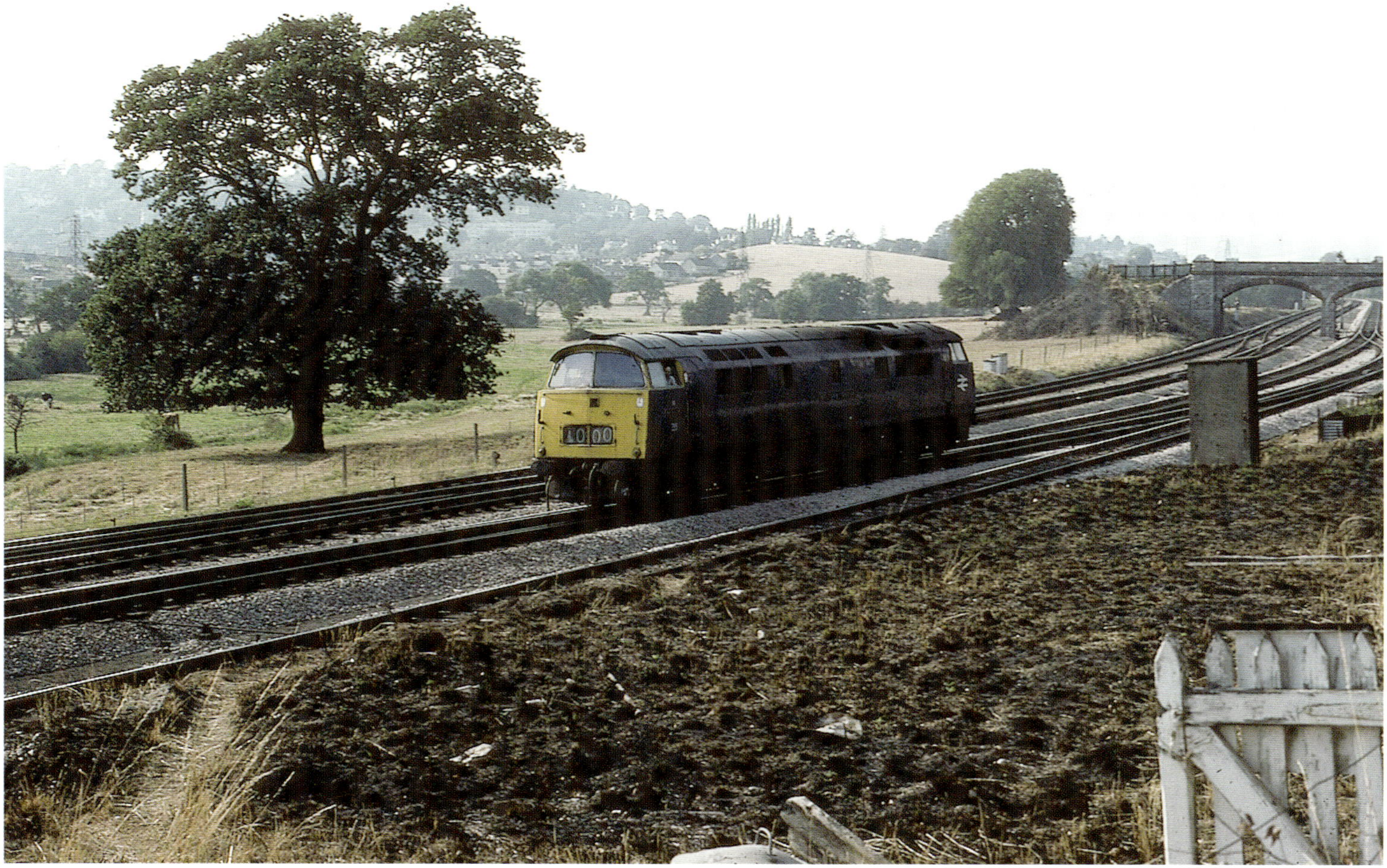

Gently meandering through the graceful pointwork at Aller Junction, D1071 *Western Renown* returns light to Laira in the evening of Saturday, 14th August 1976. *Renown* has been routed down the main line on the quadruple track section from Newton Abbot West with no difficulty in margining to Plymouth after the day's rush of holiday trains. The gate in the bottom right corner of the photograph led to the lineside allotments seen contained within corrugated iron; rather than housing an Elsan toilet, the concrete hut was used as a toolshed for the gardeners.

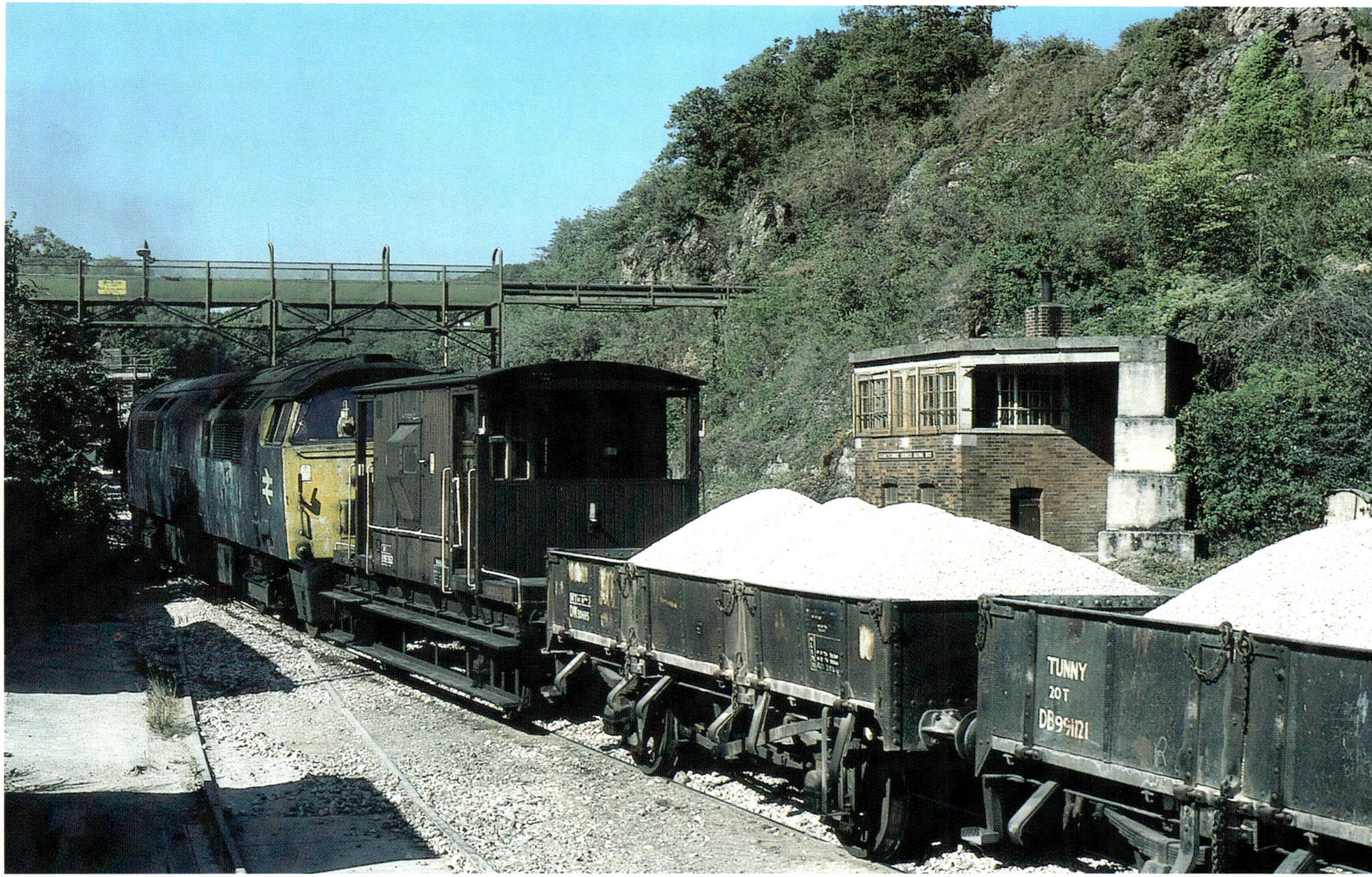

On 16th August 1976, D1015 *Western Champion* shunts at Stoneycombe Sidings, between Aller Junction and Dainton. At this time, the quarry still supplied the Western Region with ballast, as well as finer crushed stone for Taunton concrete works. The layout at Stoneycombe permitted trip workings from Hackney yard at Newton Abbot to return direct from the quarry sidings. Latterly the crossover was removed, light engines then having to crossover at Dainton and trains to run round at Totnes. The siding connection was severed prior to the introduction of multiple aspect signalling in 1987. All that was very much in the future when *Champion* was shunting a train of 'Tunny' wagons for Taunton opposite the blast protected signalbox, railburns much in evidence as the loco drivers struggled unsuccessfully for traction on the 1 in 46 gradient out of the siding.

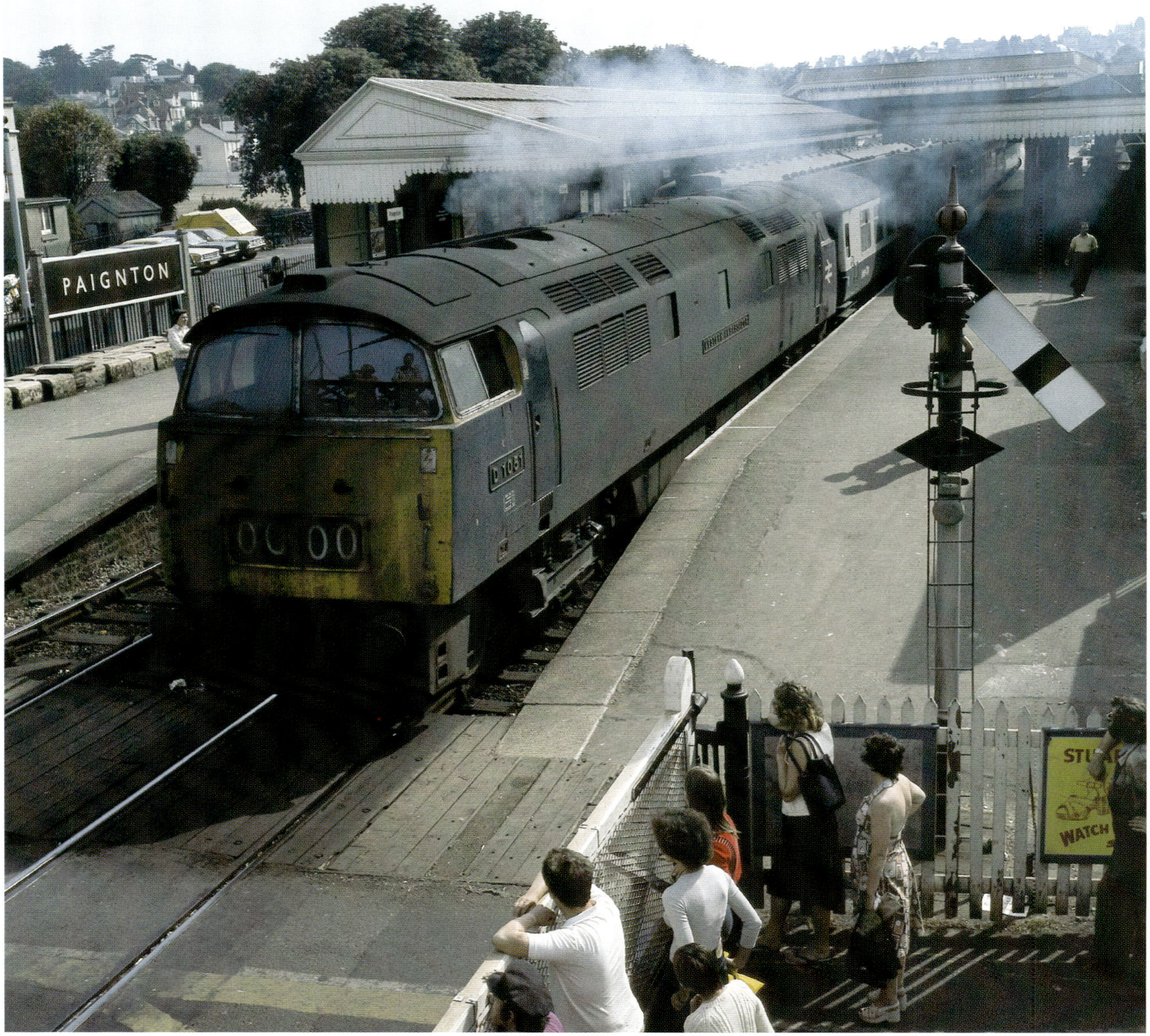
PAIGNTON
0C00
D1051
WATCH

Left: Viewed from Paignton North Signal Box on August 23rd 1976, D1051 *Western Ambassador* departs from Paignton with an up passenger working in the late afternoon. As soon as the crossing was closed to road traffic, an audience of pedestrians would accumulate at the gates, reluctant to use the overbridge and miss the spectacle of the departing train.

Below: D1053 *Western Patriarch* in the carriage sidings at Goodrington on November 6th 1976, having worked down with the 10.30 Paddington to Paignton that morning. Her next working, the 15.27 Paignton to Newton Abbot, was the last Western hauled service train we photographed.

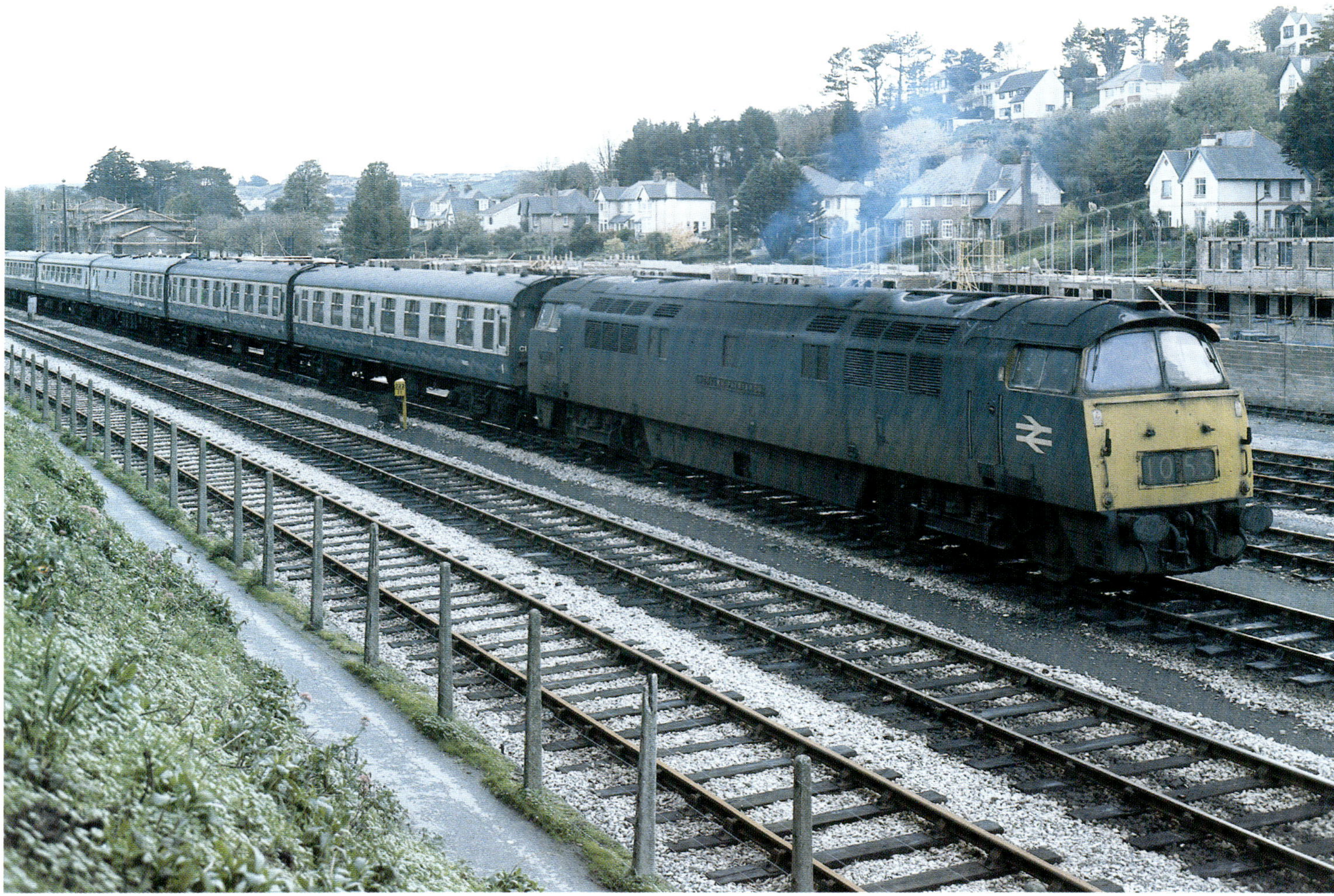

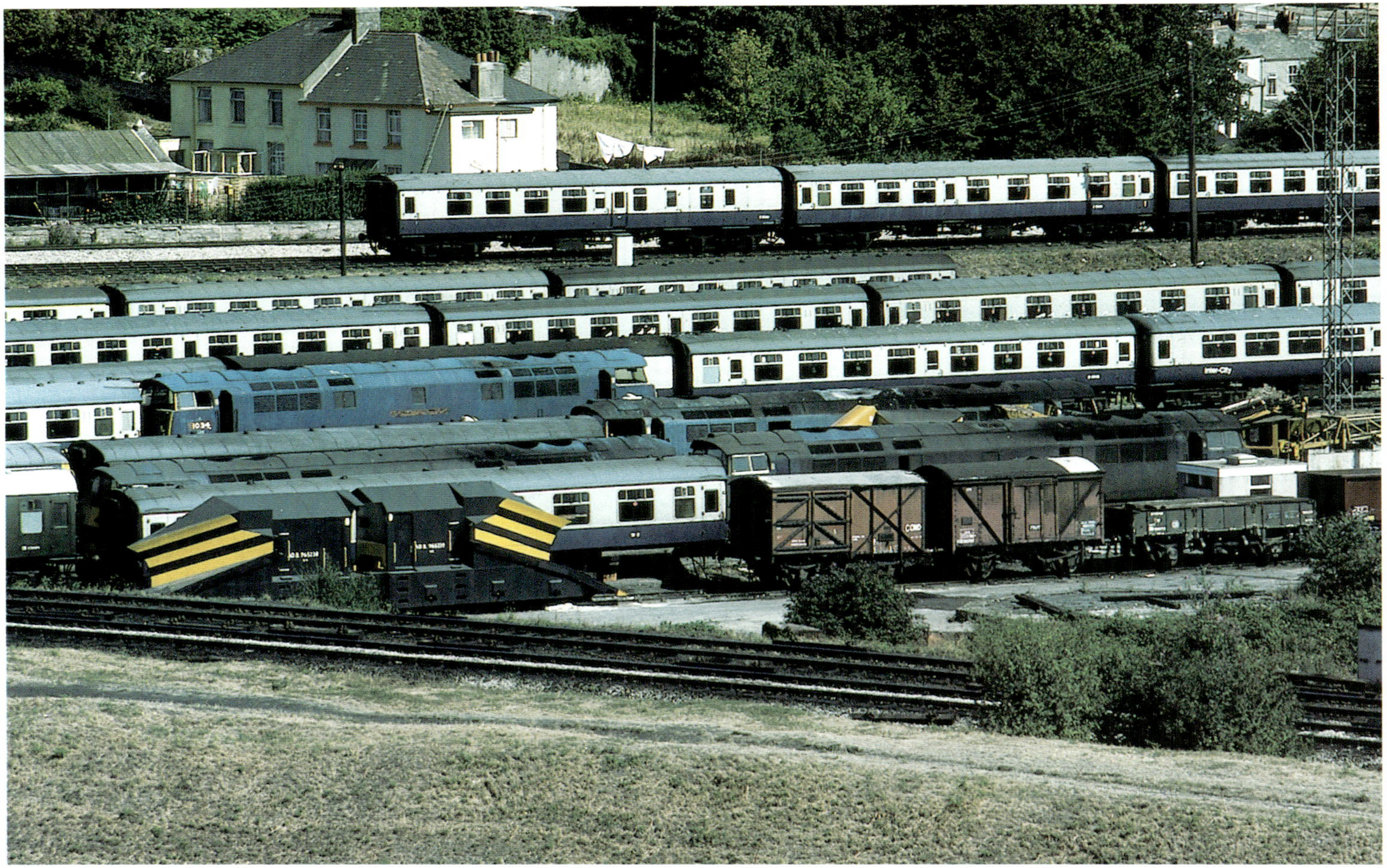

We saw D1034 *Western Dragoon,* dead in Laira yard with three other classmates amongst coaching stock and the condemned wagons. It was a sad sight and we continued into Cornwall in search of operational Westerns and the remaining mechanical signalboxes of our journey.

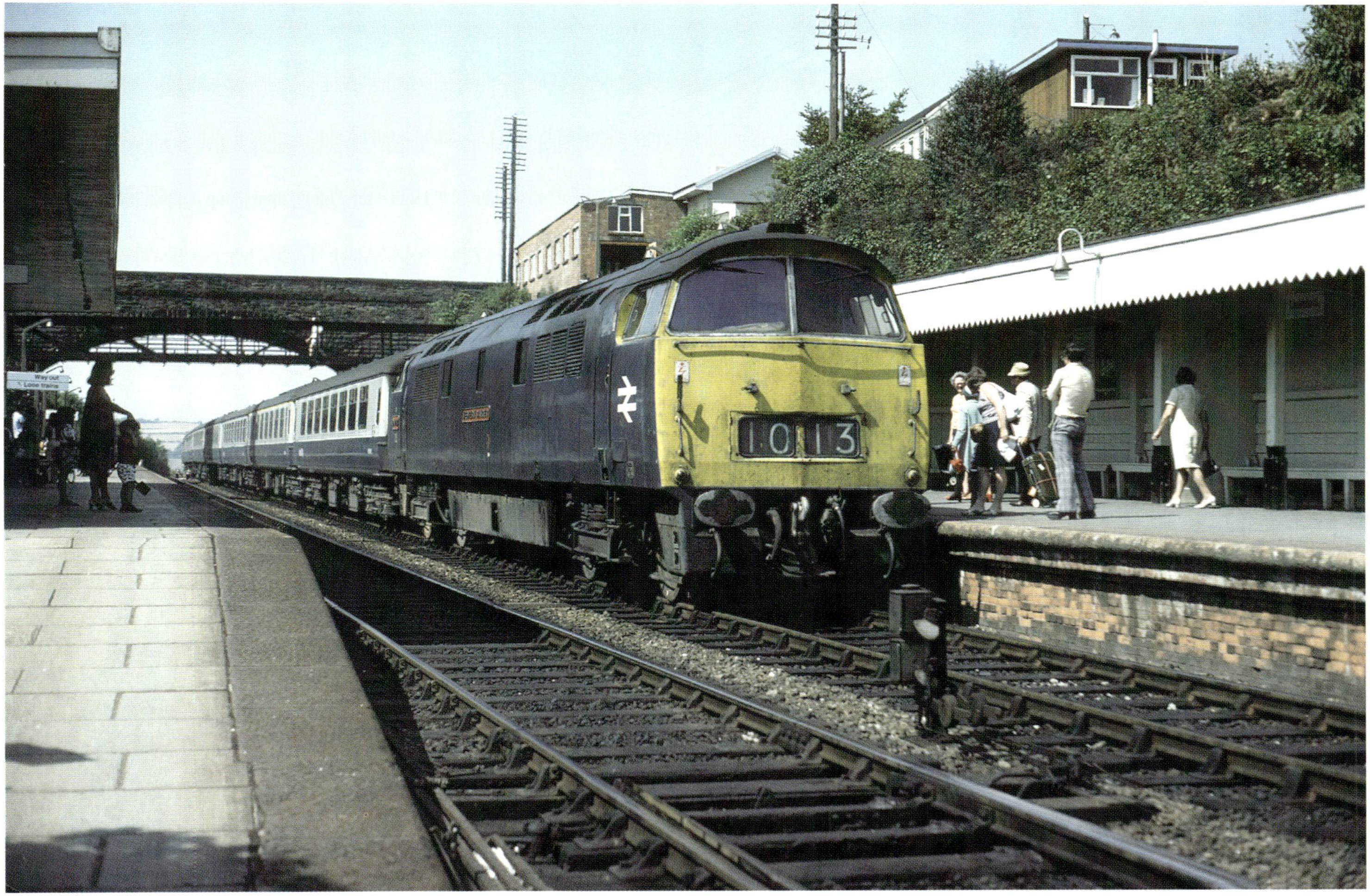

D1013 *Western Ranger* arrives in Liskeard station with an up passenger working in the middle of 16th August 1976. We saw her on several passenger workings that week whilst we were in the Duchy. The last remaining semaphore signalling on the route between Paddington and Penzance is in Cornwall - the first semaphore signals encountered by a down train these days are at Liskeard.

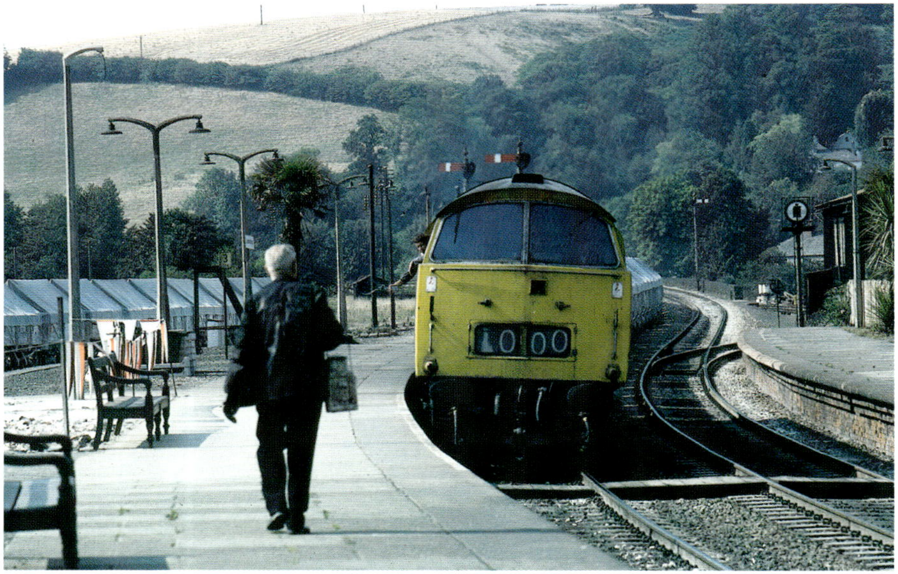

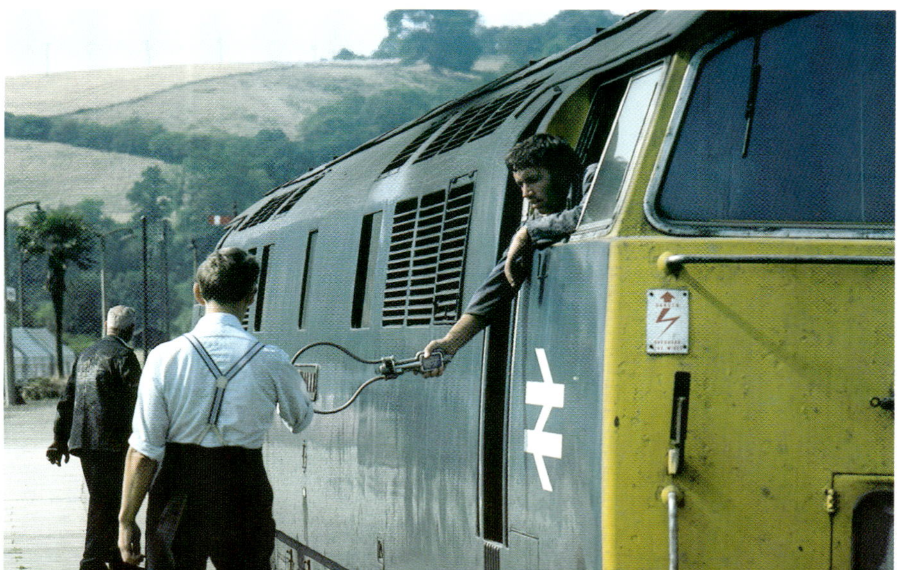

Left above: D1071 *Western Renown* arrives at Lostwithiel on 17th August 1976 with a train of empty china clay wagons comprising the 11.26 from Fowey to Burngullow. The secondman is leaning out of the cab with the token for the Carne Point branch, a little too early to hand it back to the signalman. The train has left the branch line and is running in the up direction on the down main through the station. Meanwhile, the shunter walks along the platform with a tail-lamp, ready for the run-round movement.

Left below: District Relief Signalman Tony Strong picks up the token holder or 'hoop' containing the token as the train comes to rest in the platform. The shunter is about to step into the rear cab in readiness for detaching the locomotive prior to running round the train in the down goods loop.

Opposite: Having run round the clay empties, *Renown* runs past the down main inner home signal no. 58, into the station. On this day, the locomotive also shunted milk wagons on the up side of the layout before leaving Lostwithiel at 12.03 with the return trip working of the china clay empties direct to Burngullow.

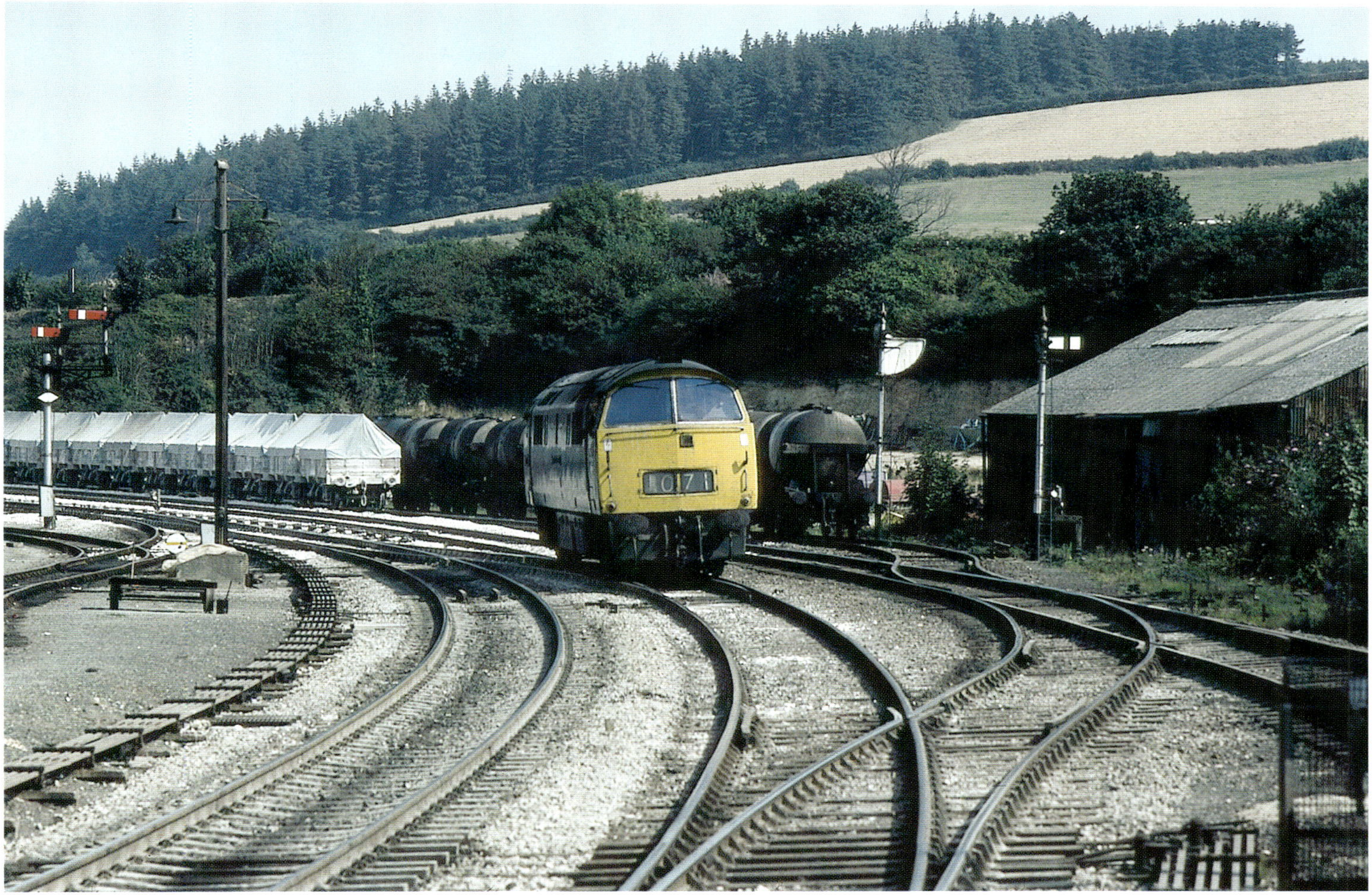

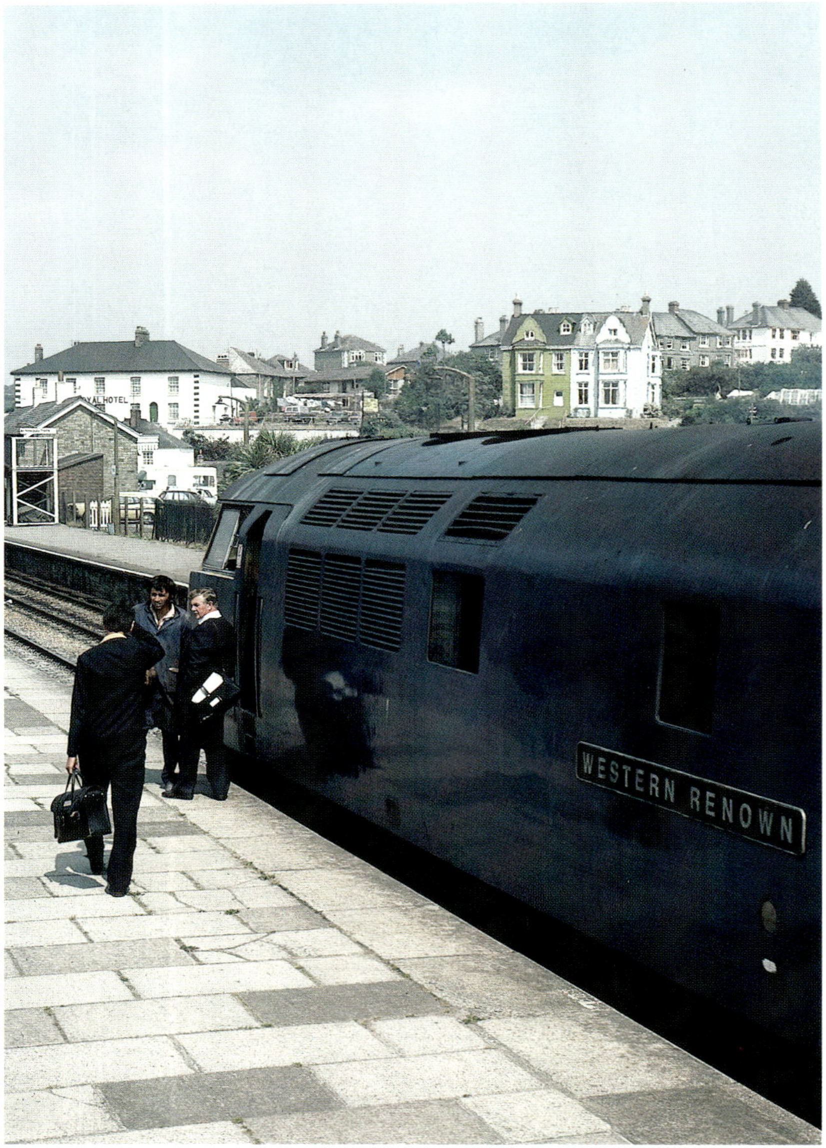

Left: Later the same day, the morning shift traincrew get relief in Par up platform at 13.45, having returned from Drinnick Mill with the late running 12.50 trip. Because this trip was running nearly an hour late, the relief crew of driver Arthur Williams and his mate were despatched from St. Blazey depot to walk over to Par, in order to avoid the morning shift men going over their time.

Opposite: The early turn were already making their way back to St. Blazey shed to book off duty as driver Williams took the long train of fifty five clay 'hoods' out under Royal Bridge, plumes of smoke characteristic of a Western roaring away from a standing start issuing forth into the Cornish sky. Once clear of the branch line junction the assisting engine would haul the formation onto the branch and around to St. Blazey, with *Renown* at the rear during this manoeuvre. This trip was booked to run-round at Par but it was commonplace for light engines to be sent down to Burngullow to attach to the rear of clay trips there, thus obviating the need to run-round, saving much time in the process. This could be quite a slick operation in the hands of professionals such as these; on this occasion Par signalman Ken Paynter asked 'Is Line Clear' to St. Blazey at 13.48, with 'Train on Line' sent at 13.51 as the train moved onto the branch. Four minutes elapsed before the block section was cleared at 13.55, barely ten minutes after changeover of the traincrew. Once at St. Blazey, *Renown* was again at the head of the train as it was not unusual for the loaded wagons to be driven into the yard, rather than propelling such a long train over short radius turnouts off the Newquay branch into the sidings.

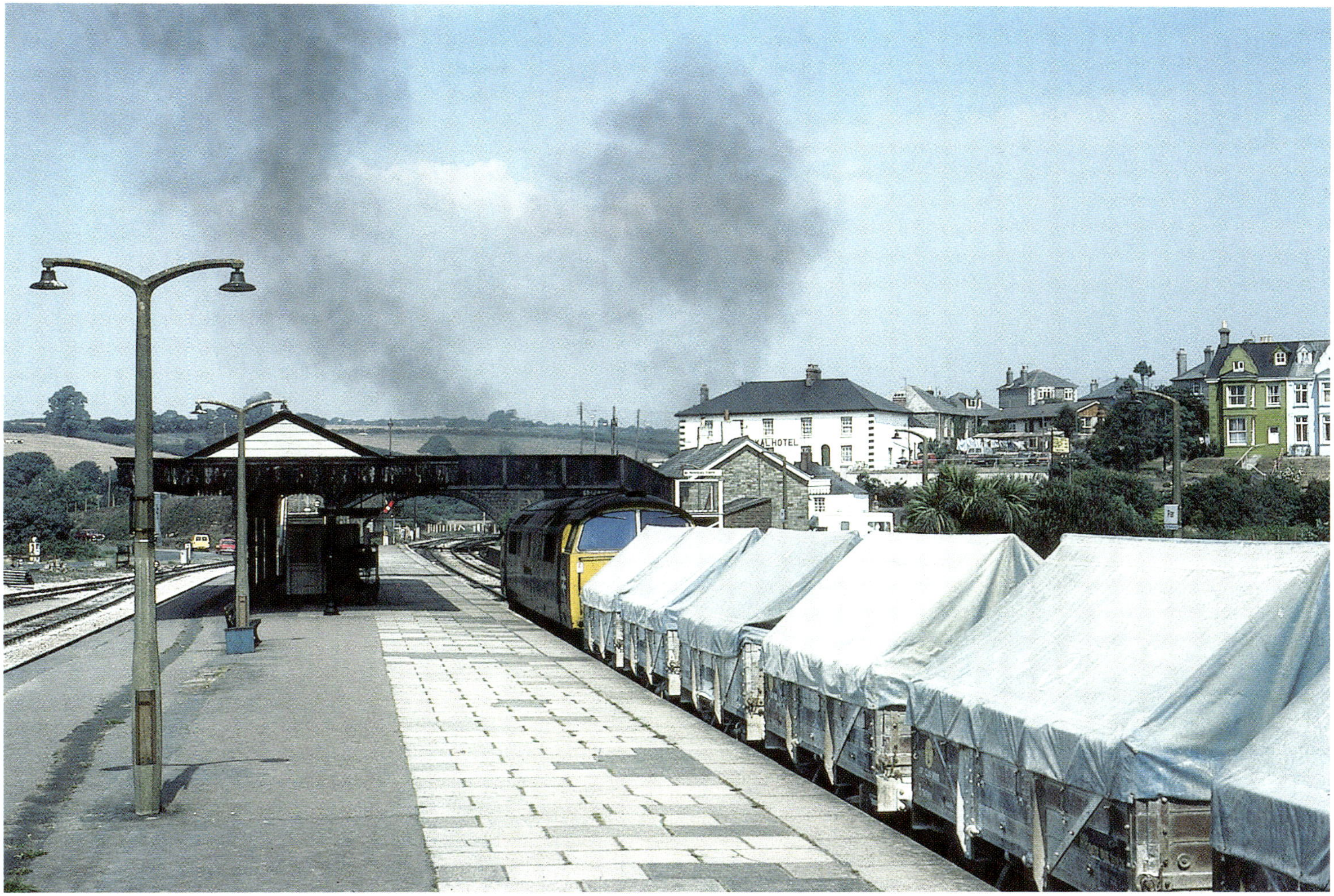

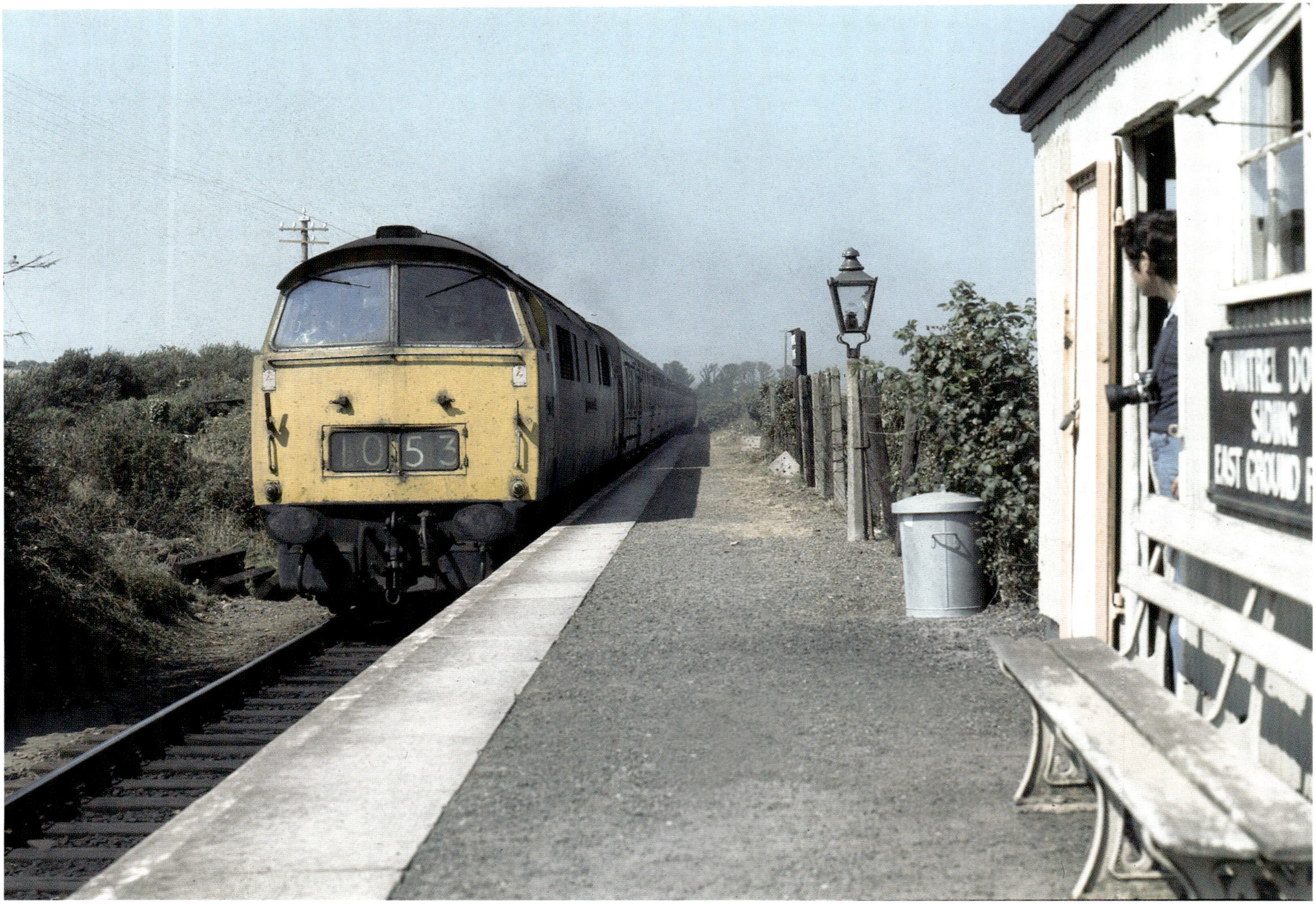

D1053 *Western Patriarch* runs through Quintrel Downs on the Newquay branch hauling the 10.30 (Saturdays Only) Newquay to Paddington on 21st August 1976. At the time, the level crossing there was protected with gates and semaphore distant signals, controlled by a tiny three lever frame in a Great Western Railway corrugated iron shed grandly titled 'QUINTREL DOWNS SIDING EAST GROUND FRAME'. The station's oil lighting can be seen on a concrete post beyond the platform dustbin. I didn't bother to photograph the train from the doorway of the ground frame, knowing my dad would get a better shot with his Mamiya, so instead I enjoyed the sight of the Western passing through the station, savouring the sight and sound of the locomotive in the last summer of operation.

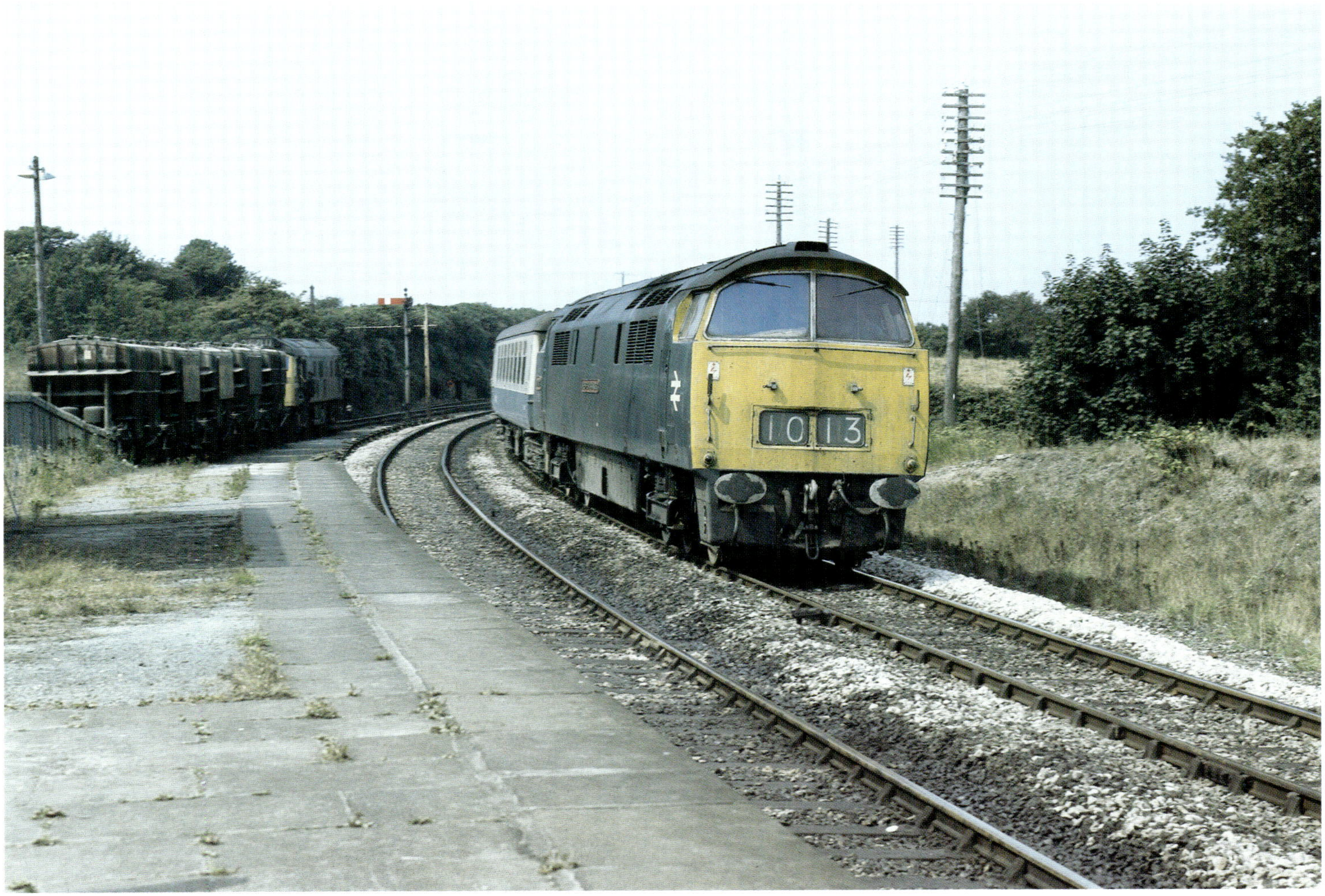

After visiting Par, St. Austell and Burngullow, we stayed overnight at Grampound Road, starting off in the morning of Wednesday, 18th August 1976 at Truro signalbox and then going on to Chacewater. Without a flat bottom rail in sight, D1013 *Western Ranger* passes Chacewater signalbox and former station with an up passenger working, whilst a class 25 shunts presflo wagons in the down siding. The signalbox closed in June the following year, being replaced by a ground frame.

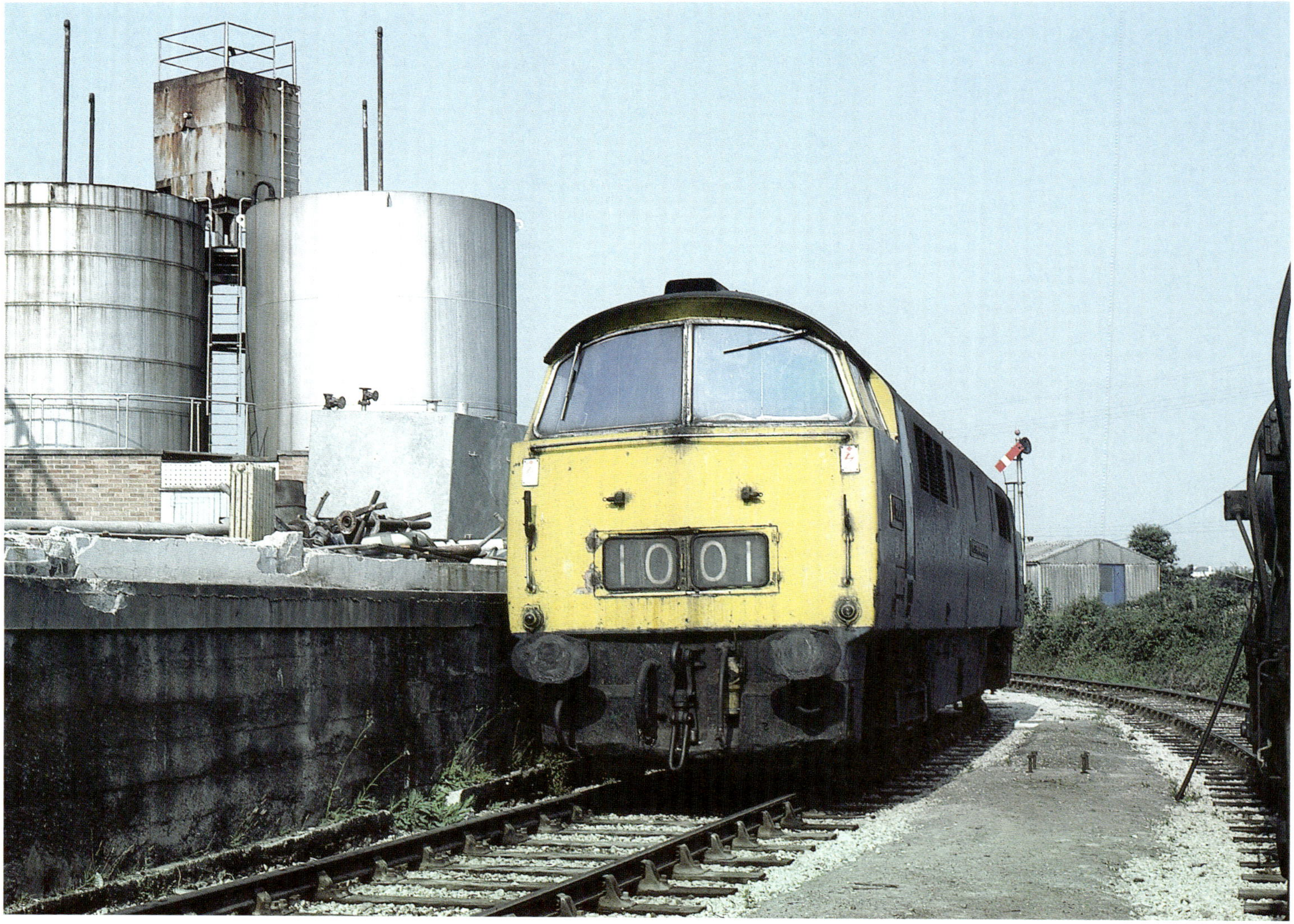

D1001 *Western Pathfinder* in splendid repose at St. Erth United Dairies Siding on 18th August 1976, before working the 16.40 milk train to Acton. Class 52s were allowed a maximum of 980 tons on this working compared with a mere 896 tons gross for the class 50s. She had worked down to Penzance with the 07.30 from Paddington earlier in the day and travelled to St. Erth after refuelling at Long Rock. The shunter's pole is leaning against the six wheeled milk wagon in readiness for the next move and the branch line signal is cleared for the next train to St. Ives.

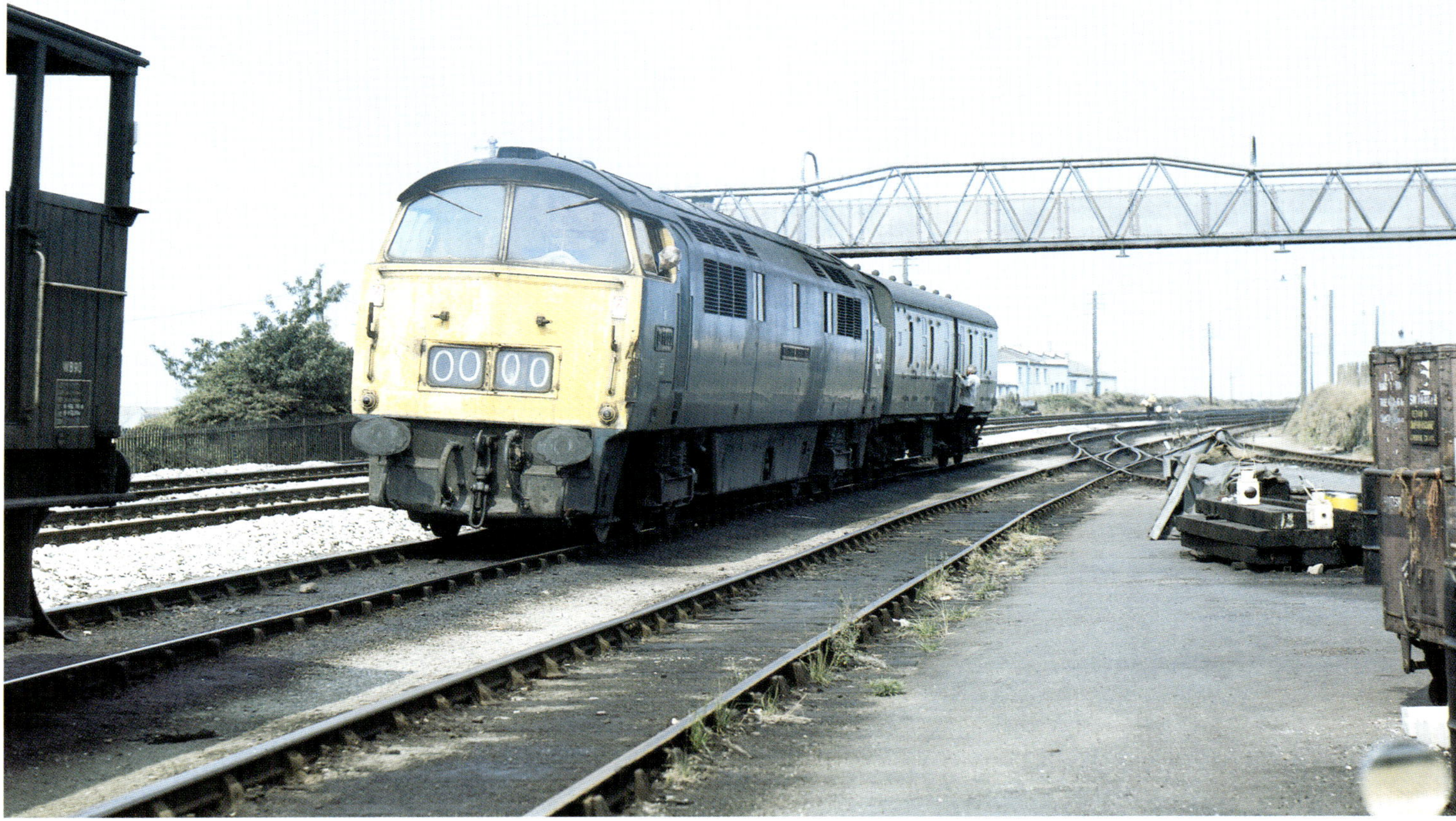

At Redruth, the town's goods depot at Drump Lane was separate to the passenger station, which was 33 chains closer to Penzance. Direct trains ran to Drump Lane from outside Cornwall as well as local trips from Truro. Here on Wednesday 18th August 1976, having left St. Blazey at 11.39 as a light engine, D1022 *Western Sentinel* shunts between the down siding and the spur. *Sentinel* shows signs of collision damage on the cabside, not serious enough to justify withdrawal but unfortunately further damage to the locomotive at Old Oak Common in January 1977 did result in her being condemned a week later.

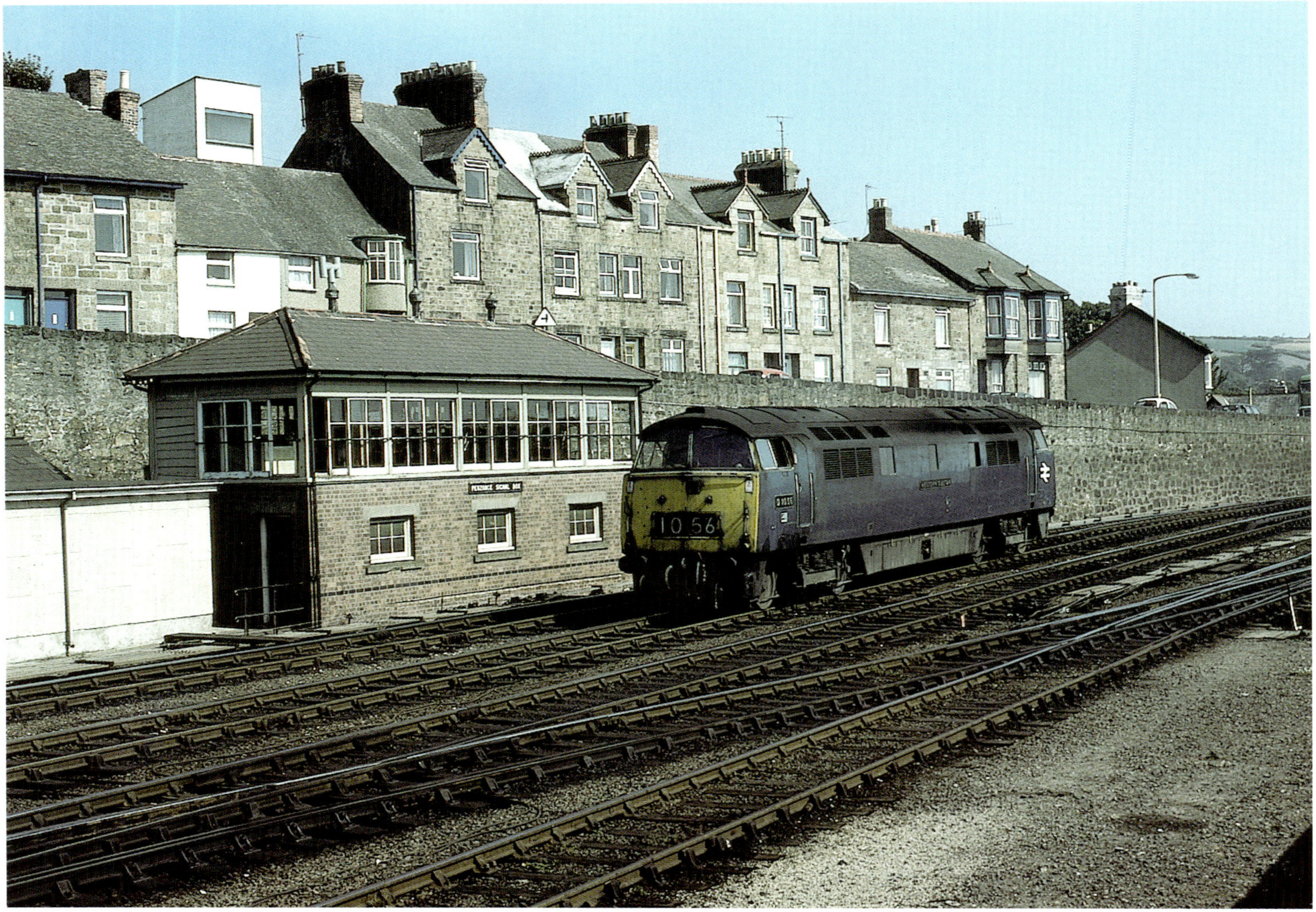

D1056 *Western Sultan* sidles into Penzance light from Long Rock, onto the stock for the 12.05 (Relief) Penzance to Paddington on Friday, 20th August 1976. The empty stock had been worked down to Penzance as 5Z97, the 03.15 ECS from Old Oak Common.

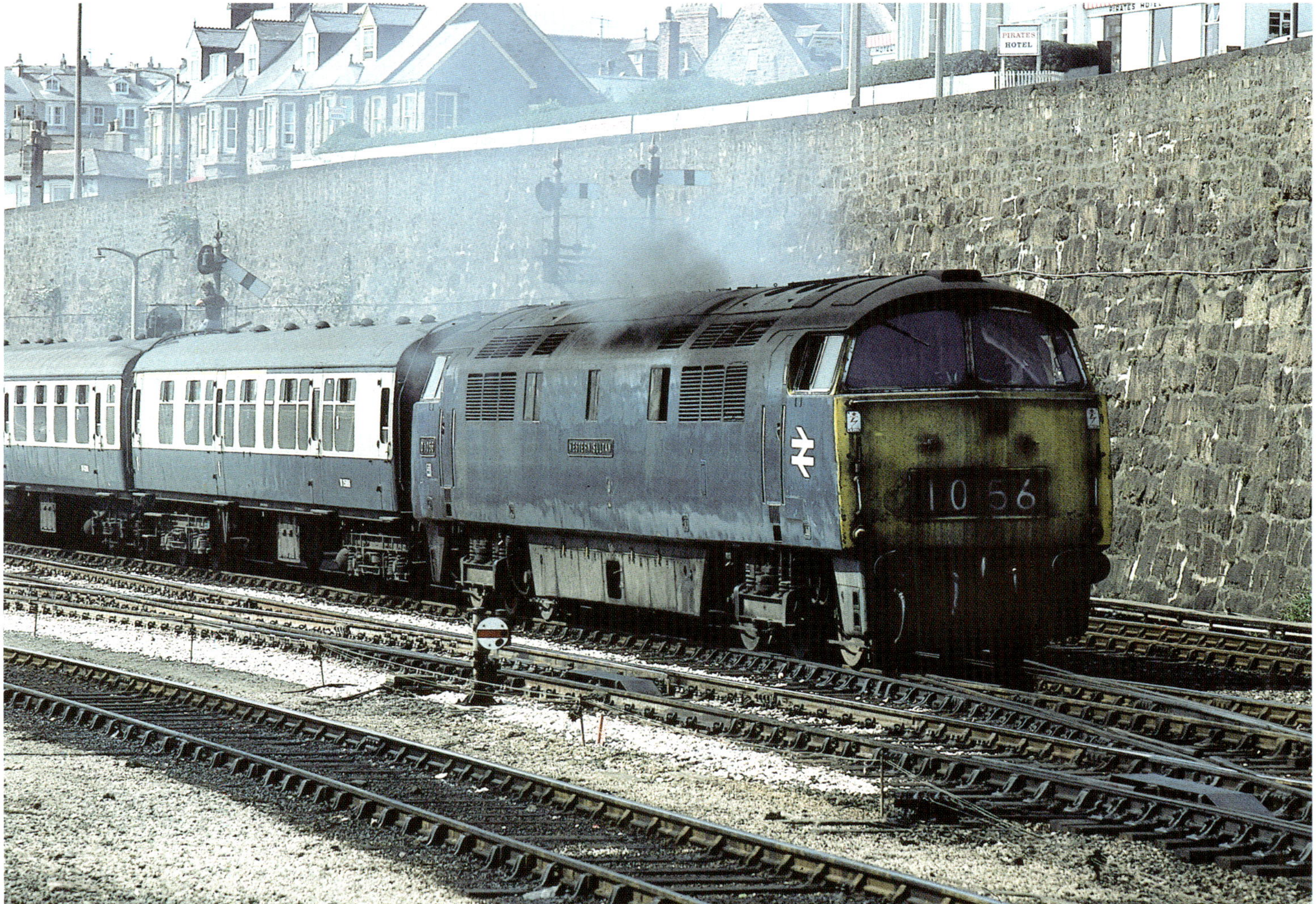

With a blast of the horn and roaring engines, D1056 *Western Sultan* departs through the station throat with the 12.05 (Relief) to Paddington. *Sultan* hauled the train to Plymouth, afterwards going to Laira for a cylinder liner change. The man clinging to the signal post looks more like a desperate photographer rather than the signal lineman. Along with a handful of other boxes in Cornwall, Penzance signalbox is still operational but now controls colour light signals instead of the semaphores seen in this view.

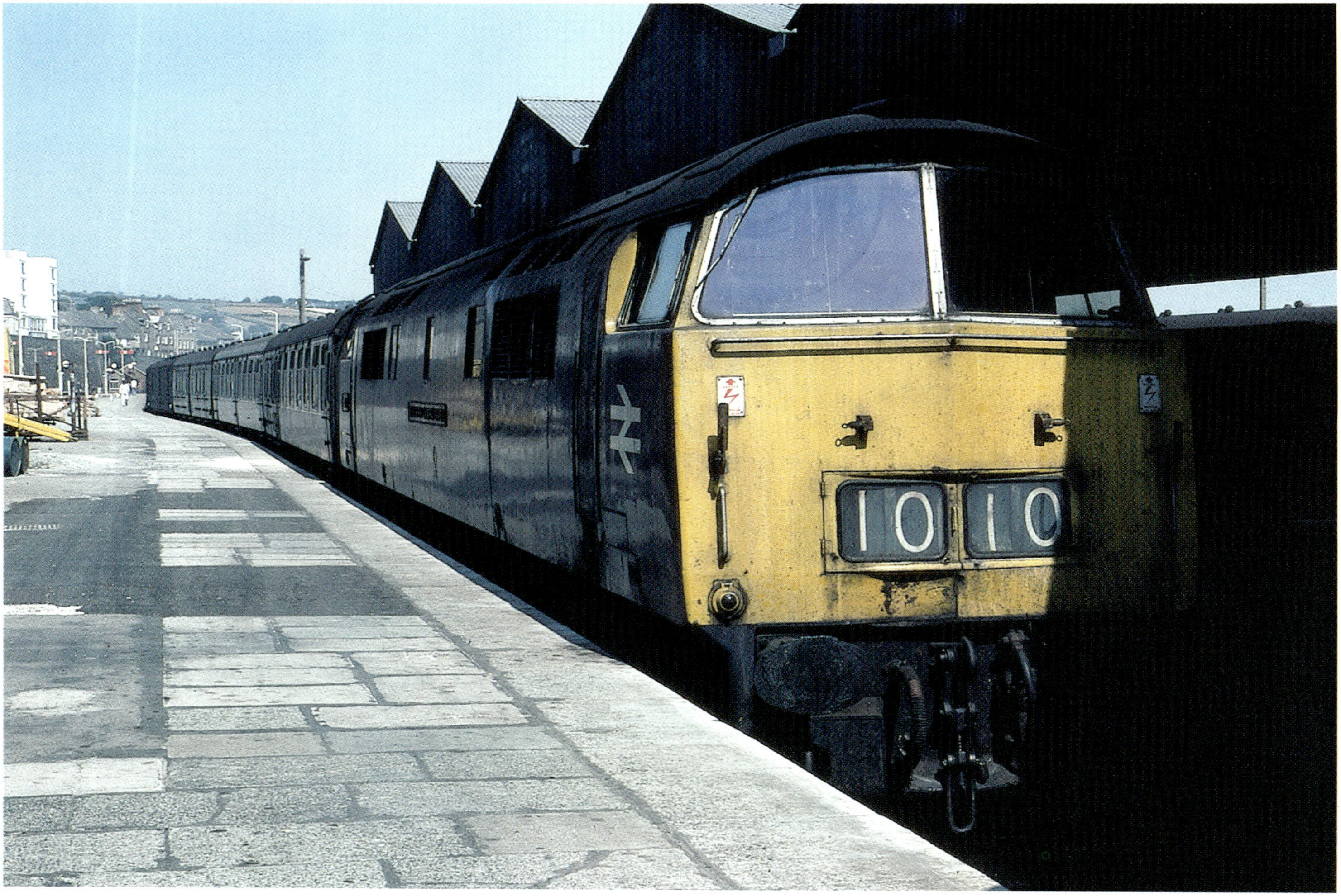

Journey's end, with D1010 *Western Campaigner* having worked down to Penzance on the 08.00 from Bristol Temple Meads. There is much evidence of parcel unloading on the platform whilst the lunchtime sun gets hotter and hotter. Photographed on Friday, 20th August 1976.

PART 3: FAREWELL

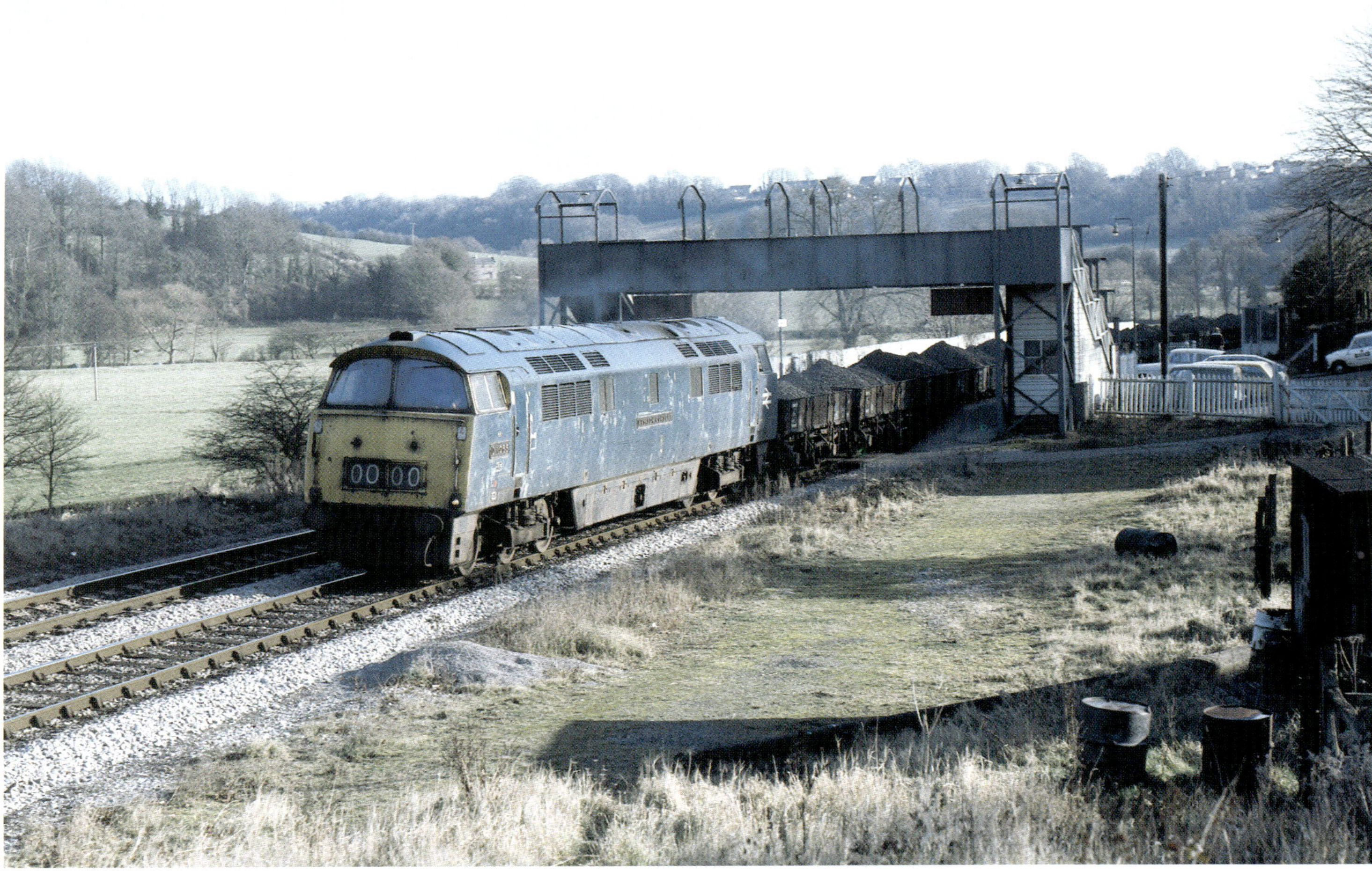

Above: On 25th January 1976, the deplorable external state of D1065 *Western Consort* is clearly seen here at Freshford as she returns to Bristol with a load of spoil from an engineering job in the Westbury area. The day was bitterly cold; we rushed back towards Frome, taking refuge by the coal fire in the signalbox at Blatchbridge Junction.

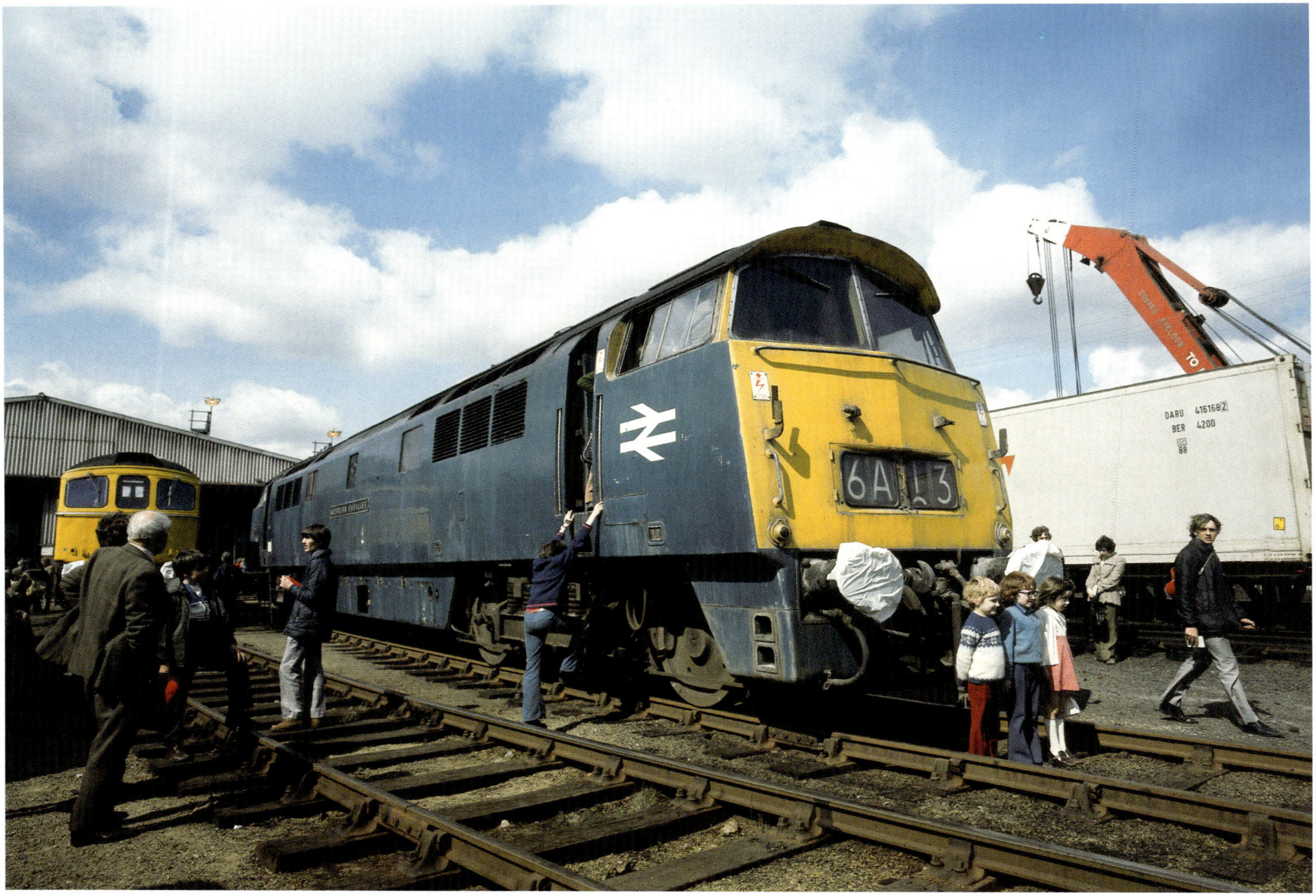

Westerns were featured more often at BR open days as their numbers declined, an official acknowledgement that they were an endangered species and therefore of interest to the enthusiast. For us, going to Eastleigh for the Works Open Day in 1975 was a sort of homecoming. My Dad had moved there from Surrey when he was three, later on in his school days seeing the first 'Spamcans' ex-works from the Campbell Road overbridge by the station. Our house was within earshot of Allbrook Junction and I can remember hearing the trains rush past until I reached the tender age of six, when we moved to Somerset. En route to the Open Day, we found a location near Romsey to photograph David Shepherd's 9F 92203 *Black Prince* on the run from Cranmore to Eastleigh. Steam on the main line wasn't quite so commonplace then as it is now. It was a bonus to see D1023 *Western Fusilier* there, and this wide-angle view captures the period dress of the mid-seventies trainspotter, as well as those three little children being photographed by their proud father beneath the type 4 bufferbeam. Where are they now?

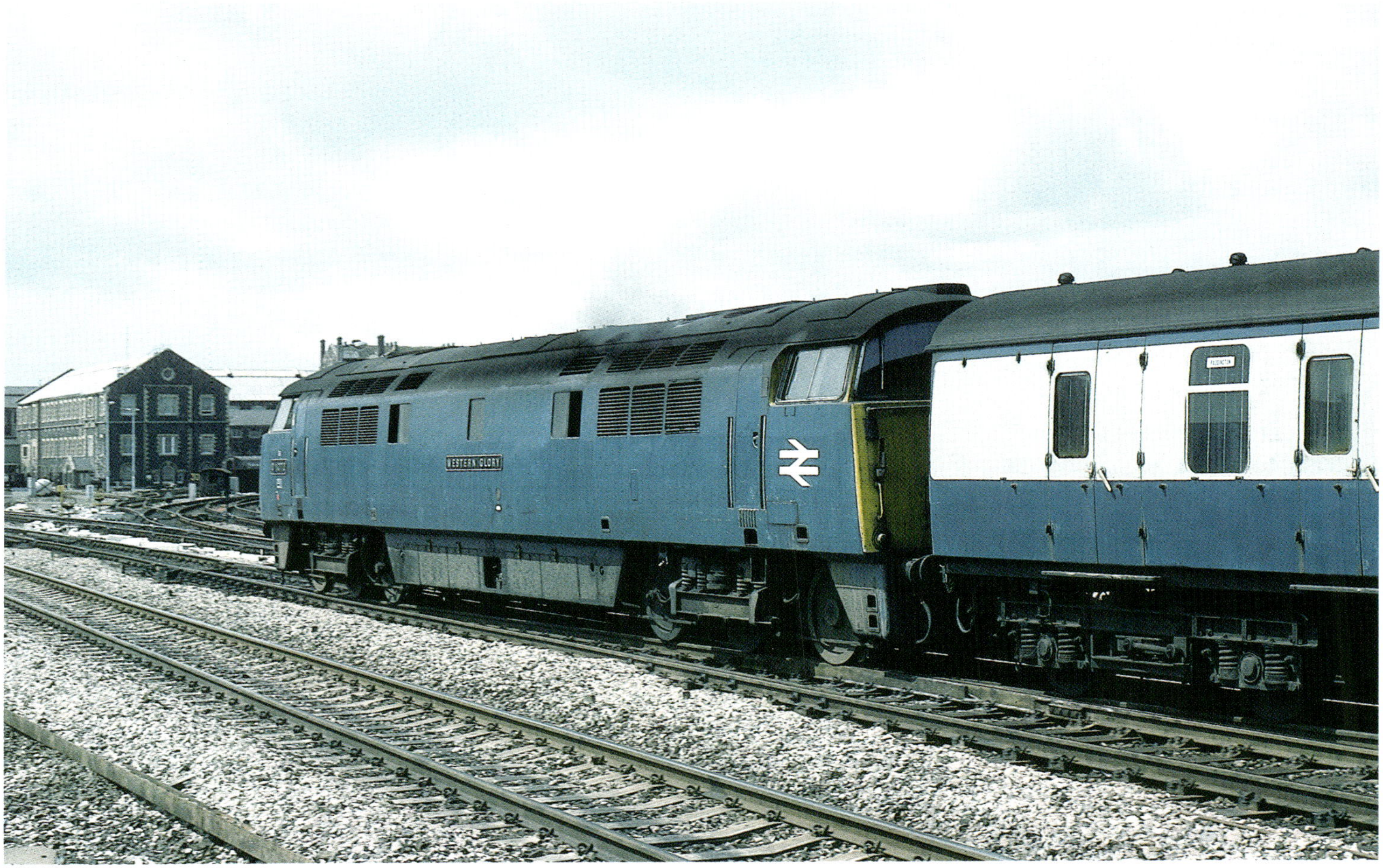

With the Chief Mechanical Engineer's building in the distance, D1072 *Western Glory* leaves Swindon on Sunday May 16th 1976. The first thirty Westerns were built here from December 1961 to July 1964. *Glory* was the penultimate Western built at Crewe, entering service in November 1963, the same day as *Western Renown*. Originally, five more Westerns had been allocated for build at Swindon but production there was slow enough to warrant construction at Crewe instead. Crewe locomotives were also cheaper!

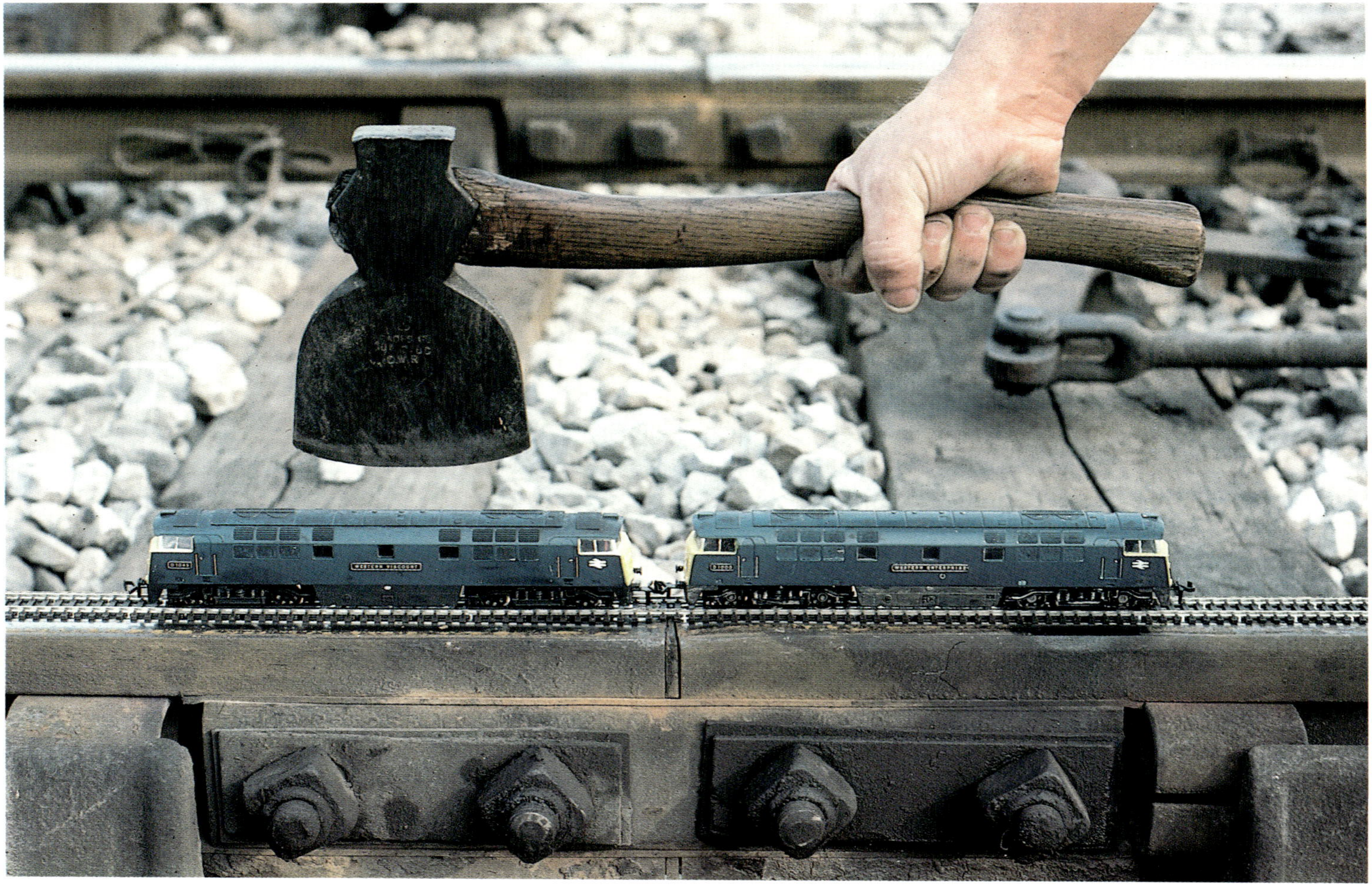

5,400 horsepower in model form. Liliput had recently re-introduced the Trix 'OO' gauge model of the Westerns and one afternoon we thought it would be fun to give them a run on the main line, so to speak. The axe hanging over them is far too symbolic but it was an accurate reflection of how we all felt in 1976. The models were of D1000 *Western Enterprise* and D1045 *Western Viscount;* the axe dated from Great Western days, like much of the railway at that time, and the hand belonged to the signalman at Blatchbridge Junction, Chris Burden.

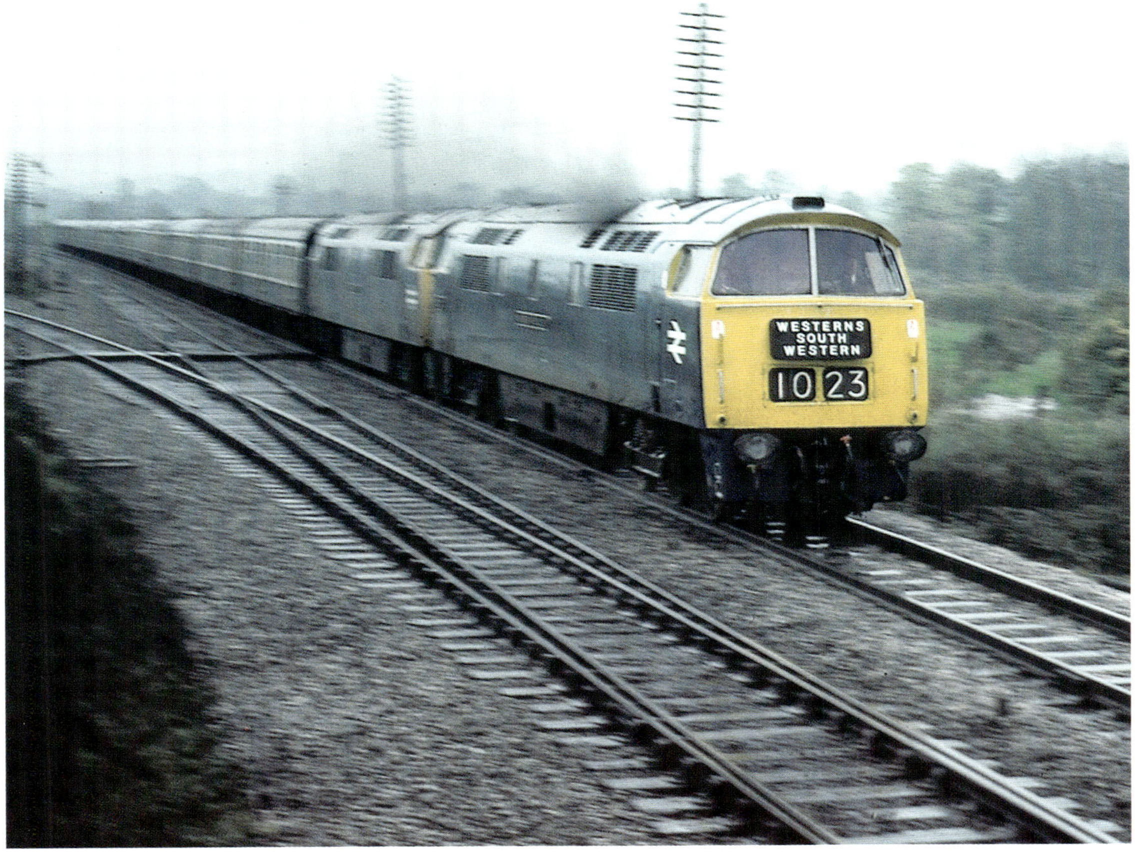

Four weeks after the end of the summer timetable and the rain had returned with a vengeance. By then Westerns were very thin on the ground. We saw this railtour at Blatchbridge Junction, en route from Paddington to Meldon Quarry on Saturday 30th October 1976, with D1023 *Western Fusilier* and D1009 *Western Invader* as haulage. *Invader* was one of the few locomotives used on the farewell railtours not to be preserved. Note how *Fusilier* has lurched to the left after the foot crossing, with the front of *Invader* still upright.

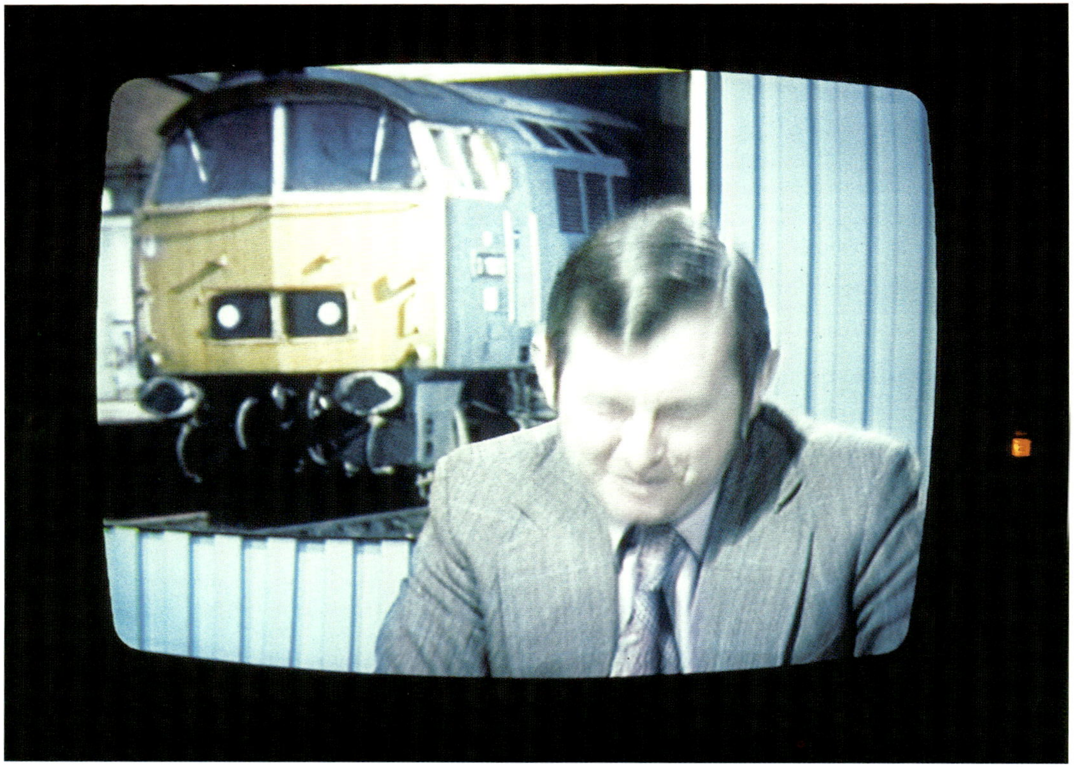

Publicity was widespread after the last Westerns were withdrawn; nevertheless we were still surprised to see HTV West devote a slot to the locomotive's demise. Bruce Hockin seems a little bemused with his script, but for Western enthusiasts there was a brief glimpse of D1023 *Western Fusilier* at Swindon, with further footage of broken up loco parts outside the works before the next news item.

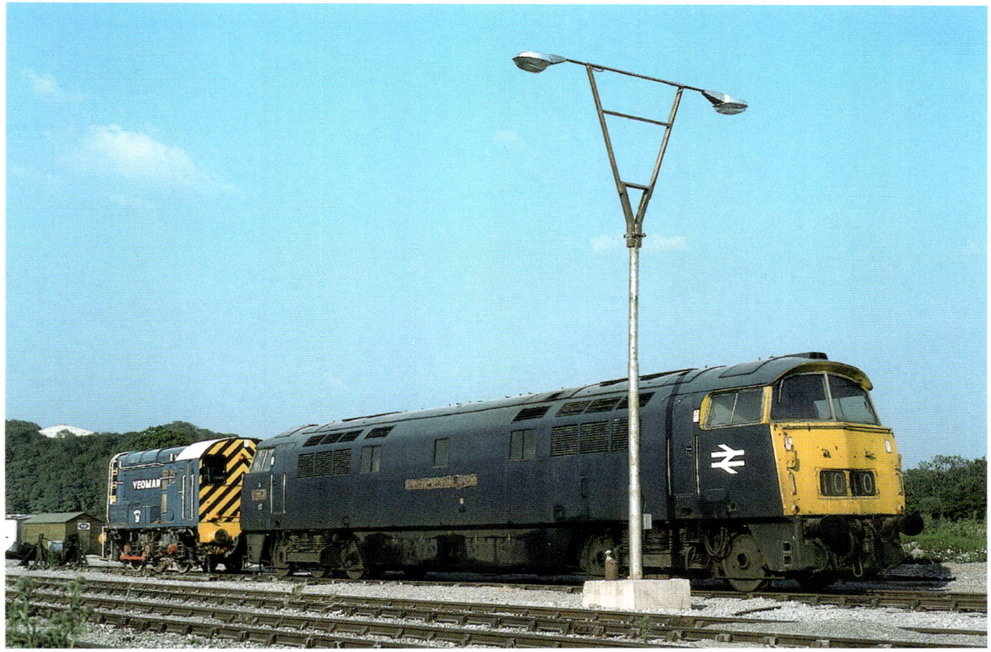

Above: D1010 *Western Campaigner* was purchased by Foster Yeoman and moved to Merehead on Thursday, 7th July 1977 and we saw her there shortly afterwards with class 08 shunter *Dulcote*. We had heard a rumour that she would be renamed *Western Yeoman* after John Yeoman, owner of Merehead Quarry. She remained there for nearly nine years with water ingress, intercooler and heat exchanger damage, rusting quietly until Foster Yeoman agreed to allow the Diesel and Electric Preservation Group to restore her at Didcot Railway Centre. 59 001 towed *Yeoman* and a brake van to Didcot on 17th May 1986 for restoration to commence. Just over a year later she moved under her own power from the 'A' engine. The 'B' engine was in too poor condition to rebuilt and a replacement engine which had seen service in *Western Nobleman* was stripped down and overhauled in time for gala days in 1990. After tyre turning at Canton and Christmas at Merehead, the move to the West Somerset Railway took place on 11th January 1991, again hauled by 59 001 but with *Yeoman* running herself from Norton Fitzwarren to Williton.Having fulfilled Foster Yeoman's desire to get D1035 operational, the DEPG were able to buy *Yeoman* for the sum of £1 in 1993. Since then, she has reverted to her original identity as *Western Campaigner* and been in operation on the WSR for running days and galas, as well as returning to Merehead for an Open Day on 28th June 1998. Having sported a variety of liveries in preservation, D1010 is now painted in 1960's maroon with a yellow buffer beam. Meanwhile, *Dulcote* became a fixture in the children's playground at the nearby village of Wanstrow.

Overleaf, opposite page: On Saturday, 23rd February 2002 the '*Western Pathfinder*' railtour became the first main line passenger outing for a Western since 1977. We found a location to the west of Bath Spa and waited for the railtour, running as the 12.09 Paddington to Gloucester via Bristol Temple Meads. It was on time and for the first time in over twenty five years I saw D1015 *Western Champion,* looking much shinier than she had in 1976. She sped through the station more quickly that I would have liked, even though the speed restriction through Bath is only 30 mph; past the small crowd at the end of the up platform, anxious to get a view after a up HST had obscured the approach. A couple of pictures later and she was gone, the chocolate and cream coaches seemingly a period piece from a different era. We decided to drive on to Bristol. Nothing could have prepared us for the sheer volume of enthusiasts on platforms 7 and 9 at Temple Meads. The loco was immaculate, but with engines ticking over much smokier than I remembered - the side windows into the engine compartment were clean enough to see inside: a unusual view in the seventies. Nick Carter, an EWS driver, drove on the Bristol to Gloucester leg of the outward journey. He chatted happily with enthusiasts on the platform, even photographing the cab interior with their cameras upon request. Seen here just before departure at 15.15, I photographed him in conversation with Tom Sawyer of the Diesel Traction Group, responsible for the splendid renovation of *Champion*.

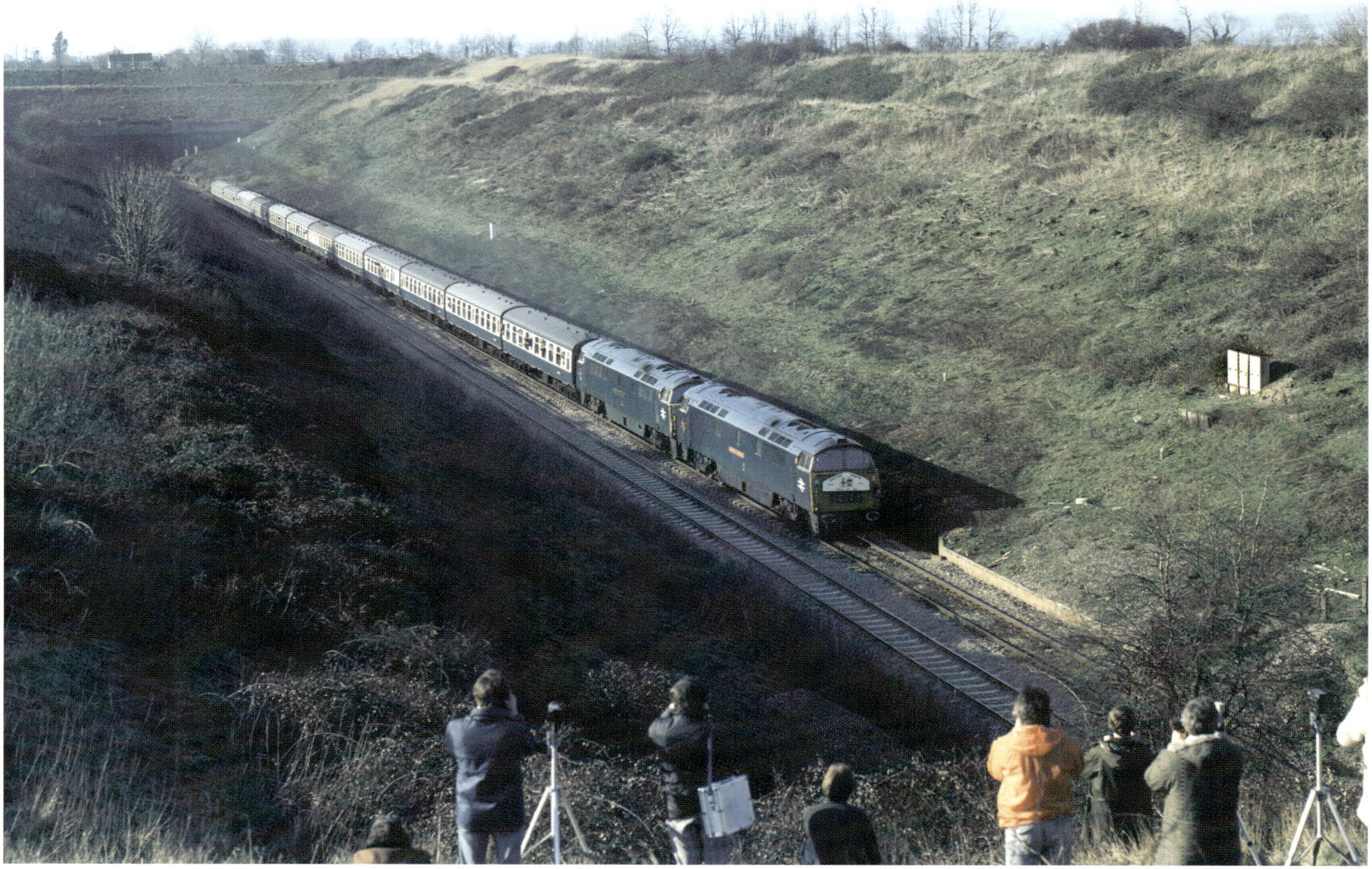

February 26th, 1977 - a sad day indeed. For the last time in BR service, Westerns emerge from the Severn Tunnel and approach Severn Tunnel East. The mania of the day can be seen by the number of still and cine cameras in evidence as enthusiasts make their last farewells. It was a wonder that some of the passengers of the train were not decapitated given the amount they were leaning out of the window. The secondman of the rear locomotive can be clearly seen, a reminder that the Westerns were not fitted for multiple working, necessitating double manning if 5,400 horsepower was required. D1013 *Western Ranger* and D1023 *Western Fusilier* head the 09.10 Paddington - Swansea - Plymouth - Paddington 'Western Tribute' charter, seen here on the Swansea to Plymouth leg of the journey, D1013 with one engine shut down due to a coolant leak - a fault rectified at Laira later the same day.

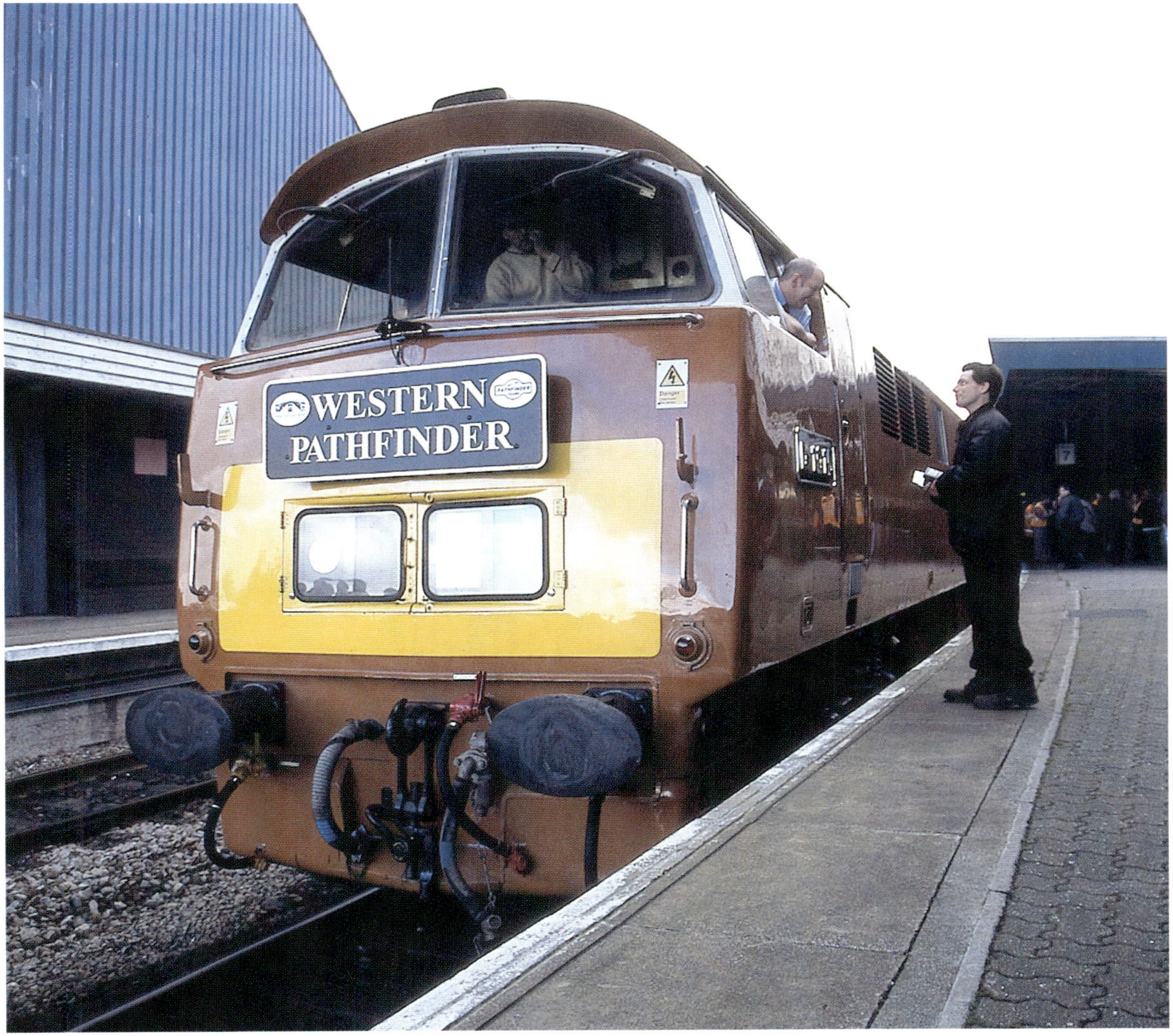
WESTERN
PATHFINDER

PHOTOGRAPHY NOTES

As noted in the introduction, Dad had bought a Mamiya Universal camera, a 'Press' type which superseded the Mamiya Super 23. He had three lenses, the standard 100 mm, the 150 mm lens which proved most useful for lineside work, and the 50 mm which was very wide-angle, useful for signalbox interiors but with limited use outside (its exaggerated angles can clearly be seen in the shot of *Western Fusilier* at Eastleigh Works). Although the Universal fitted a variety of film backs, he used only a couple of 6 x 9 film backs, giving only eight shots per 120 roll-film. The camera's operational was totally mechanical, and the paucity of double exposures and off-focus shots is a tribute to his photographic ability. I used a Rolleiflex 3.5F twin lens reflex (with a Planar lens - although Carl Zeiss snobs should note that the Schneider Xenotar is a worthy equal) but despite the superb standard focal length lens it was better for static views, being too wide-angle a view for most train shots. To solve this difficulty, we acquired a Mamiya C220, a twin lens reflex like the Rollei but with the benefit of interchangable lenses. Using 180 and 250 mm lenses helped to get a bit closer to the action. All metering was courtesy of a Weston Master V, complete with the famous invercone diffuser for transparency work. Dad would point it in the air and shout out the exposure, which was fine until clouds appeared with the onset of a train, in which case it was frantic adjustment of the aperture and a slightly grabbed shot! He was starting to become a bit of a camera collector when in late 1975 he bought a 35mm Minolta XE-1, with a variety of MC Rokkor lenses and an aperture priority automatic exposure setting. It made life a lot easier as the auto setting was pretty good, except for backlit situations, and it undoubtedly helped us record more Westerns than would otherwise have been possible. The camera still functions perfectly today. Lenses were 28 mm, 50 mm, 135 mm and 200 mm, with the medium telephoto 135 mm proving to be ideal for action shots. Film was usually Ektachrome 100 for medium format and Kodachrome 64 for 35 mm work, although we sometimes used High Speed Ektachrome on dull days in winter.

BIBLIOGRAPHY

BR Locomotives & other motive power, Williams/Percival, Ian Allan, 1974
Diesel-Hydraulic Locomotives of the Western Region, Reed, David & Charles, 1974
BR WR Working Timetable of Mandatory Train Services, Section B, 6 May 1974 to 4 May 1975;
Section PB, 5 May to 5 October 1975 & 3 May 1976 to 1 May 1976; Section PC, 5 May to 5 October 1975 & 3 May 1976 to 1 May 1977
BR WR Working Timetable of Conditional Train Services, Section PG, 5 May to 5 October 1975 & 3 May 1976 to 1 May 1977;
Section PH, 5 May to 5 October 1975 & 3 May 1976 to 1 May 1977
West of England Division, Notice of Mandatory Passenger and Parcel Train Arrangements:
Saturday 7th August to Friday 13th August 1976 & Saturday 14th August to Friday 20th August 1976.
Mum's 1976 diary
British Rail - Main Line Gradient Profiles, Ian Allan
The Coaching Stock of British Railways 1976, Mallaband/Bowles, R CTS
The Westerns, Ford/Preedy, Bradford Barton, 1976
The Power of the Westerns, Judge, OPC, 1977
Grime & Glory, Vaughan, Murray, 1985
Signalman's Nightmare, Vaughan, Murray, 1987
West Country Railway History, St John Thomas, David & Charles, 1988
Signal Box Diagrams, Vol 16: G.W.R lines in West Cornwall, Pryer
Cast of Thousands, Curtis, A&C, 2001
D1010 - A History, Tiller, 2002

INDEX

(numbers in bold indicate photographs)

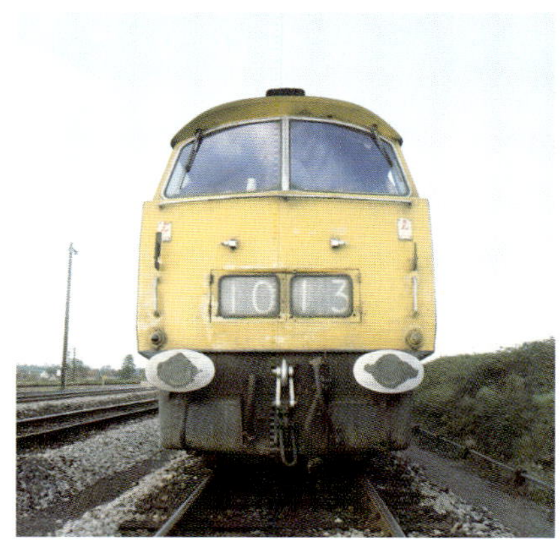
1013